SIDNEY LUMET

INTERVIEWS

CONVERSATIONS WITH FILMMAKERS SERIES
PETER BRUNETTE, GENERAL EDITOR

Photo credit: Photofest

SIDNEY
LUMET

INTERVIEWS

EDITED BY JOANNA E. RAPF

UNIVERSITY PRESS OF MISSISSIPPI / JACKSON

www.upress.state.ms.us

The University Press of Mississippi is a member of the Association of American University Presses.

Copyright © 2006 by University Press of Mississippi

Manufactured in the United States of America

First edition 2006

∞

Library of Congress Cataloging-in-Publication Data

Sidney Lumet : interviews / edited by Joanna E. Rapf.— 1st ed.
    p. cm. — (Conversations with filmmakers series)
    Includes filmography and index.
    ISBN 1-57806-723-5 (cloth : alk. paper) — ISBN 1-57806-724-3
(pbk. : alk. paper)
    1. Lumet, Sidney, 1924– —Interviews. 2. Motion picture producers
and directors—United States—Interviews. I. Rapf, Joanna E. II. Series.

PN1998.3.L86S53   2005
791.4302'33'092—dc22   2004066113

British Library Cataloging-in-Publication Data available

CONTENTS

Introduction   vii

Chronology   xvii

Filmography   xxiii

An Interview with Sidney Lumet   3
PETER BOGDANOVICH

Keep Them on the Hook   12
FILMS AND FILMING

The Insider: Sidney Lumet Talks about His Work in Films   17
ROBIN BEAN

Long Day's Journey Into Night: An Interview with Sidney Lumet   28
DALE LUCIANO

Sidney Lumet: *The Offence*   44
SUSAN MERRILL

What's Real? What's True?   53
GORDON GOW

Sidney Lumet: Letting It Happen   65
MORT SHEINMAN

Lumet: Endlessly Energetic   69
DAVID STERRITT

Colour and Concepts   73
RALPH APPLEBAUM

A Conversation with Sidney Lumet   81
MICHEL CIMENT

Interview with Sidney Lumet   104
CHANTAL DE BÉCHADE

Sidney Lumet: The Reluctant Auteur   110
DON SHEWEY

Sidney Lumet: An Interview   122
KENNETH M. CHANKO

Lumet's Morning Dawns   128
MAUREEN BURKE

Sidney Lumet: The Lion on the Left   131
GAVIN SMITH

The Law According to Lumet   145
TERRY DIGGS

Sidney Lumet: Making Movies   151
HENRY TISCHLER

Sidney Lumet: The Director Talks about Shooting in Snowstorms   157
HAROLD GOLDBERG

Critical Care and Collaboration   162
STEVEN SCHWARTZ

An Interview with Sidney Lumet   173
ANTHONY KAUFMAN

An Interview with Sidney Lumet   177
JOANNA E. RAPF

Index   195

INTRODUCTION

SIDNEY LUMET HAS MADE FORTY-TWO MOVIES in over forty years, from his first feature, *12 Angry Men* in 1957 to his most recent, *Find Me Guilty* in 2005. In 2005, he finally received an Honorary Oscar from the Academy of Motion Picture Arts and Sciences, after having been nominated for Best Director four times (for *12 Angry Men*, *Dog Day Afternoon*, *Network*, and *The Verdict*) and once for screenwriting, with Jay Presson Allen for *Prince of the City*. He has also received the D. W. Griffith Award from the Directors Guild of America for Lifetime Achievement, the Evelyn F. Burkey Award from the Writers Guild of America for "one whose contribution has brought honor and dignity to writers everywhere," and he was honored with a tribute at Lincoln Center in 2002.

Lumet has always been an independent director. When he told Don Shewey in 1982 that he liked to make films about "men who summon courage to challenge the system," about the "little guy against the system," he related this theme to himself. In fact, he is not a tall man, although he is not referring to height when he says "little guy," and he always prefers to work in New York, shunning the dominance of Hollywood. Like Woody Allen, he defines himself as a New Yorker: "I always like being in Woody Allen's world," the world of his movies and not only New York.[1] Lumet grew up in the City and can't imagine

---

1. Interview in *The Hollywood Reporter* in this volume.

living anywhere else. Hollywood, he says, wears people down, while the diversity of the City, its many ethnic neighborhoods, its art and its crime, its sophistication and its corruption, its beauty and its ugliness, all feed into what inspires him. In the interview with Michel Ciment he explains that in order to create it's important to confront reality on a daily basis. New York is filled with reality; Hollywood is a fantasyland. Because all the movies he decides to do must mean something to him personally, their genesis usually comes from the urban environment in which he lives. *The Wiz* (1978), for example, moves Dorothy's world of Kansas to Harlem.

Although he emphasizes the collaborative nature of making movies, including close work with his screenwriters, as discussed in the interview with writer Steven Schwartz, he has always insisted on complete control over his projects and since *Murder on the Orient Express* in 1974, he has had final cut. He is very much a "hands on" director who prides himself on being one of a vanishing breed who does not cater to the teen or preteen audience and who resists the current trend in Hollywood films to cut for the sake of cutting because it is what an MTV-saturated audience is used to. His fondness for the long take when it is thematically motivated may mean that young people find his movies slow, but he continues to trust the attention span of his audience. He knows he does not make the kind of movies that people line up to see, but he adds to the variety of what's out there. As he told Don Shewey, "If everybody did my kind of movie, I'd be so bored I'd never go into another movie theater in my life." His own favorites include *The Bicycle Thief, The Seventh Seal, Le Passion de Jeanne d'Arc*, and *Casablanca*, but he also loves the Indiana Jones movies and *Chicago*.

Almost inevitably for someone who has made as many movies as he has, his output has been uneven. Not every one of his projects has been a "passion," although being passionate about his work is important. Each movie he makes must mean something to him personally, and as he reiterates in a number of the interviews in this book, it is essential to care about each and every frame. But it is also important simply to keep working. Like a gymnast exercising her or his muscles, Lumet sees every project as a chance to experiment and perfect technique. For example, he considers *Daniel* (1983), an adaptation of E. L. Doctorow's *The Book of Daniel*, an intense and complex story loosely based on the lives of the children of Ethel and Julius Rosenberg, one of the best movies he's ever done. The experience of making it was so powerful, that afterwards, everything seemed "pallid."[2] Just to get back to work, he made the lighthearted, almost sentimental *Garbo Talks* (1984) about a young man who fulfills his mother's dying wish to meet the allusive Greta Garbo. Lumet admits he's not good at comedy and he does not like sentimentality, but he does like "human" stories, and *Garbo Talks* is a human story, even if it stretches credibility and borders on sentimentality. The mother in the movie, played by Anne Bancroft, embodies the kind of character to whom Lumet is attracted: a committed activist for all kinds of causes, who stands up for the rights of the oppressed, who is lively, outspoken, courageous, who refuses to conform for the sake of convenience, and whose understanding of life allows her to die with dignity. Similarly, her devoted son is single-mindedly determined to fulfill her last wish: to talk with Garbo. The search for Garbo takes him through the varied environments of New York City including the Lower East Side, Fire Island, and theatrical world in which Lumet himself grew up. Lumet once called his early film, *Stage Struck* (1958), a valentine to the theater, but *Garbo Talks* in many ways is a valentine to New York. It is not one of his favorite films, but its themes are characteristic. As he reiterates in these interviews, he is fascinated by the human cost involved in following passions and commitments, and the cost those passions and commitments inflict on others. Thematically, this is at the core of most of his movies, including his stories of corruption in the New York police department, family dramas such as *Daniel*, *Running on Empty*, and *Family Business*, up to his more recent work on television with the series *100 Centre Street*. He has stated bluntly to Don Shewey that "the pictures I'm proudest of have something to say about the human condition," and by "human" he means that the stories do not judge the characters. What Jean Renoir said of his own work applies to Lumet's: "everyone has his reasons," even the apparent bad guys, such as corrupt lieutenant detective Mike Brennan, played by Nick Nolte, in *Q & A* (1990).

Lumet suggests that his background in theater may have led him to focus on human relationships. He began his career as a child actor in

---

2. Interview with Kenneth Chanko in this volume.

New York, the son of well-known Yiddish actor Baruch Lumet who later appeared in two of his son's films, *The Pawnbroker* (1965) and *The Group* (1966). Sidney Lumet made his Broadway debut in Sidney Kingsley's *Dead End* in 1935 and continued to perform regularly on and off Broadway until he joined the Army Signal Corps in 1941. In 1949 he founded an off-Broadway acting group and began to do some directing. But it was the so-called Golden Age of television that really gave him his start as a director, and in interview after interview, he credits these television years with teaching him how to shoot quickly and efficiently, how to edit in the camera, and about the emotional meaning of lenses. Live television broadcasts taught him his craft; he is even responsible for some important practical innovations in those early TV days, such as stringing cables from the ceiling rather than running them on the floor. He is so thoroughly prepared, works so quickly and efficiently that some of his co-workers sometimes find him impatient, but the result is that he stays on schedule and generally comes in under budget. He talks a lot about how important the rehearsal period is before shooting starts; he probably spends more time in preproduction and rehearsal than most directors. But beyond his skill as a technician, Lumet also brought to his early television projects the humanity that has been at the core of everything he has done since. In an essay for *Cue* written in 1952, he said of his work on the live anthology series *Danger* that he wanted it to be "human, honest and occasionally illustrative of some major point about living."[3]

Lumet has suggested that the key to his talent as a director may well be his origins as an actor. He's known as an "actor's director," and he writes with exceptional sensitivity about actors in his book *Making Movies*, stressing mutual trust and the importance of listening. He loves actors, respects their privacy, and is impressed by the high degree of self-knowledge the best of them possess. And he has worked with the best of them over the years, a roster, probably unequaled by any other director, that includes Henry Fonda, Joan Greenwood, Sophia Loren, Marlon Brando, Anna Magnani, Joanne Woodward, Paul Newman, Maureen Stapleton, Katharine Hepburn, Ralph Richardson, Jason Robards, Jr., Walter Matthau, Rod Steiger, Sean Connery, Ossie Davis,

3. "Notes on TV," *Cue* (July 19, 1952): 6.

Candice Bergen, James Mason, Simone Signoret, Maximilian Schell, Lynn Redgrave, Colin Redgrave, Vanessa Redgrave, Omar Sharif, Lotte Lenya, Alan King, James Coburn, Al Pacino, Tony Roberts, Anthony Perkins, Albert Finney, Lauren Bacall, Ingrid Bergman, John Gielgud, Faye Dunaway, William Holden, Peter Finch, Robert Duvall, Beatrice Straight, Richard Burton, Joan Plowright, Diana Ross, Michael Jackson, Lena Horne, Myrna Loy, Michael Caine, Christopher Reeve, Anne Bancroft, Hermione Gingold, Richard Gere, Julie Christie, Gene Hackman, Jane Fonda, River Phoenix, Dustin Hoffman, Matthew Broderick, Nick Nolte, Melanie Griffith, Don Johnson, Richard Dreyfuss, Andy Garcia, James Spader, Helen Mirren, Albert Brooks, Wallace Shawn, Sharon Stone, Glenn Close, and Vin Diesel, among others.

His background as an actor may also be why he has done so many adaptations from plays, although he suggests that all movies are in some ways adaptations because they are artificially created. He likes theater for he loves words, and as a director he is not afraid of long speeches. But always he avoids what he calls "rubber ducky" dialogue, talk that explains the psychology of a character rather than showing it. A wonderful example of showing psychology rather than stating it is in *Prince of the City* (1981) when the embattled, whistle-blowing special investigator (played by Treat Williams) finds himself a victim and, like so many of the characters in Lumet's movies, connects with something deeper in himself which is shown as he starts to wear a cross again. Another example is in *The Verdict* (1982). An ambulance-chasing, alcoholic lawyer (Paul Newman in one of his finest roles) finds some redemption and a connection with the idealism of his youth: he is drinking coffee rather than alcohol at the end. Lumet likes these kinds of details, even though they may go unnoticed. They are true to life. He has often said that the best style is "unseen," just like the lens plots that structure his movies. The audience should feel, but they should not be aware of the technique. The movie he is proudest of in this respect is probably *Long Day's Journey Into Night* (1962), an almost a word-for-word adaptation of Eugene O'Neill's autobiographical play, but still one of the most "cinematic" movies he has ever made. He discusses why in several of the interviews in this book.

Because Lumet insists that the style of a movie, in addition to not showing, should also serve its story, he is adamantly anti-auteurist. He is that rare director who refuses possessory credit: "a film by . . ." He finds it "pretentious," and he hates pretentiousness, including the fad-dish word "cinema," a word, he tells Henry Tischler that he does not understand "except at the top of Spanish movie houses." "Film," like "cinema," belongs to critics and scholars looking for what my students often call "deep meaning." Lumet thinks there is too much talk about "meaning" in movies today, and when asked about "meaning" in his own work, he usually says simply that he does not think about it much. His metaphor to Don Shewey describing the search for meaning in movies is to the point: "I don't want to pour ten quarts of water into a two quart pail." He prefers to talk technique. Yet certain ideas about meaning do emerge in these interviews.

As a child of the Depression, growing up poor in New York City with poverty and corruption all around him, Lumet became concerned with the importance of justice to a democracy. He says he likes questioning things, people, institutions, what is considered by society as "right" and "wrong." He told Gavin Smith in 1988 that he regarded many of his films up to that time as ideological critiques of postwar American society, films such as *The Anderson Tapes* (1971), which presciently sees the omnipresence of surveillance in modern life, *Network* (1976), which reveals the dangerous potential of television, or *Power* (1985), which examines how media can come to replace human reality in politics. He is interested in how destructive modern life can be, but he does not believe that art itself has the power to change anything. Yet it is still important to him to make movies that "matter." There is, as he says, a lot of "shit" to deal with in the entertainment industry, but the secret of good work is to maintain your honesty and your passion. The difference between what he describes as "good" work and "great" work—and "great" is not a word he uses very often—is "honest moments." He now finds an early film such as *The Pawnbroker* (1965) too hysterical. It is not necessary to scream in order to convey emotion. Every human being struggles towards self-knowledge in a world that doesn't help very much. Almost all Lumet's movies are about this struggle.

Today he is doing more and more work in television, returning to where his directing career really began. His reasons for returning to television some forty years after he left it are mixed. One is what he simply calls "the age thing."[4] Hollywood is nervous about hiring older directors and Lumet's last three features before *Find Me Guilty* (2005), *Night Falls in Manhattan* (1997), *Critical Care* (1997), and *Gloria* (1999) were not big successes. But another reason is more positive. Allen Sabinson, who for a short seven months had been president of Miramax's film division and who in 2001 was looking to upgrade A&E from its *Biography* lethargy, read a pilot script that Lumet had been commissioned to write for NBC called *100 Centre Street*. Lumet was not looking for small screen work at the time, but the network made him an offer he could not refuse. NBC eventually passed on it but Sabinson decided to make the pilot to test the waters with a dramatic series on A&E. Lumet had been offered a TV directing job when George Clooney decided to remake *Fail-Safe* as a live broadcast in the spring of 2001, but he turned it down: "I just couldn't get my motor going about redoing something I had done so many years ago."[5] The job went to Stephen Frears. But the new technology of HD video did get his motor going. "I saw a test of this new Sony 24-frame-per-second high definition video camera. It put me away. It was the most extraordinary color I'd ever seen. Absolutely natural. Exactly what your eye saw. Which, God knows, movie color is not. I was in love."[6]

As the interviews in this book make clear, Lumet has always favored naturalism and/or realism. He does not like the "decorator's look"; rarely does he want the camera to call attention to itself; the editing must be unobtrusive. As his cinematographer on *100 Centre Street*, Ron Fortunato, jokingly says, "Sidney flips if he sees a look that's too artsy."[7] So what thrilled him about HD video "was that it gave me what my eye saw. . . . Being primarily a realistic director, and not a high-style direc-tor, that reality has always been important to me."[8]

---

4. Bruce Fretts, "Film Vet Sidney Lumet Steps Back into the TV Spotlight for A&E's First Drama Series," *Entertainment Weekly* (January 19, 2001).

5. David Everitt, "A Return to the Small Screen, and to Some Old Ideas," *New York Times* (January 7, 2001): 40.

6. Denis Hamil, "Justice-Seeking Sidney: Director Lumet Goes Back to Court—43 Years After *12 Angry Men*," *New York Daily News*. Showtime Section (December 10, 2000): 19.

7. Eric Rudolph, "A Favorable Verdict for 24p," *American Cinematographer*, 84.4 (April 2001): 64.

8. Everitt, 40.

He agreed to do the series for A&E on the condition that he could shoot it in HD video in a modified live-television style, taping scenes with three cameras, as he did in live TV in the 1950s. This enabled him to direct and cut from one angle to the other and to use master shots, reaction shots, and close-ups all in one take. During a typical, three-camera court scene on *100 Centre Street*, each camera would have a shot list with five to twenty shots per five-minute scene. Fortunato comments in amazement that he "would sit in the truck and watch Sidney as he live-switched what was close to a final cut [on the fly]."[9]

The live technique created a "kind of energy" for the actors and also a sharper texture to the image, a little like that of a news broadcast, which made "the action feel more alive."[10] Lumet did not want this show to look like film; he wanted it to look "real." He said to Fortunato, "Don't be discouraged because it doesn't look like film. I want it to look like a live event," and "24p HD gave me the look I wanted."[11] Yet with all its technical innovations, *100 Centre Street* was human drama: no sappy endings, no Perry Mason moments, just the people in the system, "the DAs, public defenders, defendants, witnesses, judges, clerks, cops."[12] Lumet is sorry it did not continue for another season. He had plenty of ideas for it.

He once told Michel Ciment that people tend to do their best work at the beginning and middle of their careers, not at the end. But these are people who have been struggling in Hollywood all their lives. One of the directors Lumet admires most, Akira Kurosawa, made *Dreams* at the age of eighty. Still intensely energetic, youthful, and passionate about life, Sidney Lumet continues to work out of his small office in New York City. He has new projects on the table and is excited by the new technology of HD video. He says he will never shoot on film again, but it is not finally the technology that matters to him. It is, rather, those "real" people and "real" situations, and the stories he can tell about them, "human, honest and occasionally illustrative of some

---

9. Rudolph, 58.

10. Caryn James, "The Scales of Justice and How They Tilt," *New York Times* (January 15, 2001): E12.

11. Rudolph, 57.

12. James.

major point about living." As he said to *The Hollywood Reporter* in 1997, "There is nothing better than directing."

Following the pattern of the other books in the Conversations with Filmmakers series, the interviews in this volume are presented chronologically and in their entirety, with minimal editing. The inevitable repetition of ideas as Lumet talks about his work over a career that spans more than forty years reveals a remarkable consistency in terms of how he feels about the role of the director, about style, technique, his background in acting and television, melodrama (he loves it!), and the importance of making movies that matter personally. He concluded his own book, *Making Movies*, by saying that his job "is to care about and be responsible for every frame of every movie I make." But his last words are for young people, "dreaming of finding out what matters to *them*." Whether they become moviemakers or cops, doctors or soldiers, he wants them to say "to themselves and to anyone who will listen, 'I care.' "[13]

For my own work on this volume, I am especially indebted to my friend and colleague, Benjamin Harris who, as a graduate student, started a personal project on Sidney Lumet a number of years ago and encouraged me with my own. I would also like to thank Walter Bernstein, Peter Brunette, Ryan J. Tan, Chris Tubbs, my son, Alex Eaton, and at the University Press of Mississippi, for their advice and patience, Seetha Srinivasan and Anne Stascavage. But my biggest debt of gratitude is, of course, to Sidney Lumet, for his time, artistry, inspiration, and caring.

JER

---

13. Sidney Lumet, *Making Movies* (New York: Vintage Books, 1996), p. 218.

CHRONOLOGY

1924	Born on June 25 in Philadelphia, Pennsylvania.
1926	Lumet family moves to New York City.
1928	Lumet makes his acting debut with his father in a Yiddish Theatre production and on radio, where his father served as actor-writer-director.
1928–32	Continues to do children's roles in the Yiddish Theatre and on radio. Appears on a weekly radio show, in Yiddish, *The Rabbi from Brownsville* between 1931–32.
1935	Makes his Broadway debut at the Belasco Theater in Sidney Kingsley's *Dead End*.
1937	Plays one of the lead parts, that of young Jesus, in Max Reinhardt's *The Eternal Road*. His father and Lotte Lenya, wife of the play's composer, Kurt Weill, are also in the cast.
1938	Plays Stanley in *Sunup to Sundown*, directed by Joseph Losey at the Hudson Theatre, and Mickey in *Schoolhouse on the Lot* at the Ritz.
1939	Is seen as Johnny in William Saroyan's *My Heart's in the Highlands,* and Leo in *Christmas Eve* at the Henry Miller Theatre. Also does a movie role as Joey Rogers, the brother of Sylvia Sidney's character, in *One Third of a Nation*.
1940	Plays Hymie Tashman in *Morning Star* at the Longacre Theatre and appears in *George Washington Slept Here*. He is also Joshua, the young Jesus in *Journey to Jerusalem* at the National Theatre. At the end of this year this play is

	filmed with its original cast, the first photographed play made available on 16 mm exactly as produced by the Theatre Guild in New York.
1941	Appears as Willie Berg, a young hoodlum, in *Brooklyn, U.S.A.* at the Forrest Theatre. For one term, attends Columbia University's extension division to study dramatic literature, then enlists in the Army Signal Corps.
1946	Succeeds Marlon Brando in the role of David in Ben Hecht's *A Flag Is Born*, produced by the Alvin Theatre in New York.
1948	Plays Tonya in Arthur Goodman's experimental play, *Seeds in the Wind*, directed by Paul Tripp, at the Empire Theatre. Lumet's friend, Yul Brynner, offers him a job as an assistant director at CBS.
1949	Founds an off-Broadway acting group and begins to do some directing.
1949	Is promoted to staff director at CBS. Marries actress Rita Gam.
1951–1953	Lumet directs about 150 episodes of *Danger*, a thirty-minute weekly program for CBS. During this time he also does episodes of *You Are There* and begins directing live programming, including teleplays for such series as *Playhouse 90*, *Kraft Television Theatre*, and *Studio One*.
1954	Divorces Rita Gam.
1955	Directs the off-Broadway revival of George Bernard Shaw's *The Doctor's Dilemma*.
1956	Directs Kermit Bloomgarden's production of *Night of the Auk* at the Playhouse Theatre. Marries Gloria Vanderbilt. Reginald Rose and Henry Fonda commission Lumet to direct *12 Angry Men*.
1957	*12 Angry Men* is released and for his direction, Lumet wins the Director's Guild of America Award (DGA) and is nominated for an Academy Award.
1958	*Stage Struck* is released in March. Directs *All the King's Men* for TV.
1959	*That Kind of Woman*, starring Sophia Loren, is released in September. *The Fugitive Kind* is released December 1.

1960 Directs Albert Camus's *Caligula* on Broadway. In June a two-part, semi-documentary, *The Sacco and Vanzetti Story*, for NBC, airs. Lumet earns an Emmy nomination for direction. In November he directs Jason Robards, Jr. in *The Iceman Cometh* for WNTA-TV. For this he wins an Emmy. He directs a theatrical version of *Rashomon* for WNTA-TV in December.

1961 *A View from the Bridge* is released.

1962 *Long Day's Journey Into Night* is released. Lumet still regards it as one of the best films he has ever made, and he again wins the DGA Award. Later this year he directs *Nowhere to Go But Up* at the Winter Garden.

1963 Divorces Gloria Vanderbilt. Marries Gail Jones, daughter of Lena Horne.

1964 *Fail-Safe* is released in October. *The Hill* is shot. Daughter Amy Lumet is born in London.

1965 *The Pawnbroker* is released in April 1965. It is Lumet's first big commercial success. He wins the British Academy Award for his direction. *The Hill* is released in October and marks the first time he films in Europe.

1966 *The Group*, based on Mary McCarthy's novel, is released in March.

1967 *The Deadly Affair* is released in February. Daughter Jenny Lumet born.

1968 *Bye, Bye, Braverman* is released in April and *The Seagull* in December.

1969 *The Appointment* is released, and in September, Lumet assists Ely Landau with the compilation documentary, *King: A Filmed Record . . . Montgomery to Memphis*.

1970 *The Last of the Mobile Hot-Shots* is released in January.

1971 *The Anderson Tapes* is released in June.

1972 *Child's Play* is released on December 12.

1973 *The Offence* is released in May.

1974 *Serpico* is released in February, *Lovin' Molly* in March, and *Murder on the Orient Express* in December.

1975 *Dog Day Afternoon* is released in October. Lumet receives an Academy Award nomination for Best Director and the film is nominated for Best Picture.

1976	*Network* is released in December. The Motion Picture Academy again nominates him for Best Director, and the film is nominated for Best Picture. He wins a Golden Globe for his direction.
1977	*Equus* is released in November.
1978	*The Wiz* is released on October 24. Divorces Gail Jones.
1980	*Just Tell Me What You Want* is released on January 18. Marries Mary Gimbel.
1981	*Prince of the City* is released. With Jay Presson Allen, he is nominated for a screenwriting Academy Award for this film and wins a New York Film Critics Circle Award for direction.
1982	*Deathtrap* is released on March 19, and *The Verdict* is released on December 8. For *The Verdict*, Lumet again receives an Oscar nomination for Best Director, along with a Golden Globe nomination.
1983	*Daniel* is released on August 26.
1984	*Garbo Talks* is released on October 12.
1986	*Power* is released in January. *The Morning After* is released on December 25.
1988	*Running on Empty* is released on November 10.
1989	*Family Business* is released on December 15.
1990	*Q & A* is released.
1992	*A Stranger Among Us* is released on July 17.
1993	*Guilty as Sin* is released on June 4. Lumet receives the D. W. Griffith Award from the Director's Guild of America for Lifetime Achievement.
1995	Publishes *Making Movies*.
1997	*Night Falls in Manhattan* is released on May 16.
1997	*Critical Care* is released in October. He receives the Evelyn F. Burkey Award from the Writers Guild of America.
1998	The Independent Film Producers (IFP) honors Lumet with a Lifetime Achievement Award.
1999	*Gloria* is released on January 22.
2001	Lumet produces *100 Centre Street*, a television series for A&E, and writes and directs a number of the episodes. The series is shot in HD-video. For "New Technology" the

Motion Picture Producers Association (PGA) honors him with a Golden Laurel Award.

2002   The Academy of Motion Picture Arts and Sciences, with the participation of the Film Society of Lincoln Center, presents a Tribute to Sidney Lumet at the Walter Reade Theater on June 4.

2004   *Strip Search* airs on HBO in April. Lumet receives the Joseph L. Mankiewiecz Award for Excellence in Filmmaking.

2005   Directs a new feature, *Find Me Guilty*. He receives an Honorary Oscar from the Academy of Motion Picture Arts and Sciences on February 27.

FILMOGRAPHY

1957
12 ANGRY MEN
Producers: Henry Fonda and Reginald Rose
Director: **Sidney Lumet**
Screenplay: Reginald Rose, from his original teleplay
Director of Photography: Boris Kaufman
Art Direction: Robert Markell
Editor: Carl Lerner
Music: Kenyon Hopkins
Sound: James Gleason
Cast: Henry Fonda (Juror No. 8, "Davis"), Lee J. Cobb (Juror No. 3),
Ed Begley (Juror No. 10), Jack Warden (Juror No. 7), Marin Balsam (Juror
No. 1), John Fielder (Juror No. 2), Jack Klugman (Juror No. 5), Edward
Binns (Juror No. 6), Joseph Sweeney (Juror No. 9), George Voskovec
(Juror No. 11), Robert Webber (Juror No. 12), Rudy Bond (Judge), James
A. Kelly (Guard), Bill Nelson (Court Clerk), John Savoca (Defendant)
B&W
95 minutes

1958
STAGE STRUCK
Producer: Stuart Millar
Director: **Sidney Lumet**
Screenplay: Ruth and Augustus Goetz, based on the play *Morning Glory*
by Zoe Akins
Directors of Photography: Franz F. Planer and Maurice Hartzband
Art Direction: Kim Edgar Swandos

Costumes: Moss Mabry
Editor: Stuart Gilmore
Music: Alex North
Sound: James Gleason and Terry Kellum
Cast: Henry Fonda (Lewis Easton), Susan Strasberg (Eva Lovelace), Joan
Greenwood (Rita Vernon), Herbert Marshall (Robert Hedges),
Christopher Plummer (Joe Sheridan), Daniel Ocko (Constantine), Pat
Herrington (Benny), Frank Campenella (Victor), John Fielder (Adrian),
Patricia Englund (Gwen Hall), Jack Weston (Frank), Sally Gracie
(Elizabeth), Nina Hansen (Regina), Harold Grau (Stage Doorman)
Color
95 minutes

1959
THAT KIND OF WOMAN
Producers: Carlo Ponti and Marcello Giroso
Director: **Sidney Lumet**
Screenplay: Walter Bernstein, from a story by Robert Lowry
Director of Photography: Boris Kaufman
Art Direction: Hal Pereira and Roland Anderson
Costumes: Edith Head
Editor: Howard Smith
Music: Daniele Amfitheatrof
Sound: James Gleason and Charles Grenzbach
Cast: Sophia Loren (Kay), Tab Hunter (Red), George Sanders (The Man),
Jack Warden (Kelly), Barbara Nichols (Jane), Keenan Wynn (Harry)
B&W
92 minutes

1959
THE FUGITIVE KIND
Producers: Martin Jurow and Richard A. Shepherd
Director: **Sidney Lumet**
Screenplay: Tennessee Williams and Meade Roberts, based on Williams's
play *Orpheus Descending*
Director of Photography: Boris Kaufman
Art Direction: Richard Sylbert

Costumes: Frank Thompson
Editor: Carl Lerner
Music: Kenyon Hopkins
Sound: James Gleason and Philip Gleason
Cast: Marlon Brando (Val Xavier), Anna Magnani (Lady Torrance),
Joanne Woodward (Carol Cutrere), Maureen Stapleton (Vee Talbot),
Victor Jory (Jabe Torrance), R. G. Armstrong (Sheriff Talbot), Emory
Richardson (Uncle Pleasant, the Conjure Man), Spivy (Ruby Lightfoot),
Sally Gracie (Dolly Hamma), Lucille Benson (Beulah Binnings), John
Baragrey (David Cutrere), Ben Yaffee (Dog Hamma), Joe E. Brown, Jr.
(Pee Wee Binnings), Virgilia Chew (Nurse Porter)
B&W
135 minutes

1961
A VIEW FROM THE BRIDGE
Producer: Paul Graetz
Director: **Sidney Lumet**
Screenplay: Norman Rosten, based on Arthur Miller's play
Director of Photography: Michel Kelber
Art Direction: Jacques Saulnier
Editor: Françoise Javet
Music: Maurice Leroux
Sound: Jo de Bretagne
Cast: Raf Vallone (Eddie Carbone), Jean Sorel (Rodolpho), Maureen
Stapleton (Beatrice Carbone), Carol Lawrence (Catherine), Raymond
Pellegrin (Marco), Morris Carnovsky (Mr. Alfieri), Harvey Lembeck
(Mike), Mickey Know (Louis), Vincent Gardenia (Lipari), Frank
Campanella (Longshoreman)
B&W
114 minutes

1962
LONG DAY'S JOURNEY INTO NIGHT
Producer: Ely Landau
Director: **Sidney Lumet**
Screenplay: Eugene O'Neill's play

Director of Photography: Boris Kaufman
Art Direction: Richard Sylbert
Costumes: Motley
Editor: Ralph Rosenblum
Music: Andre Previn
Cast: Katharine Hepburn (Mary Tyrone), Ralph Richardson
(James Tyrone, Sr.), Jason Robards, Jr. (Jamie Tyrone), Dean Stockwell
(Edmund Tyrone), Jeanne Barr (Kathleen the Maid)
B&W
Originally 174 minutes, cut to 136 minutes

1964
FAIL-SAFE
Producer: Max E. Youngstein
Director: **Sidney Lumet**
Screenplay: Walter Bernstein, based on the novel by Eugene Burdick
and Harney Wheeler
Director of Photography: Gerald Hirschfeld
Art Direction: Albert Brenner
Costumes: Anna Hill Johnstone
Editor: Ralph Rosenblum
Sound: Jack Fitzstephens and William Swift
Cast: Henry Fonda (The President), Dan O'Herlihy (General Black),
Walter Matthau (Groeteschele), Frank Overton (General Bogan), Edward
Binns (Colonel Grady), Fritz Weaver (Colonel Cascio), Larry Hagman
(Buck), William Hansen (Secretary Swenson), Rullel Hardie (General
Stark), Russell Collins (Knapp), Sorrell Booke (Congressman Raskob),
Nancy Berg (Ilsa Wolfe), John Connell (Thomas), Frank Simpson
(Sullivan), Hildy Parks (Betty Black), Janet Ward (Mrs. Grady),
Dom DeLouise (Sgt. Collins), Dana Elcar (Foster), Stuart Germain
(Mr. Cascio), Louise Larabee (Mrs. Cascio), Frieda Altman (Jennie),
Bob Gerringer (Fly)
B&W
112 minutes

1965
THE PAWNBROKER
Producers: Roger H. Lewis and Philip Langner

Director: **Sidney Lumet**
Screenplay: David Friedkin and Morton Fine, based on the novel by
Edward Lewis Wallant
Director of Photography: Boris Kaufman
Art Direction: Richard Sylbert
Costumes: Anna Hill Johnstone
Editor: Ralph Rosenblum
Music: Quincy Jones
Sound: Dennis Maitland
Cast: Rod Steiger (Sol Nazerman), Geraldine Fitzgerald (Marilyn
Birchfield), Brock Peters (Rodriquez), Jaime Sanchez (Jesus Ortiz),
Thelma Oliver (Ortiz's Girl), Marketa Kimbrell (Tessie), Baruch Lumet
(Mendel), Juano Hernandez (Mr. Smith, the Philosopher), Linda Geiser
(Ruth), Nancy R. Pollock (Bertha), Raymond St. Jacques (Tangee),
John McCurry (Buck), Charles Dierkop (Robinson), Eusebia Cosme
(Mrs. Ortiz), Warren Finnerty (Savarese), Jack Ader (Morton), Marianne
Kanter (Joan), E. M. Margolese (Papa)
B&W
115 minutes

1965
THE HILL
Producer: Kenneth Hyman
Director: **Sidney Lumet**
Screenplay: Ray Rigby, based on a play by Rigby and R. S. Allen
Director of Photography: Oswald Morris
Art Direction: Herbert Smith
Editor: Thelma Connell
Sound Editor: Peter Musgrave
Cast: Sean Connery (Joe Roberts), Harry Andrews (Regimental Sergeant
Major Wilson), Ian Bannen (Harris), Alfred Lynch (George Stevens),
Ossie Davis (Jacko King), Roy Kinnear (Monty Bartlett), Jack Watson
(Jock McGrath), Ian Hendry (Williams), Sir Michael Redgrave (Medical
Officer), Norman Bird (Commandant), Neil McCarty (Burton), Howard
Goorney (Walters), Tony Caunter (Martin)
B&W
123 minutes

1966
THE GROUP
Producer: Sidney Buchman
Director: **Sidney Lumet**
Screenplay: Sidney Buchman, based on the novel by Mary McCarthy
Director of Photography: Boris Kaufman
Production Designer: Gene Callahan
Costumes: Anna Hill Johnstone
Editor: Ralph Rosenblum
Sound: Jack Fitzstephens and Dennis Maitland
Cast: Candice Bergen (Elinor Eastlake, "Lakey"), Joan Hackett (Dorothy
Renfew), Elizabeth Hartman (Priss Harshorn), Shirley Knight (Polly
Andrews), Joanne Pettet (Kay Strong), Mary-Robin Redd (Pokey
Prothero), Jessica Walter (Libby MacAusland), Kathleen Widdoes (Helena
Davison), James Broderick (Dr. James Ridgeley), James Congdon (Sloan
Crockett), Larry Hagman (Harald Peterson), Hal Holbrook (Gus Leroy),
Richard Mulligan (Dick Brown), Robert Emhardt (Mr. Andrews), Carrie
Nye (Norine), Philippa Bevans (Mrs. Hartshorn), Leta Bonynge
(Mrs. Prothero), Marion Brash (Radio Man's Wife), Sara Burton
(Mrs. Davison), Flora Campbell (Mrs. MacAusland), Bruno DiCosmi
(Nils), Leora Dana (Mrs. Renfrew), Bill Fletcher (Bill), George Gaynes
(Brook Latham), Martha Greenhouse (Mrs. Bergler), Russell Hardie
(Mr. Davison)
Color
150 minutes

1967
THE DEADLY AFFAIR
Producer: **Sidney Lumet**
Director: **Sidney Lumet**
Screenplay: Paul Dehn, based on the novel *Call the Dead* by John
le Carré
Director of Photography: Freddie Young
Art Direction: John Howell
Costumes: Cynthia Tingay
Editor: Thelma Connell
Music: Quincy Jones

Sound: Les Hammond
Cast: James Mason (Charles Dobbs), Simone Signoret (Elsa Fennan),
Maximilian Schell (Dieter Frey), Harriet Anderson (Ann Dobbs), Harry
Andrews (Inspector Mendel), Kenneth Haigh (Bill Appleby), Lynn
Redgrave (Virgin), Roy Kinnear (Adam Scarr), Max Adrian (Adviser),
Robert Flemyng (Samuel Fennan), Colin Redgrave (Director), Les White
(Harek), The Royal Shakespeare Company in *Edward II* by Christopher
Marlowe, directed by Peter Hall
Color
107 minutes

1968
BYE, BYE BRAVERMAN
Producer: **Sidney Lumet**
Director: **Sidney Lumet**
Screenplay: Herbert Sargent, based on the novel *To an Early Grave* by
Wallace Markfield
Director of Photography: Boris Kaufman
Art Direction: Ben Kasazkow
Costumes: Anna Hill Johnstone
Editor: Ralph Rosenblum
Music: Peter Matz
Sound: Dick Vorisek
Cast: George Segal (Morroe Rieff), Jack Warden (Barnet Weiner), Jessica
Walter (Inez Braverman), Phyllis Newman (Myra Mandelbaum),
Godfrey Cambridge (taxi cab driver), Joseph Wiseman (Felix
Ottensteen), Sorrell Booke (Holly Levine), Zohra Lampert (Etta Rieff),
Anthony Holland (Max Ottensteen), Susan Wyler (Pilar), Lieb Lensky
(Custodian), Alan King (The Rabbi)
Color
94 minutes

1968
THE SEA GULL
Producer: **Sidney Lumet**
Director: **Sidney Lumet**
Screenplay: Mour Budberg, from the play by Anton Chekhov

Director of Photography: Gerry Fisher
Production Designer: Tony Walton
Costumes: Tony Walton
Editor: Alan Heim
Cast: James Mason (Trigorin), Vanessa Redgrave (Nina), Simone
Signoret (Arkadina), David Warner (Konstantin), Harry Andrews (Sorin),
Denholm Elliot (Dorn), Eileen Herlie (Polina), Alfred Lynch
(Medveddenko), Ronald Radd (Shamraev), Kathleen Widdoes (Masha),
Frej Lindquest (Yakov), Karen Miller (Housemaid)
Color
141 minutes

1969
THE APPOINTMENT
Producer: Martin Poll
Director: **Sidney Lumet**
Screenplay: James Salter, from an original story by Antonio Leonviola
Director of Photography: Carlo Di Palma
Art Direction: Piero Gherardi
Costumes: Alda Marussig
Editor: Thelma Connell
Music: John Barry
Sound: David Hildyard
Cast: Omar Sharif (Federico Fendi), Anouk Aimee (Carla), Lotte Lenya
(Emma Valandier), Paola Barbara (Mother), Didi Perego (Nany), Luigi
Proiette (Fabre), Fausto Tozzi (Renzo), Inna Alexeieff (old woman on
train), Ennio Balbo (Ugo Perino), Linda De Felice (fisherman's wife),
Sandro Dori (Cutter), Cyrus Elias (apprentice lawyer), Gabriella Grimaldi
(Anna), Isabella Guidotti (Perino's secretary), Angelo Infanti (Antonio)
Color
100 minutes

1969
KING: A FILMED RECORD . . . MONTGOMERY TO MEMPHIS
Producer: Ely Landau
Directors of Connecting Sequences: **Sidney Lumet** and Joseph
L. Mankiewicz

Cast: Paul Newman, Joanne Woodward, James Earl Jones (commentators), Ruby Dee, Clarence Williams III, Ben Gazzara, Charlton Heston, Harry Belafonte, Sidney Poitier (narrators), Burt Lancaster (as himself), Martin Luther King (himself in archival footage)
B&W
153 minutes

1970
THE LAST OF THE MOBILE HOT-SHOTS
Producer: **Sidney Lumet**
Director: **Sidney Lumet**
Screenplay: Gore Vidal, based on *The Seven Descents of Myrtle* by Tennessee Williams as produced on stage by David Merrick
Director of Photography: James Wong Howe
Production Design: Gene Callahan
Costumes: P. Zipprodt
Editor: Alan Heim
Music: Quincy Jones
Sound: Nat Boxer
Cast: James Coburn (Jeb), Lynn Redgrave (Myrtle), Robert Hooks (Chicken), Perry Hayes (George), Reggie King (Rube)
Color
108 minutes

1971
THE ANDERSON TAPES
Producer: Robert M. Weitman
Director: **Sidney Lumet**
Screenplay: Frank R. Pierson, based on the novel by Lawrence Sanders
Director of Photography: Arthur Ornitz
Art Direction: Philip Rosenberg
Costumes: Gene Coffin
Editor: Joanne Burke
Music: Quincy Jones
Sound: Dennis Maitland, Jack Fitzstephens, and Al Gramaglia
Cast: Sean Connery (Duke Anderson), Dyan Cannon (Ingrid Everleigh), Martin Balsam (Tommy Haskins), Ralph Meeker (Captain Delaney),

Alan King (Pat Angelo), Christopher Walken (the Kid), Val Avery (Socks Parelli), Dick Williams (Spencer), Garrett Morris (Everson), Stan Gottlieb (Pop), Paul Benjamin (Jimmy), Anthony Holland (Psychologist), Conrad Bain (Dr. Rubicoff), Richard B. Schull (Werner), Margaret Hamilton (Miss Kaler), Judith Lowry (Mrs. Hathaway), Max Showalter (Bingham), Norman Rose (Longene), Med Miles (Mrs. Longene), Ralph Stanley (D'Medico), John Call (O'Leary), John Bradon (Vanessi), Paula Trueman (nurse)
Color
98 minutes

1972
CHILD'S PLAY
Producer: David Merrick
Director: **Sidney Lumet**
Screenplay: Leon Prochnik, based on the play by Robert Marasco produced on the Broadway stage by David Merrick
Director of Photography: Gerald Hirschfeld
Production Design: Philip Rosenberg
Costumes: Ruth Morley
Editors: Edward Warschilka and Joanne Burke
Music: Michael Small
Sound: William Edmondson
Cast: James Mason (Jerome Malley), Robert Preston (Joseph Dobbs), Beau Bridges (Paul Reis), Ronald Weyland (Father Mozian), Charles White (Father Griffin), David Rounds (Father Penny), Kate Harrington (Mrs. Carter), Jamie Alexander (Sheppard), Brian Chapin (O'Donnell), Bryant Fraser (Jennings), Mark Hall Haefeli (Wilson), Tom Leopold (Shea), Julius Lo Iacono (McArdle), Christopher Man (Travis), Paul O'Keefe (Banks), Robert D. Randall (Medley), Robbie Reed (class president)
Color
100 minutes

1973
THE OFFENCE
Producer: Denis O'Dell
Director: **Sidney Lumet**

Screenplay: John Hopkins, based on his play *This Story of Yours*
Director of Photography: Gerry Fisher
Art Direction: John Clark
Costumes: Vangie Harrison
Editor: John Victor Smith
Music: Harrison Birtwhistle
Sound: Simon Kaye
Cast: Sean Connery (Detective Sergeant Johnson), Trevor Howard
(Cartwright), Vivien Merchant (Maureen Johnson), Ian Bannen
(Baxter), Derek Newark (Jessard), John Hallam (Panton), Peter Bowles
(Cameron), Ronald Radd (Lawson), Anthony Sagar (Hill), Howard
Goorney (Lambeth), Richard Moore (Garrett), Maxine Gordon (Janie)
Color
113 minutes

1974
SERPICO
Producer: Martin Bregman
Director: **Sidney Lumet**
Screenplay: Waldo Salt and Norman Wexler, based on the book by
Peter Maas
Director of Photography: Arthur Ornitz
Art Direction: Douglas Higgins
Production Design: Charles Bailey
Costumes: Anna Hill Johnstone
Editor: Dede Allen
Music: Mikis Theodorakis
Sound: John J. Fitzstephens, Edward Beyer, Robert Reitano, and Richard
Cirincione
Cast: Al Pacino (Serpico), John Randolph (Sidney Green), Jack Kehoe
(Tom Keough), Biff McGuire (Inspector McClain), Barbara Edayoung
(Laurie), Corneilia Sharpe (Leslie), Tony Roberts (Bob Blair), John
Medici (Pasquale), Alan Rich (D.A. Tauber), Norman Ornellas (Rubello),
Ed Grover (Lonbardo), Al Henderson (Peluce), Hank Garre (Malone),
Damien Leake (Joey), Joe Bova (Potts), Gene Gross (Captain Tolkin),
John Stewart (Waterman), Woodie King (Larry), James Tolkin (Steiger),
Ed Crowley (Barto), Bernard Barrow (palmer), Sal Carollo (Mr. Serpico),

Mildred Clinton (Mrs. Serpico), Nathan George (Smith), Gus Fleming
(Dr. Metz), Richard Foronjy (Corsaro), Alan North (Brown)
Color
130 minutes

1974
LOVIN' MOLLY
Director: **Sidney Lumet**
Producer: Stephen Friedman
Screenplay: Stephen Friedman, based on the novel *Leaving Cheyenne* by
Larry McMurtry
Director of Photography: Edward Brown
Art Direction: Robert Drunheller and Paul Hefferan
Production Design: Gene Coffin
Costumes: Gene Coffin
Editor: Joanne Burke
Music: Fred Hellerman
Sound: Jack Fitzstephens and John Sabat
Cast: Anthony Perkins (Gid), Beau Bridges (Johnny), Blythe Danner
(Molly), Edward Binns (Mr. Fry), Susan Sarandon (Sarah), Conrad
Fowkes (Eddie White), Claude Traverse (Mr. Tayler), John Henry Faulk
(Mr. Grinson)
Color
98 minutes

1974
MURDER ON THE ORIENT EXPRESS
Producers: John Brabourne and Richard Goodwin
Director: **Sidney Lumet**
Screenplay: Paul Dehn, from the novel by Agatha Christie
Director of Photography: Geoffrey Unsworth
Art Direction: Jack Stephens
Production Design: Tony Walton
Costumes: Tony Walton
Editor: Anne V. Coates
Music: Richard Rodney Bennett
Sound: Peter Handford and Bill Rowe

Cast: Albert Finney (Hercule Poirot), Lauren Bacall (Mrs. Hubbard), Martin Balsam (Bianchi), Ingrid Bergman (Greta Ohlsson), Jacqueline Bisset (Countess Andrenyi), Jean-Pierre Cassel (Pierre Paul Michel), Sean Connery (Colonel Arbuthnot), John Gielgud (Beddoes), Wendy Hiller (Princess Dragomiroff), Anthony Perkins (Hector McQueen), Vanessa Redgrave (Mary Debenham), Rachel Roberts (Hildegarde Schmidt), Richard Widmark (Ratchett), Michael York (Count Andrenyi), Colin Blakely (Hardman), George Coulouris (Doctor Constantine), Der Quilley (Foscarelli), Vernon Dobtcheff (concierge)
Color
128 minutes

1975
DOG DAY AFTERNOON
Producers: Martin Bregman and Martin Elfand
Director: **Sidney Lumet**
Screenplay: Frank Pierson, based on magazine articles by P. F. Kluge and Thomas Moore
Director of Photography: Victor J. Kemper
Art Direction: Doug Higgins
Costumes: Anna Hill Johnstone
Editor: Dede Allen
Sound: Jack Fitzstephens, Richard Cirincione, Sanford Rackow, and Stephen A. Rotter
Cast: Al Pacino (Sonny Wortzik), John Cazale (Sal), Penny Allen (Sylvia, the head teller), Sully Boyar (Mulvaney), Beulah Garrick (Margaret), Carol Kane (Jenny), Sandra Kazan (Deborah), Marcia Jean Kurtz (Miriam), Amy Levitt (Maria), John Marriott (Howard), Estelle Omens (Edna), Gary Springer (Bobby), James Broderick (Shelton), Charles Dunning (Moretti), Carmine Foresta (Carmine), Lang Henriksen (Murphy), Floyd Levine (Phone Cop), Thomas Murphy (policeman with Angie), Dominic Chianese (Sonny's father), Marcia Haufrecht (Vi's friend), Judith Malina (Vi, Sonny's mother), Susan Peretz (Angie), Chris Sarandon (Leon), Dick Williams (limo driver), Lionel Pina (pizza boy), Charles Mackensie (doctor), Jay Gerber (Sam)
Color
130 minutes

1976
NETWORK
Producer: Howard Gottfried
Director: **Sidney Lumet**
Screenplay: Paddy Chayefsky
Director of Photography: Owen Roizman
Production Design: Philip Rosenberg
Costumes: Theoni V. Aldredge
Editor: Alan Heim
Music: Elliot Lawrence
Sound: Jack Fitzstephens, Sanford Rackow, and Marc M. Laub
Cast: Faye Dunaway (Diana Christensen), William Holden (Max
Schumacher), Peter Finch (Howard Beale), Robert Duvall (Frank
Hackett), Wesley Addy (Nelson Chaney), Ned Beatty (Arthur Jensen),
Arthur Burghardt (Great Ahmed Khan), Kathy Cronkite (Mary Ann
Gifford), William Prince (Edward George Ruddy), Beatrice Straight
(Louise Schumacher), Marlene Warfield (Laurene Hobbs), Jerome
Dempsey (Walter C. Amundsen)
Color
121 minutes

1977
EQUUS
Producers: Lester Persky and Elliot Kastner
Director: **Sidney Lumet**
Screenplay: Peter Shaffer, from his play
Director of Photography: Oswald Morris
Production Design: Tony Walton
Art Direction: Simon Holland
Costumes: Tony Walton
Editor: John Victor-Smith
Music: Richard Rodney Bennett
Sound: Jimmy Sabat
Cast: Richard Burton (Dr. Martin Dysart), Peter Firth (Alan Strang), Colin
Blakely (Frank Strang), Joan Plowright (Dora Strang), Harry Andrews
(Harry Dalton), Eileen Atkins (Magistrate Hester Saloman), Jenny Agutter
(Jill Mason), John Wyman (the horseman), Kate Reid (Margaret Dysart)

Color
137 minutes

1978
THE WIZ
Director: **Sidney Lumet**
Producers: Rob Cohen, Kenneth Harper, Burtt Harris
Screenplay: Joel Schumacher, from the play by William F. Brown,
adapted from L. Frank Baum's novel, *The Wonderful Wizard of Oz*
Director of Photography: Oswald Morris
Production Design: Philip Rosenberg and Tony Walton
Art Direction: Philip Rosenberg
Set Decoration: Robert Drumheller and Edward Stewart
Costumes: Tony Walton and Miles White
Editor: Dede Allen
Music: Nick Ashford, Quincy Jones, Valerie Simpson, and Luther
Vandross
Supervising Sound Editor: Jack Fitzstephens
Cast: Diana Ross (Dorothy), Michael Jackson (Scarecrow), Nipsey Russell
(Tinman), Ted Ross (Lion), Mabel King (Evillene), Theresa Merritt (Aunt
Em), Thelma Carpenter (Miss One), Lena Horne (Glinda the Good),
Richard Pryor (The Wiz), Stanley Greene (Uncle Henry), Clyde J. Barrett
(subway peddler), Derrick Bell (The Four Crows), Roderick-Spencer
Sibert (The Four Crows), Kashka Banjoko (The Four Crows), Ronald
"Smokey" Stevens (The Four Crows)
Color
134 minutes

1980
JUST TELL ME WHAT YOU WANT
Producers: Burtt Harris, **Sidney Lumet**, and Jay Presson Allen
Director: **Sidney Lumet**
Screenplay: Jay Presson Allen, from her novel
Director of Photography: Oswald Morris
Production Design: Tony Walton
Art Direction: John Jay Moore
Costumes: Gloria Gresham and Tony Walton

Editor: Jack Fitzstephens
Music: Charles Strouse
Sound: Peter C. Frank
Cast: Ali MacGraw (Bones Burton), Alan King (Max Herschel),
Myrna Loy (Stella Liberti), Keenan Wynn (Seymour Berger), Tony
Roberts (Mike Berger), Peter Weller (Steven Routledge), Sara Truslow
(Cathy), Judy Kaye (Baby), Dina Merrill (Connie Herschel), Joseph
Maher (Dr. Coleson), John Walter Davis (Stan), Stanley Greene
(Bones's Lester)
Color
112 minutes

1981
PRINCE OF THE CITY
Producers: Burtt Harris, Jay Presson Allen, Raymond Hartwick
Director: **Sidney Lumet**
Screenplay: Jay Presson Allen and **Sidney Lumet**, from the book by
Robert Daley
Director of Photography: Andrzej Bartkowiak
Production Design: Tony Walton
Costumes: Anna Hill Johnstone
Editor: Jack Fitzstephens
Music: Paul Chihara
Sound: Peter C. Frank
Cast: Treat Williams (Daniel Ciello), Jerry Orbach (Gus Levy), Richard
Foronjy (Joe Marinaro), Don Billett (Bill Mayo), Kenny Marino (Dom
Bando), Carmine Caridi (Gino Mascone), Anthony Page (Raf Alvarez),
Norman Parker (Rick Cappalino), Paul Roebling (Brooks Paige), Bob
Balaban (Santimassino), James Tolkan (District Attorney Polito), Steve
Inwood (Mario Vincente), Lindsay Crouse (Carla Ciello), Tony Turco
(Socks Ciello), Ronald Maccone (Nick Napoli), Ron Karabatsos (Dave
DeBennedeto), Tony DiBenedetto (Carol Alagretti), Tony Munafo
(Rocky Gazzo), Robert Christian (The King), Lee Richardson (Sam
Heinsdorff), Lane Smith (Tug Barnes), Peter Michael Goetz (Attorney
Charles Deluth), Cynthia Nixon (Jeannie), Harry Madsen (Bubba Harris)
Color
167 minutes

1982
DEATHTRAP
Producers: Burtt Harris, Jay Presson Allen, Alfred De Liagre, Jr.
Director: **Sidney Lumet**
Screenplay: Jay Presson Allen, based on the play by Ira Levin
Director of Photography: Andrzej Bartkowiak
Production Design: Tony Walton
Art Direction: Edward Pisoni
Costumes: Tony Walton
Editor: Jack Fitzstephens
Music: Johnny Mandel
Sound: Al Nahmias, Rick Shaine, Jess Soraci
Cast: Michael Caine (Sidney Bruhl), Christopher Reeve (Clifford
Anderson), Dyan Cannon (Myra Bruhl), Irene Worth (Helga Ten Dorp),
Henry Jones (Porter Milgrim), Joe Silver (Seymour Starger), Tony
DeBenedetto (Burt, the bartender), Al LeBreton (handsome actor),
Stewart Klein (himself), Jeffrey Lyons (himself), Joel Siegel (himself),
Francis B. Creamer Jr. (the minister), Jenny Lumet (stage newsboy),
Jayne Heller (stage actress), George Peck (stage actor), Perry Rosen (stage
actor)
Color
116 minutes

1982
THE VERDICT
Producers: Burtt Harris, David Brown, and Richard D. Zanuck
Director: **Sidney Lumet**
Screenplay: David Mamet, from the novel by Barry Reed
Director of Photography: Andrzej Bartkowiak
Production Design: Edward Pisoni
Art Direction: John Kasarda
Costumes: Anna Hill Johnstone
Editor: Peter C. Frank
Music: Johnny Mandel
Sound: Louis Cerborino and Maurice Schell
Cast: Paul Newman (Frank Galvin), Charlotte Rampling (Laura Fischer),
Jack Warden (Mickey Morrissey), James Mason (Edward J. Concannon),

Milo O'Shea (Judge Hoyle), Lindsay Crouse (Kaitlin Costello), Ed Binns (Bishop Brophy), Julie Bovasso (Maureen Rooney), Roxanne Hart (Sally Doneghy), James Handy (Kevin Doneghy), Wesley Addy (Dr. Robert Towler), Joe Seneca (Dr. Lionel Thompson), Lewis J. Stadlen (Dr. David Gruber), Kent Broadhurst (Joseph Alito), Colin Stinton (Billy), Burtt Harris (Jimmy, the bartender)
Color
129 minutes

1983
DANIEL
Producers: E. L. Doctorow, **Sidney Lumet**, Burtt Harris
Director: **Sidney Lumet**
Screenplay: E. L. Doctorow, from his novel *The Book of Daniel*
Director of Photography: Andrzej Bartkowiak
Production Design: Philip Rosenberg
Costumes: Anna Hill Johnstone
Editor: Peter C. Frank
Music: Bob James
Sound: Peter Odabashian and Maurice Schell
Cast: Timothy Hutton (Daniel Isaacson), Mandy Patinkin (Paul Isaacson), Lindsay Crouse (Rochelle Isaacson), Edward Asner (Jacob Ascher), Ellen Barkin (Phyllis Isaacson), Amanda Plummer (Susan Isaacson), John Rubinstein (Robert Lewin), Maria Tucci (Lise Lewin), Julie Bovasso (Frieda Stein), Tovah Feldshuh (Linda Mindish), Joseph Leon (Selig Mindish), Carmen Matthews (Mrs. Ascher), Rita Zohar (Grandmother), Ilan Mitchell-Smith (Young Daniel), Jena Grecco (Young Susan), Dael Cohen (Daniel as a little boy), Colin Stinton (Dale), Isaac Patinkin (Infant Daniel), Joyce R. Korbin (Sadie Mindish)
Color
130 minutes

1984
GARBO TALKS
Producers: Burtt Harris and Elliot Kastner
Director: **Sidney Lumet**

Screenplay: Larry Grusin
Director of Photography: Andrzej Bartkowiak
Production Design: Philip Rosenberg
Costumes: Anna Hill Johnstone
Editor: Andrew Mondshein
Music: Cy Coleman
Sound: Harry Peck Bolles
Cast: Anne Bancroft (Estelle Rolfe), Ron Silver (Gilbert Rolfe), Carrie
Fisher (Lisa Rolfe), Catherine Hicks (Jane Mortimer), Steven Hill (Walter
Rolfe), Howard Da Silva (Angelo Dokakis), Dorothy Loudon (Sonya
Apollinar), Harvey Fierstein (Bernie Whitlock), Hermione Gingold
(Elizabeth Rennick), Richard B. Shull (Shepard Plotkin)
Color
103 minutes

1986
POWER
Producers: Reene Schisgal and Mark Tarlov
Director: **Sidney Lumet**
Screenplay: David Himmelstein
Director of Photography: Andrzej Bartkowiak
Production Design: Peter S. Larkin
Art Direction: William Barclay
Costumes: Anna Hill Johnstone
Editor: Andrew Mondshein
Music: Cy Coleman
Sound: Louis Cerborino
Cast: Richard Gere (Pete St. John), Julie Christie (Ellen Freeman),
Gene Hackman (Wilfred Buckley), Kate Capshaw (Sydnet Betterman),
Denzel Washington (Arnold Billings), E. G. Marshall (Sen. Sam
Hastings), Beatrice Straight (Claire Hastings), Fritz Weaver (Wallace
Furman), Michael Learned (Washington Governor Andrew Stannard),
J. T. Walsh (Jerome Cade), E. Katherine Kerr (Irene Furman), Polly Rowles
(Lucille DeWitt), Matt Salinger (Phillip Aarons), Tom Mardirosian
(Sheikh)
Color
110 minutes

1986
THE MORNING AFTER
Producers: Bruce Gilbert and Faye Schwab
Director: **Sidney Lumet**
Screenplay: James Hicks and David Rayfiel (uncredited)
Director of Photography: Andrzej Bartkowiak
Production Design: Albert Brenner
Art Direction: Kandy Stern
Costumes: Ann Roth
Editor: Joel Goodman
Music: Paul Chihara
Sound: Maurice Schell
Cast: Jane Fonda (Alex Sternbergen), Jeff Bridges (Turner Kendall), Raul
Julia (Joaquin Manero), Diane Salinger (Isabel Harding), Geoffrey Scott
(Bobby Korshack), Richard Foronjy (Sergeant Greenbaum), James
"Gypsy" Haake (Frankie), Kathleen Wilhoite (Red), Don Hood (Hurley),
Kathy Bates (woman on Mateo Street)
Color
103 minutes

1988
RUNNING ON EMPTY
Producers: Naomi Foner, Burtt Harris, Griffin Dunne, and Amy
Robinson
Director: **Sidney Lumet**
Screenplay: Naomi Foner
Director of Photography: Gerry Fisher
Production Design: Philip Rosenberg
Art Direction: Robert Guerra
Costumes: Anna Hill Johnstone
Editor: Andrew Mondshein
Music: Tony Mottola
Sound: James Sabat and Tom Fleischman
Cast: Christine Lahti (Annie Pope), River Phoenix (Danny Pope), Judd
Hirsch (Arthur Pope), Jonas Abry (Harry Pope), Martha Plimpton (Lorna
Phillips), Ed Crowley (Mr. Phillips), L. M. Kit Carson (Gus Winant),
Steven Hill (Donald Patterson), Augusta Dabney (Abigail Patterson),

David Margulies (Dr. Jonah Reiff), Marcia Jean Kurtz (school clerk),
Jenny Lumet (music girl)
Color
111 minutes

1989
FAMILY BUSINESS
Producers: Burtt Harris, Jennifer Ogden, and Lawrence Gordon
Director: **Sidney Lumet**
Screenplay: Vincent Patrick, from his novel
Director of Photography: Andrzej Bartkowiak
Production Design: Philip Rosenberg
Art Direction: Robert Guerra
Costumes: Ann Roth
Editor: Andrew Mondshein
Music: Cy Coleman
Sound: Maurice Schell
Cast: Sean Connery (Jessie McMullen), Dustin Hoffman (Vita
McMullen), Matthew Broderick (Adam McMullen), Rosanna DeSoto
(Elaine), Janet Carroll (Margie, waitress at Doheny's), Victoria Jackson
(Christine), Bill McCutcheon (Danny Doheny), Deborah Rush (Michele
Dempsey), Marilyn Cooper (Rose Gruden), Salem Ludwig (Nat Gruden),
Rex Everhart (Ray Garvey), Luis Guzmán (Julio Torres)
Color
110 minutes

1990
Q & A
Producers: Burtt Harris, Patrick Wachsberger, and Arnon Milchan
Director: **Sidney Lumet**
Screenplay: **Sidney Lumet**, from the book by Edwin Torres
Director of Photography: Andrzej Bartkowiak
Production Design: Philip Rosenberg
Art Direction: Beth Kuhn
Costumes: Ann Roth and Neil Spisak
Editor: Richard P. Cirincione
Music: Rubén Blades and Jay Livingston

Sound: Maurice Schell
Cast: Nick Nolte (Detective Lieutenant Mike Brennan), Timothy Hutton (Asst. District Attorney Al Reilly), Armand Assante (Bobby Texador), Patrick O'Neal (Kevin Quinn), Lee Richardson (Leo Bloomenfeld), Luis Guzmán (Detective Luis Valentin), Charles Dutton (Homocide Detective Sam Chapman), Jenny Lumet (Nancy Bosch/Mrs. Bobby Texador), Paul Calderon (Roger Montalvo), International Chrysis (Jose Malpica), Dominic Chianese (Larry Pesch aka Vito Francone), Leonardo Cimino (Nick Petrone), Maurice Schell (Detective Zucker), Burtt Harris (Phil)
Color
137 minutes

1992
A STRANGER AMONG US
Producers: Steve Golin, Sandy Golin, Carol Baum, Howard Rosenman, Sigurjon Sighvatsson, Robert J. Avrech, Susan Tarr, Burtt Harris, and Lilith Jacobs
Director: **Sidney Lumet**
Screenplay: Robert J. Avrech
Director of Photography: Andrzej Bartkowiak
Production Design: Philip Rosenberg
Art Direction: W. Steven Graham
Costumes: Ann Roth and Gary Jones
Editor: Andrew Mondshein
Music: Jerry Bock
Sound: Richard Cirincione, Maurice Schell
Cast: Melanie Griffith (Emily Eden), Eric Thal (Ariel), John Pankow (Levine), Tracy Pollan (Mara), Lee Richardson (Rebbe), Mia Sara (Leah), Jamey Sheridan (Nick), Jake Weber (Yaakov), David Rosenbaum (Mr. Klausman), Ruth Vool (Mrs. Klausman), David Margulies (Lt. Oliver), Maurice Schell (Detective Marden), Edward Rogers III (Detective Tedford), James Gandolfini (Tony Baldessari), Burtt Harris (Emily's father), Ira Rubin (French Rebbe), Françoise Granville (French Rebbetzen), Rene Sofer (Shayna)
Color
110 minutes

1993
GUILTY AS SIN
Producers: Don Carmody, Bob Robinson, Martin Ransohoff, Lilith
Jacobs, and Jolene Moroney
Director: **Sidney Lumet**
Screenplay: Larry Cohen
Director of Photography: Andrzej Bartkowiak
Production Design: Philip Rosenberg
Costumes: Gary Jones
Editor: Evan A. Lottman
Music: Howard Shore
Sound: Ron Bochar
Cast: Rebecca De Mornay (Jennifer Haines), Don Johnson (David
Greenhill, aka Edgar Greenhill), Stephen Lang (Phil Garson), Jack
Warden (Moe), Dana Ivey (Judge Tompkins), Ron White (Diangelo),
Norma Dell'Agnese (Emily), Sean McCann (Nolan), Luis Guzmán (Lt.
Martinez), Robert Kennedy (Caniff), Christina Baren (Miriam Langford),
James Blendick (McMartin), Tom Butler (Heath), Lynn Cormack (Esther
Rothman)
Color
107 minutes

1997
NIGHT FALLS ON MANHATTAN
Producers: Josh Kramer, Thom Mount, and John H. Starke
Director: **Sidney Lumet**
Screenplay: **Sidney Lumet**, from Robert Daley's novel, *Tainted Evidence*
Director of Photography: David Watkin
Production Design: Philip Rosenberg
Art Direction: Robert Guerra
Costumes: Joseph G. Aulisi
Editor: Sam O'Steen
Music: Mark Isham
Sound: Ron Bachar
Cast: Andy Garcia (Sean Casey), Ian Holm (Liam Casey), James
Gandolfini (Joey Allegretto), Lena Olin (Peggy Lindstrom), Shiek
Mahmud-Bey (Jordan Washington), Colm Feore (Harrison), Ron

Liebman (Morganstern), Richard Dreyfuss (Sam Vigoda), Dominic
Chianese (Judge Impelliteri), Paul Guilfoyle (McGovern), Bonnie Rose
(instructor), Norman Matlock (detective), Sidney Armus (judge), Marcia
Jean Kurtz (Eileen), Bobby Cannavale (Vigoda assistant #1)
Color
118 minutes

1997
CRITICAL CARE
Producers: Don Carmody, **Sidney Lumet**, and Steven Schwartz
Director: **Sidney Lumet**
Screenplay: Steven Schwartz, from the novel by Richard Dooling
Director of Photography: David Watkin
Production Design: Philip Rosenberg
Art Direction: Dennis Davenport
Costumes: Dona Granata
Editor: Tom Swartwout
Music: Michael Convertino (uncredited)
Sound: Fred Rosenberg
Cast: James Spader (Dr. Werner Ernst), Kyra Sedgwick (Felicia Potter),
Helen Mirren (Stella), Anne Bancroft (Nun), Albert Brooks (Dr. Butz),
Jeffrey Wright (Bed Two), Margo Martindale (Constance "Connie"
Potter), Wallace Shawn (furnace man), Philip Bosco (Dr. Hofstader),
Colm Feore (Richard Wilson), Edward Herrmann (Robert Payne), James
Lally (Poindexter), Harvey Atkin (Judge Fatale), Al Waxman (Sheldon
Hatchett), Hamish McEwan (Dr. Hansen), Jackie Richardson
(Mrs. Steckler)
Color
107 minutes

1999
GLORIA
Producers: Chuck Binder, G. Mac Brown, Gary Foster, Lee Rich,
Josie Rosen
Director: **Sidney Lumet**
Screenplay: Steven Antin, from John Cassavetes's 1980 screenplay
Director of Photography: David Watkin

Production Design: Mel Bourne
Art Direction: Carols A. Menéndez
Costumes: Dona Granata and Judianna Makovsky
Editor: Tom Swartwout
Music: Howard Shore
Sound: Bob Chefalas and Philip Stockton
Cast: Sharon Stone (Gloria), Jean-Luke Figueroa (Nicky Nuñez), Jeremy Northam (Kevin), Cathy Moriatry (Diane), George C. Scott (Ruby), Mike Starr (Sean), Bonnie Bedelia (Brenda), Barry McEvoy (Terry), Don Billett (Raymond), Jerry Dean (Mickey), Tony DiBenedetto (Zach), Teddy Atlas (Ian), Bobby Cannavale (Jack Jesus Nunez), Sarita Choudhury (Angela), Miriam Colon (Maria), Desiree Casado (Luz)
Color
108 minutes

2005
FIND ME GUILTY
Producers: Oliver Hengst, Bob Yari, Bob DeBrino, Vin Diesel, Robert Greenhut, **Sidney Lumet**, T. J. Mancini, George Zakk
Director: **Sidney Lumet**
Screenplay: T. J. Mancini, Robert McCrea
Production Design: Christopher Nowak
Art Direction: Emily Beck
Editor: Tom Swartwout
Sound: Coll Anderson
Cast: Vin Diesel (Jack DiNorscio), Frank Pietrangolaare (Carlo Mascarpone), Rose Pasquale (Carlo's Wife), Paul Borghese (Gino Mascarpone), Michalina Almindo (Gino's Girlfriend), James Biberi (Frank Brentano), Vinny DeGennaro (Danny Roma), Peter Dinklage (Ben Klandis), John Louis Fischer (D.E.A. Agent), Jerry Grayson (Jimmy Katz), Ben Lipitz (Henry Kelsey), Domenick Lombardozzi (Jerry McQueen), Richard Portnow (Max Novardis), Alex Rocco (Nick Calabrese)
Color

SIDNEY LUMET

INTERVIEWS

An Interview with Sidney Lumet

PETER BOGDANOVICH/1960

Lumet was a child actor on Broadway, appearing in such plays as
My Heart's in the Highlands, Dead End, *and* The Eternal Road.

After the Army, he did some off-Broadway directing, then in
1950 moved to television, where he has directed hundreds of shows,
including such two-part "spectaculars" as All the King's Men *and*
The Sacco-Vanzetti Case. *On the New York stage he has directed*
Shaw's The Doctor's Dilemma, *Arch Oboler's* Night of the Auk,
and Camus's Caligula. *His four films, which have all been made*
on the East Coast, are 12 Angry Men *(1957),* Stage Struck
(1958), That Kind of Woman *(1959), and* The Fugitive Kind
(1960).

Lumet is one of a group of young directors trained in television
and stage work (Mann and Ritt are two others) who have been
looked upon as likely to bring a new directness and sophistication
to film. While the contributions of these men have not measured up
to early expectations, their attitude toward film remains an interest-
ing one. The following interview has been somewhat abridged for
publication.

PB: *Could you say something about the problems of making* Fugitive Kind?
SL: They were always the original ones that came up in rehearsal or in
the initial discussion of the script which we were all aware of—Tennessee

---

From *Film Quarterly*. Winter 1960: 18–23. Copyright © 1960 by the Regents of the
University of California. Reprinted by permission of *Film Quarterly*.

[Williams], Anna [Magnani], myself, Marlon [Brando]—which was that the boy's character disappeared over the last half of the picture. This was true of the play [*Orpheus Descending*] as well. And constantly the problem was how to activate him, how to make him a driving force in the picture, because it is *Orpheus* descending, and it's very hard to do *Orpheus Descending* without Orpheus.

PB: *Wasn't there anything Williams could do about that?*
SL: He wanted to. His problem was that he started off wanting a play about Orpheus, and dramatically it's always a fuller thing for him to write a woman protagonist—his great parts have been women's parts. Whatever solutions I'd come up with would not work for Tennessee, and you can't force a situation, you know, it has to fit organ-ically into what he had in mind and into what flows easily for him to write. And that we never found, and to me it's the failing of the picture. I love the picture; I think it's got some remarkable things in it and some of his most beautiful writing. And thematically it's, to me, the finest of his pieces—thematically. I'm not talking about the dramatic completion of it.

PB: *Do you rehearse extensively before you start shooting?*
SL: Yes, I like to rehearse a minimum of two weeks before I shoot. Now that was another problem—Anna has never rehearsed; she's never done a play. I like to stage it before I start shooting, and it was physi-cally impossible for her to work with a table that was supposed to be a counter, with two chairs supposed to be a door—she literally could not visualize a set. The sheer theatrical process is an alien one to her, so as a result some of the subsequent problems that came up normally would have come up in rehearsal.

PB: *You have directed extensively on television; what are the biggest differences you found between directing for films and television?*
SL: Scale. It's the difference between working on a 21-inch canvas and a 75-foot canvas, and that's a tremendous difference. That doesn't mean that there aren't things that can work in both—there's a certain level of drama that works in everything—but directorially it's a shift in the eye; it's a shift in the instruments, the tools that you use to focus dramatic attention and so on. And it's also a difference internally—for

instance, I've seen some Shakespeare on TV and it's been disastrous. I wonder if the sheer physical size of the screen isn't something that automatically rules out tragedy, for example. In other words, maybe TV is irrevocably stuck with drama, melodrama—one may never be able to do genuine tragedy on TV.

PB: *Then you must be against the showing of movies on television.*

SL: Yeah, it's incredible. It's one of the reasons I don't think pay-TV is going to be the panacea that the Hollywood people think it's going to be. Take a picture like *Red River*—now, I know, nonsense story-line—it's a superb film. Cinematically it's an extraordinary piece of work. And what [Howard] Hawks did in terms of the reality of a cattle drive, it's, to me, on the level with what [John] Ford did with *Stagecoach*. But you see it on television and it's just shots of cows going by—it's pointless, it's meaningless, it seems as if it's overlong, its majesty is lost.

PB: *Now what are the differences you found in directing for the stage and movies?*

SL: To begin with, they're even farther apart than television and motion pictures. To me, far more things can be interchanged between television and motion pictures than between theater and motion pictures. The theater, for all its attempts at realism for the past thirty years, is a totally unreal medium—its essence is really poetic rather than literal. The screen *can* become poetic but, God knows, the majority of the good work has been devoted to literal and realistic, representational art. So it's an enormous difference—the difference between poetry and prose.

PB: *What have you found to be your main obstacle in film work?*

SL: For myself the main obstacle is the set-up, the film in America. The financial set-up, the method of making motion pictures, and the method of distribution is one that *conspires* to defeat freedom and good work. And I suppose it's the age-old complaint, there's no solution that I know of. I know every once in a while somebody just takes a camera and goes off into the street, but what if you had a piece that doesn't belong in the street? What if your piece needs a sumptuousness and a sensuousness as part of its dramatic meaning? And, you know, documentaries and semi-documentaries are not the only method of work in film. And as soon as you get past that level, financially you're caught in a miserable situation. *12 Angry Men* cost $343,000, which is ridiculously cheap, but that's a rarity; it had one set, twelve actors, and a very tight shooting schedule of twenty days.

PB: *Many fine directors—Huston, Wilder, Bergman, Welles, Kubrick—either write their own screenplays or collaborate extensively with others on scripts. To date you haven't done either; do you think you'd find it more satisfying to work on scripts rather than just do the best you can with material you are given?*

SL: It's not "either/or." I *can't* write. And I have such respect for writers—I don't understand how two writers collaborate, for instance—so that the method for myself is one simply of letting them do their work, then going *back* into work in terms of whatever specifics are needed, whether it's structural or dialogue. On *Fugitive Kind*, for instance, there was a good deal of re-writing between the original draft and what wound up on the screen.

PB: *Did you have a say in that?*

SL: Oh, yeah. And the working procedure was that Tennessee and Meade [Roberts] brought in the first draft, then all of us together talk, talk, talk, talk, talk—back, another draft, talk, talk, talk, talk, talk—back, another draft—I think it was the fourth draft we used.

PB: *Boris Kaufman was your photographer on every film except* Stage Struck; *how large do you feel is his contribution when an evaluation of the final work is made?*

SL: Well, Boris is a rarity, because there are loads of brilliant technical people—and he *is* brilliant technically—but his real artistry comes through in the fact that I don't know of another cameraman who has the sense of dramatic interpretation that Boris has. When Boris and I have worked together there's never been any instance where we haven't done something outrageously new—though they don't jump out at you in the films, thank God. The camera becomes *another* leading actor. There are two basic philosophies—and traps—that I think directors fall into: one of well-just-let-me-lay-back-and-just-show-what's-going-on, just-let-me-*record*-it, or the converse, the shooting-through-the-crotch,

and gimme-that-eyeball-being-in-the-front school. They are both falla-
cious because the camera—like everything else in a piece—has to relate
to what's going on dramatically. You have to cast your camera the way
you cast an actor.

PB: *Many critics either eulogize the death of Hollywood or constantly refer*
to the great dearth of talent out there. What do you think are the reasons for
the cultural desert on the West Coast?
SL: This is gonna sound spooky—I think it goes back much farther
than Hollywood. That place has no reason for being. It seems to me—as
far as I know—I'm not the most erudite person in the world—but all
the great centers of art have been centers of *other* things. They've either
been a geographical center of the country or they've been a seaport—
whether it's been Venice, Florence, Rome, London, Paris, New York,
Berlin—they've had other functions; the life of the place has been connected to the main stream of life of that nation, of those people, and
art came as a flower of that. Now, Los Angeles [laugh], I'm sorry, it's not
a seaport, it's lousy land for farming, it's got no reason for being. Right
now it's got aircraft factories, and maybe in five hundred years aircraft
factories'll be a reason for having a city. But up till now there hasn't
been. It seems to me that it's extremely difficult for any creative work to
latch itself on to an unorganic place. I think it's interesting that San
Francisco's always had the artistic excitement—certainly in terms of
literature and painting—Los Angeles never.

PB: *They're isolated in Hollywood, in other words.*
SL: Yeah, I feel that in order to get some sunlight they went to a completely dead spot. And it's interesting because all the directors that I
respect have gotten away from there as fast as they could. Zinnemann
hasn't made a picture in Hollywood I don't think in five years, Gadge
[Elia Kazan] hasn't made a picture in Hollywood in seven years.
[George] Stevens has, and I think it's showing in the work.

PB: *How would you explain then the great films that have been made in*
Hollywood, say in the twenties and thirties?
SL: When you hire the most talented people alive—literally—
assembled from all over the world, to work there, of course you're

gonna have some good ones. And also good work is possible *any* place.
I don't mean that Hollywood kills work; I just think it makes it tougher
to do good work.

PB: *Now that the autocracy of the major studios is over, do you think the*
independents have raised the level of films in America?
SL: No, because basically they're the same guys who just didn't have a
chance when the studios were tight and strong. With all due respect
and affection for United Artists, they're not risking a bloody thing; you
still come into UA with a star versus a budget. And it is basically the
same procedure at Metro. [Sam] Spiegel every once in a while—because
he'll produce a winner like *River Kwai*—is allowed to try something off-
beat. But he knows full well that he has to keep returning financial win-
ners. I know I'm very pressured by this. I hope *Fugitive Kind* makes a lot
of money because none of my pictures have made a lot of money and
I *need* one. I know my employment will be directly affected by it. So it
isn't really independent production—nobody gets together and says,
"Hey, let's make a movie about . . ." What's basically happened, I feel, is
that because of financial reasons the actors have begun to dominate the
market completely, and that's a good move only because as long as it's a
roulette game I'd just as soon see the people who are actually spinning
the wheel get the largest share of the dough. I don't think it's accomplished anything creatively. I think most of the actors who kept saying,
"Oh, God, if I ever have my own independent company, boy, will I do
good stuff . . ." have turned out the same crap that Louis B. Mayer used
to do—only not as well.

PB: *Do you think there is a cinematic movement in America coming to com-*
pete with the French "New Wave"?
SL: No, I don't. I hate to be pessimistic, I don't at all. Reggie Rose and
I've been trying for a year and a half to get done a piece that he wrote, a
brilliant piece called *Black Monday*, which is the story of a Southern
town on the first day of integration of schools. And we're just not
gonna get it done, it's that simple. Out of the very nature of the subject
matter, it's gotta be big. The financial problem is getting extremely
severe now in terms of getting money to do a picture. I think, by the
way, that in five years it's going to be absolutely marvelous, because

we're going to have financing the way plays are financed: a bunch of people get together, put up money, and you rise or fall with the quality of the piece.

PB: *What do you think are the advantages or disadvantages of wide screen, Cinemascope, stereophonic sound, and the like?*
SL: I think they're ridiculous, I think they're pointless, I think they're typical Hollywood products. And typical Hollywood mentality, because the essence of *any* dramatic piece is people, and it is symptomatic that Hollywood finds a way of photographing people directly opposite to the way people are built. Cinemascope makes no sense until people are fatter than they are taller.

PB: *Why then do serious directors like Kazan or Stevens choose to work in Cinemascope?*
SL: They don't choose; there's no choice. When Stevens does a picture for 20th Century-Fox he *has* to shoot in Cinemascope. On *Anne Frank*, he fought for six months trying not to shoot it in Cinemascope and then had to. Spent all his time with the art director trying to figure out beams and girders to cut down the sides of the screen, and how to isolate what he wanted.

PB: *What filmmakers, if any, have most influenced your work in movies?*
SL: I don't think any. I have great respect for about, I guess, seven or eight directors—Jean Vigo, Carl Dreyer, René Clair, De Sica, Wyler, Zinnemann.

PB: *Having been an actor, what do you think a stage performer finds most difficult in adjusting to pictures?*
SL: Probably the toughest problem is for him to keep a knowledge of the point of development or the point of transition that his character is at because of the out-of-sequence problem and the working in small sections. So that the growth, the tiny motivating rivulets that go into the big stream of the entire character, tend to get lost and he tends to become general and act attitudes, because his concentration is scattered and he doesn't quite know where he's at. It's one of the reasons I like the rehearsal procedure so, because it gives him a very clear idea of the

sweep of the man. On every picture except *Fugitive Kind* the last four days of rehearsal were run-throughs just like a play or a television show.

PB: *Do you think the recent loosening of the Production Code has really helped Hollywood films toward attaining greater maturity?*
SL: Oh, no, they're just exploiting it for box office. William Wyler's films have always been mature whether he could say "bastard" on the screen or not. You know, it's like Cinemascope. They're using it so that they can start putting on the screen some of the things they've got in the ads.

PB: *Almost every director is occasionally exposed to withering critiques of his work, and it would be interesting to know what a director would answer, what he thinks when he reads such a notice.*
SL: There's just nothing you can do because you're talking from such completely different frames of reference, you know, you just gotta let it go. And some of the greatest significances as well as some of the greatest attacks are attributed to complete accidents. On *All the King's Men* I read a review which loved the show and which called me a genius because in the first scene when Willie Stark was on his way up, talking *to* the people, I'd shot reactions of the crowd in the stand, the wildness of the faces and so on—and then in the second part, which came on a week later, when he'd been in power for six years, he was making an outdoor address and I played it in the rain with umbrellas—visually it was quite exciting—and how wasn't this marvelous that on his way up he was related to the people and looking them in the eye, and here he was now like standing over their graves and they're covered with umbrellas. The reason for it was very simple—I used up all the money for extras on the first show and on the second show I needed a crowd of fifty and I could only afford twenty people so I gave them umbrellas which spread everybody out [laugh]. So, go figure.

PB: *Complete freedom granted, would you rather work in films, television, or the theater?*
SL: I never want to give up any one of them. I guess I'd spend the majority of time in the movies simply because it takes the longest. I mean, to me the ideal set-up would be a picture a year, a play a year,

and about three months of television a year—because each one gives you such a shaking-up for the other, they all help one another *because* the problems are so totally different.

PB: *Joseph Mankiewicz has been quoted as saying that he fails to see any basic difference between the theater and the movies; what would you say to that?*
SL: Well, I don't agree. He should do a play again and see.

PB: *What do you think leads a director to say a thing like that?*
SL: I haven't the remotest idea. People say strange things in interviews, myself included. I'm always horrified by them when I read them back.

Keep Them on the Hook

FILMS AND FILMING/1964

THE BASIC LINE taken in *The Pawnbroker* is that regardless of how brutal life is one must go on. Everyone has rights: you have a right to kill yourself if you want to, but as long as you can stay alive you cannot exist in a half world as the central character in our film tries to. He is Sol Nazerman, a Jewish pawnbroker who lives in Harlem amongst what he considers as the lowest form of life, despising all around him; seemingly emotionless he has almost cut himself off from life, while trying to blot from his mind the memory of his past—his happy marriage, his children, and the loss of both in a Nazi concentration camp.

The thing that I am happy about with this film is that it is a real breaking of the conventional hero idea; the man is an absolute bastard, the people around him are in general totally unpleasant, there is no sentimentalizing about Jews or Negroes (no sweet white man helps a Negro medical student into medical college because he thinks the Negro is bright and has a chance). The Negroes are shown for whatever they happen to be; if they are pimps and whores then that is how they are shown.

There is no easy way out in the film for an audience; Sol has nothing to redeem him. The total intent is to make you take him on the human level for whatever he is. People have told me, "You can't keep that music at the end because it is so loud." I know what they are complaining about, but it was a deliberate intent on the part of the composer (Quincy Jones) and myself. I don't want anybody to cry; I don't want that kind of sentimentality on it. The kind of insane joy that starts with

---

From *Films and Filming.* October 1964: 17–20. Adapted from a tape-recorded interview.

the music at the end with its wildness, is joy in the sense that Sol's alive again . . . and in my eyes it's a happy ending! We worked very hard and specifically with that final result, so as not to give the audience the conventional catharsis, not to let them off the hook in the sense of "Have a good weep . . . but now let's go and have a cup of coffee fellows." I think the picture stays with you much longer because of the ending.

The Pawnbroker is the first time that there has really been a Negro "heavy" in a film: everybody has been so self-conscious about their relationships with Negroes in American films, and I daresay the same is true of British films. It is usually "the marvellous colored man." He's so noble, always perfect . . . that's basically as chauvinistic as the way they used to play him in the thirties. It has to be moved onto the level where they are shown as whatever the dramatic situation dictates. Some of the biggest attacks on the picture I feel are going to come from the so-called liberal press because they will be so shocked—"Look at this portrait of the Negro race! They're not all good."

The only area of social significance in terms of the American situation specifically (there certainly was no attempt to show Harlem as a modern concentration camp—it's quite the reverse, Harlem in the film is meant to have an enormous life about it with all its sadness) is that I wanted the corruption, and this isn't just for America, basically white. There is a specific attack in the uniformity of the white world, and the Negro (Brock Peters) who runs the whore house has everything white about him: his house is white, his telephone is white, his boy friend is white. He's one of the Negroes who wants to live in the white world and has made it!

Sol has buried himself in this area because he needs to be with people that he can despise, to be among people that make the contempt easy for him because he is not even strong enough to have the energy of a good healthy hate. Life, Harlem, with its total catastrophic future with the no-future of it, that brutal horrible way of living, has actually more life in it than Sol could ever have imagined. This is represented in the youth he has as an assistant, Jesus: in the most degrading human circumstances this little flower grows (he's a hell of a flower . . . he's been a dope pusher, a thief and lives off a whore—but he is charming, alive, there's life in him). And it is as if Sol buried himself in a graveyard and suddenly the graveyard livens up and kicks him out.

The author of the novel, Edward Lewis Wallant, was a brilliant talent—he died in 1962 at the age of thirty-six, an enormous loss because something very great was going to come from him. His uncle ran a pawnshop and the area of involvement for Wallant himself was interesting on just a religious level, which is true of a great many young Americans today. It's an extraordinary kind of religion because it is not intellectual at all and is based on a literal translation of the Bible. You find it amongst nearly all the young Negroes in the south and it manifests itself completely in political—not religious—activity. Wallant, being involved in Negro life, made the point of departure in the book religious. But this we changed, it's the only area of intentional change I made. The book originally takes place over Easter, and Wallant really treated it as a story of a resurrection. But I felt that to do this in the film would be a pretension, partially because I was working on it . . . I didn't feel it was pretension on Wallant's part because that is the way he felt; but not having that kind of stimulation myself I knew that if I used it this would wind up as a pretension because it is not part of me.

Unfortunately, I had come into the project rather late, in fact only two weeks before it was due to shoot. It had originally been offered to me by the two men who produced it, Roger Lewis and Philip Langner, who at the time had a deal with Metro. Metro had wanted to do it as an Eady plan picture, with a script where it all took place in Soho, to be shot in England! It was ridiculous. I had read the book before, loved Wallant's work, and was furious at the kind of treatment it had been given, so turned it down. Then the producers took the property to Ely Landau (at the time I was doing *Fail-Safe*) and another director was assigned, another script was written, with the setting moved back to New York. Then literally two weeks before shooting the other director had to leave because he was physically ill. So I came in two weeks before the film was due to be shot.

The only actor who had been set up to them was Rod Steiger as Sol. I cast everyone else and found the location in just two weeks . . . thankfully it is an area I know. When you go for unnatural-naturalism, as I have in the film, it is very important when casting to get artists most people don't know about. So the problem was to find people who had not worked that much, and in fact for about twenty of the people it is their first film, like Jaime Sanchez who plays Jesus Ortiz.

The technique we used for showing the intrusion into Sol's memory of the horrors of the concentration camp he was in, the way he lost his family and his hopes, is based on quick shock cuts. For me it works marvelously—it is not used as a technique just for the sake of itself. I began with the basis that for Sol the past is not past, it is much more present than what is going on at the moment around him. This is a man who is in such agony that he must feel nothing or he will go to pieces. Then, knowing the way my own memory works, when it is something that I do not want to remember I will fight it and fight it; but it keeps intruding itself in larger and larger bursts, and if it is important enough, it finally breaks through and takes over completely and then recedes in the same way. These sequences are laid out using one frame, two frame, three frame cuts of increasing rapidity, finally up to six frame cuts and then eventually into a sequence.

The old idea was that it took three frames for an image to register on the eye, that the eye could not retain an image for less than three frames. So the first time we used this quick cutting device was when it was a question of taking an idea and moving it from an intellectualization to a good technique, to make it something that will work for an audience. In the first sequence the cuts are not nearly as short as later, they are six frames because I knew that the first time I used it the shock to an audience would be enormous anyway, and clarity was the important thing; the following time I used four then two frames, and by the third sequence I was using just two and one frame cuts . . . and you *see* it, which shows that the eye can absorb this if it is led into it gently enough.

The most interesting thing was that finally I was using this technique in a completely natural sequence, in the scene between Sol and the Negro (Brock Peters), where Sol discovers the latter runs a whore house. At the end of this Sol is weeping and the Negro leans over to him with his "Yes . . . Yes . . . ," and we used just two frames on Brock and you'd swear it is a normal cut because you have become orientated to it by then.

We did a lot of this kind of insane cutting in the early days in TV, when often television technique was far in advance of movies. I'm always amused by avant-garde critics who'll probably sit down and say about this film, "Well the two frame cut came from *Last Year in Marienbad*, and this came from . . ." which is nonsense. There's one general premise: almost anything that any of us has done you can find in a John Ford film.

But in the early television days we were doing cuts as fast as a finger could move. John Frankenheimer, who was my AD, can bear me out: there was one sequence on a live show where John had sixty-four cues to give in a one-minute period. John had three cues for each camera cut, which is just about as fast as a switcher's fingers can move. So I think the main thing that a lot of us had to offer film when we came in was, "Why have you always done it this way; why don't you try new ways." Generally the kind of liberating force came from our own ignorance in photographic techniques—we found equivalents for them and these we moved over into motion pictures with an eye on the change in scale we were working on.

The Insider: Sidney Lumet Talks about His Work in Films

ROBIN BEAN/1965

THERE WAS A TIME WHEN the film industry regarded television as some giant preying mantis about to liquidate the cinema's audiences. Now, a little late perhaps, it has come to accept the fact that it
can live pretty peacefully with it while of course producing a good deal
of the filmed programmes for television. The major film producing
companies went in for television series in a big way—Warners, 20th
Century–Fox, MGM (which recently announced an extension to its studio,
presumably to take in more TV films), and Columbia (its television side,
Screen Gems, makes more money now for the studio than its theatrical
films). Maybe it is because of this expanding studio interest in TV that
the quality of television films has now deteriorated to the level of some
of the old movies that are dug up on Sundays which preferably should
have been left to rest where they were: forgotten, and rightly so. One
can't think of a worse advertisement to lure people back into cinemas
than much of this tripe. Television hasn't gained much from the movies,
but on the other hand the cinema, particularly that in America, has
gained an enormous new impetus from television . . . not from filmed
television but from the live shows which unfortunately have now
almost become extinct.

During the mid and late fifties, television in America was going
through an extraordinarily interesting period. *Danger, Play of the Week,
Playhouse* 90 and so on were to provide a thorough and rigorous training ground for a group of young directors, who were later to inject into

From *Films and Filming*. June 1965: 9–13.

American cinema a revitalizing force which has been far more effective in creative and visual terms than the more highly publicized *nouvelle vague, cinema véritè*, neo-realism or neo-boredom. In live television the director not only had to be good with actors or know how to handle his camera; he had to be technician and editor as well, to be able to improvise, adapt with split second thinking. He learnt by experiment; there were no rules as to what you could or could not do as there were in filmmaking at the time. He had to have a dynamic enthusiasm, a sharp visual eye, and probably a good amount of stamina. These qualities came out in the foremost of the directors to migrate from television to films during the late fifties when live television began to be replaced by pre-filmed shows. The majority of the younger directors in America had their main grounding in television; the three most talented being Franklin Schaffner, John Frankenheimer and Sidney Lumet. So far we have only seen two feature films from Schaffner, *A Woman of Summer* and *The Best Man*, but quite a number from Frankenheimer and Lumet. The most notable feature about the work of these three is that there has been a steady creative development through their work, each film has been a progressive step from the last. They have another important quality too: although all three have a visual flair for images, through creating a feeling through movement, of using technique for emotional impact, they each have an absorbing interest in the characters they are dealing with; they know how to touch an audience on its emotional funny bone, how to involve the spectator as an unseen participant; a quality very few postwar directors possess (of non-TV directors one would include Elia Kazan and Desmond Davis).

Of the three, Lumet's work has been the more erratic. His first film, *12 Angry Men*, showed promise; but his next three seemed to lack a complete dramatic form—*Stage Struck, That Kind of Woman* and *The Fugitive Kind*. Since then his direction has become more fluid, using technique to underline characterisation (and in his handling of actors he has rarely been at fault) rather than treating them as separate entities as too many directors have done for decades.

Lumet has never worked in Hollywood except for the studio work on *View from the Bridge* and his last film, *The Hill*, he has worked entirely in New York. Born in 1925, he began his career as a child actor, appearing in many plays on Broadway. After being in the army, he appeared in two more plays, "then I dropped it and started directing. I was directing off-Broadway, then I went into television as an assistant director, and later as a director." Lumet directed many, many shows with John Frankenheimer acting as his assistant director on quite a few of them. "It was the marvelous period in American television. Philco used to do some extraordinary shows. . . . Then Johnny went out to the coast to do some shows. Later on we did some beauties on *Play of the Week* . . . The best shows? Really, they'd be too numerous to mention. I can think of fifteen to twenty that I think are important pieces of work. The out-pouring at the time was enormous because it was taking a bunch of young people with varying degrees of talent but *all* talented; at least eight to ten writers, five to six directors, maybe twenty-five to thirty actors and all of them working every week. It was an extraordinarily high output."

What was the subsequent value of this television work? "Enormous. There were two big single contributions from a sheerly technical point of view.

"The first was the emotional meaning of lenses. A lens in itself has a certain kind of impact. If one takes, let's say, a close up, the same size head shot on an 18 mm lens has a very different emotional feeling than shot on a 75 mm lens. The opening up of lenses, and focal lengths, is a dramatic tool. This was one tremendous advantage of television—your eye became terribly sensitized to what the lens itself was doing. Very often the cutting would be coming so heavily that you wouldn't have time to refer to your script notes as to whether or not the cameraman was on a 40 mm or 28 mm; you'd just have to be able to spot it off the monitor.

"The second enormous technical help was editing. This became no problem because you were actually editing as you went. The technical rules of editing, that is when you've got the wrong reverses looking camera right camera left and so on, which really takes a little time to find out in movies; all that was solved in advance because you know what shoulder the camera should be over otherwise a person will be looking the wrong way and so on. By the time I did *12 Angry Men*, which had enormous technical problems in being done in one room, in three-hundred and eighty-five set-ups there was not one single techni-cal error . . . and that was all due to the television training."

How did *12 Angry Men* materialize as a film? "I didn't do the television show; Franklin Schaffner did that. But I had done everything else of the writer's (Reginald Rose). So when he came to do the film (he and Fonda were producing) he asked me to direct. We had done some shows together. One was *Crime in the Streets* with John Cassavetes, which was an extraordinarily powerful show. We did another called *Tragedy in a Temporary Town* with Lloyd Bridges; an interesting thing about the emotional instability that comes with migratory work—these were migratory industrial workers who lived in aluminium trailer camps and just drifted from job to job with seasonal layoffs—it won all sorts of awards. I had done another two with Reggie which had both turned out very well because I understood very clearly the kind of writer he is, what his strengths are, what his weaknesses are, so I have always gotten very good results from his work."

After *12 Angry Men* Lumet went on to direct *Stage Struck* and *That Kind of Woman*. *Stage Struck* was a remake of *Morning Glory*, with Susan Strasberg in the role originally played by Katharine Hepburn—that of the girl who tries to get on Broadway by proving that she has a wonderful gift to offer the stage. Susan Strasberg, as it turned out, was not the happiest of choices, for her acting lacked a feeling of insecurity, was too assured, and overplayed for effect. This was the major flaw in an otherwise enchanting film. "It was a lovely sort of Valentine to the theatre, the genuine feeling of romance about it. The photographic level I thought was terribly exciting—it was the first time I had ever used color. I found out a great deal on this film."

That Kind of Woman again used New York to striking effect and had Sophia Loren giving the best performance of her American made films. The story was simple, in the romantic tradition: millionaire (George Sanders), his two women (Sophia Loren and Barbara Nichols) and the bodyguard (Keenan Wynn) entrusted to look after the Boss's interests, i.e. the women. Young GI (Tab Hunter) falls for Sophia, who is left with the choice of honest love or wealth. But it was surprisingly witty, well controlled and avoided all the old sentimental cliches. "It was a totally romantic piece and treated as such. The problems there were studio problems—Ponti and I didn't get along."

Did this transition from the more confined television atmosphere to the wider canvas raise more complications for Lumet? "People always think that the smaller the thing is the simpler it is. It is quite the reverse. There are a million things you no longer have to worry about directorially. There is immediate visual relief; there is an immediate change of tempo automatically. There is probably a heightening of interest. I'm sure that when you go to the theatre and see in the program that it is set in 'The Living Room of So and So's house' your heart sinks a little. But when you see that there are to be twelve set changes your whole interest and energy comes up, and the top of each scene always holds more promise. It is the same in movies. Every time that cut takes place and you are some place else, a great deal of dramatic work has been done for the director automatically. It is the thing that irritated me so about some of the criticism leveled on *Long Day's Journey Into Night*, because there was a total lack of understanding of cinema technique . . . despite the fact that that was what all the reviews were about, and the pretentions of what people thought was cinema technique. All their eyes were capable of seeing was scenery; they didn't know cinema technique from a hole in the wall. There was more sheer physical technique in that movie, in its editing and its camerawork, than anything you are liable to see for twenty years. In the University of Southern California they use it to illustrate a certain level of camera work.

"So the problems of 'opening up' actually come as an enormous relief . . . and then you find the ignorance falls over the other side. You have a three-hundred foot dolly shot, which is all built on the fact that you are dollying for ever and ever, then you turn your film over to Paramount, Ponti and Chuck West (who is the head of the editing department). You come back three weeks later to see it . . . and they've found a way to cut it up, to intercut it with other shots. Which is their technique but not mine."

The main reasons for his making *That Kind of Woman* and *Stage Struck*, says Lumet, was "that I could do them both in New York. It seems like a stupid excuse for doing a movie, but at the time it wasn't. I have no regrets about it. I'm sorry the pictures weren't better . . . they both could have been a lot better than they were.

"There was a very active campaign on my part to try to get more production shifted to New York. I think that not only had personal advantages but that it would eventually have an enormous creative advantage. Kazan and I were the only ones working there. There were so many possibilities at the time. Both he and I had spoken at some length to Billy Rose and others about creative studio space for them . . . and real estate in New York is an enormous problem. One of the things we had to be able to bring them was of course some guarantee that the space would be used, it would take up enormous areas and they would have to have some kind of financial return. So we were both interested in just sheerly getting pictures there . . . if we could manage three a year between us then we could guarantee to some great real estate entrepreneur a certain income that would be worthwhile for him to build us a decent studio, because New York doesn't have any. At any rate, those were largely motivating forces for those two films." Apart from Lumet and Kazan, New York only has the few amateur groups which made a dismal attempt at becoming America's film protege. "And," adds Lumet, "they are *amateur* groups."

Lumet then went on to Tennessee Williams, filming his play *Orpheus Descending* under the title of *The Fugitive Kind*, with Marlon Brando, Anna Magnani and Joanne Woodward. The problems in adapting Williams? "The problems were many because thematically we wanted the piece to be about the boy, and it was built for that. Yet in the actual text it was all the woman's. That we never resolved; it was largely my fault. I was a little awed and cowed by him and also I knew that as a play this was his favorite. It was the first play he ever wrote (it was originally called *Battle of Angels* and had failed eighteen years before—it had been brought back as *Orpheus Descending* and had failed again). This was now his third attempt to make it work. I don't know whether it was a question of not having the heart or the courage, but I could never tell him "Tennessee it doesn't work because of this, this and this . . ." I just couldn't be that honest with him . . .

"I don't think there is any problem in doing Tennessee Williams's work as a movie, because I am a great believer in words in films, and I think that the idea of literature being dead so far as cinema is concerned is one of those temporary little fads. . . . The biggest problem about his work is that it is almost romantic drama in the sense that the emotions are keyed so high, the language is so lush and in finding the cinematic equivalent of that I think (I say this without having seen what Huston did on *Iguana*) that Max Ophuls would have been the perfect director for a Tennessee Williams film.

"There is a conflict in the sense that I know the South, particularly the area that Tennessee came from. What one thinks is lush verbage is sheer reportage. The richness of speech in that section of the country is unbelievable, and it has an enormous literary heritage behind it. The Greenville Press in Mississippi was the small press that gave us Faulkner. They are an incredible bunch of people. His language is sheer reportage: there is a streetcar named Desire; Cat on a hot tin roof is a common expression. So his dramas have to be done realistically because they are certainly true even if they aren't quite real. It's how to find that style . . .

"I think that the world he's grown up in is peopled with those characters. I've met his mother, and *Glass Menagerie* is no overdrawing. . . ."

Then from Williams to Arthur Miller, when Lumet directed *A View From the Bridge*, with Raf Vallone, Maureen Stapleton and Carol Lawrence. Although the location work was done in Brooklyn, the studio interiors were shot in Paris. "That was sheerly financial. The man who bought it had a few dollars and many francs. So we spent the dollars doing the exteriors in America and the francs on the interiors in Paris. But it worked out marvelously. The art director was an incredibly sensitive man who didn't speak a word of English. He went to America and for two weeks I took him in and out of houses in Brooklyn and what his eye saw was absolutely perfect.

"I think the film was better than the play in that we eliminated the pretensions in the script. In the play everybody was terribly aware of Greek tragedy, the Greek-chorus and all that nonsense . . . it's a very simple story really. A man kills himself because he cannot get the woman he wants. If it can hit a tragic level, fine. But don't make that a requisite for the piece.

"I didn't know Raf Vallone's work, I just remembered him from *Bitter Rice* in which he ran around like an Italian Yul Brynner, snorting and being very masculine. But he'd been in the Paris production of the play, and Arthur Miller said he was the most extraordinary Eddie Carbone he'd ever seen. Within five minutes of working with him you could see in him the fabulous talent, the wild temperament. You have to go-get-him because his own mechanism is so powerful and gravitates so around its own reality, that once you have him hooked into the character you have something very special on film."

In America the film was released by a small art house distributor. "Because it was doing incredibly well in New York he immediately booked it for the next three weeks all over the country not realizing that he didn't have a damned thing to 'sell.' He had Arthur and I do the trailer . . . and if you've ever seen a tall dude and a short dude doing a trailer . . . it's the most unappetizing thing!"

Lumet turned again to the theatre for his next film, *Long Day's Journey Into Night*, probably the most brilliant adaptation of a play, for although it was shot word for word almost entirely on one set without any "expansion" or opening out of the story, it is a purely cinematic interpretation of O'Neill's work. He uses his camera to intensify the atmosphere evoked by the author's dialogue, examining in minute detail the character, feelings and reactions of the Tyrone family; each hesitant glance or slight movement having a very special purpose. The occasional pause, or silence, engulfing the audience, playing on the mind and senses of the spectator. The excrutiating pain that is aroused by the growing void between the characters—they let their masks slip to reveal their deepest feelings about themselves and about each other but still drift further apart. Each character is etched deeply on the mind. The mother who tries to fool her family, and herself, that she is not a drug addict. The father, the ex-actor who lives in past glories he never achieved outside his own imagination, a skinflint who counts the seconds an electric light bulb burns, who keeps a mental note of the level in the whisky bottle, and values the younger son's life in terms of how much it would cost him to save it. The older son, Jamie, a self-determined failure who finds his escape in the bottle and whores, a deep jealousy of his brother's obvious talent and dreams. The younger son Edmund, a consumptive, frail, deeply sensitive towards the feelings of others, searching for a reason to life (O'Neill's autobiographical character, it has many of the writers' failings when dealing with themselves, making it the most difficult to explore).

The cast, Katharine Hepburn as the mother, Ralph Richardson as the father, Jason Robards Jr. as Jamie and Dean Stockwell as Edmund, blends so well into the piece that it is very difficult to pick out one individual performance as being greater than another, though Hepburn is allowed a few lapses in which her own personality dominates that of the character.

"It was just *the* best cast for the film," says Lumet. "Everybody was our first choice. When I met Kate, I couldn't have disliked her more, and I imagine she felt the same way about me. Ely Landau (the producer) sensed this and as we left the house he said, 'Sidney, you didn't get along too well.' 'No, it wasn't exactly one of those total rapport meetings.' He said, 'Well, let's get somebody else.' I said, 'No, what ever hell it is going to be it is going to be worth it, because she is the best person in the world for that part.' And of course it didn't turn out to be hell at all. She's a great, great woman, and it wound up just as happily as anything ever could.

"We didn't think we would have Ralph Richardson as he had another picture due, and I started looking around for other people. Then, God bless him, he had a little out in his contract which was that he didn't have to say yes until he saw the second script and when they said, 'We've got a re-write,' he said 'Ah . . .' As soon as the re-write came in, he turned it down and all the money that went with that and came with us.

"Jason Robards—you couldn't have kept him away! And Dean we had like a shot, he was so eager right away."

On the part of Edmund, which has been criticized as being the easiest part to play, a mistake often made when dealing with autobiographical characters, Lumet reckons that "it was in fact the most difficult to play. O'Neill always wrote himself badly. In *Iceman Cometh* the part of the young boy had the same problems that Edmund has in this. It is full of self-pity; he is the listener primarily. It is always the most passive part—the self-pitying victim. O'Neill had such self-hatred that he almost didn't dare to write himself in any sort of active way because I am sure that he felt that any time he did anything it turned out terribly, and hurt or injured someone. So as a result you find very often parts that are the most autobiographical in all of his works are terribly passive.

"Edmund can be played almost as an observer. I felt thematically that we would lose a great deal if we did that because in the stage production in New York the play was about the father and the brother. I felt that it was about the mother and Edmund. As a result we really had to activate it in the most extraordinary way. We got a sort of level of pain going; in other words got the passivity coming out of what I said

I felt about O'Neill, which is active, restraining oneself; not acting because if you do you'll kill something . . . which is a very different thing from passive."

Lumet rehearsed the film for three weeks before shooting, "I won't do a film any more without rehearsing," and shot it in thirty-seven days. It originally ran for 190 minutes, though the version shown in Britain had been cut by some fifty-four minutes, which seemed an illogical thing to do.

Long Day's Journey Into Night was set up by Ely Landau. "It was all Ely's project. He used to sell film to television, then buying and selling television stations . . . it's a way of life! And he wound up rather wealthy.

"He started out with what I think is a totally valid idea, and it is still to be seen whether it is going to work or not. His point was that there was a vacuum on the market for pictures of extremely high quality made for under a million dollars, which could then make back, not eight or ten million, but make back . . . a million. The interesting thing is how few of the people who have always talked about this thing actually would go to work for it once it was on the line. If my commercial salary is six figures, I don't work for Ely for that . . . we did *Long Day's Journey* for a fraction of our salaries." *Long Day's Journey* cost $435,000.

Lumet's next film, *Fail-Safe*, deals with the dangers of the nuclear arms race and of its control by automation. Although made two years ago, it is only now being released—having been held up because of the similarity in story to *Dr. Strangelove.*

"*Fail-Safe* was part of another project actually. As you see, I keep looking for isolated little people to work with to stay away from studios as long as possible. Max Youngstein, a marvellous man who used to be one of the powers at United Artists, wanted to launch a company on the most logical basis I have ever heard. This was that we would all take just as much money as we needed to live on, which isn't much, you can struggle along on a thousand a week if you watch cabs, tips and things like that. Max was going to do the profit participation, but not the way the big studios do it. The big thing he was going to break was the distribution fee, by having his own distribution company. He was going to begin at 22 percent, as opposed to the companies' thirty-five, and within three years hope to be down to 18 percent which is what it should be costing. He got me involved, together with Johnny Frankenheimer and another . . . about three of us were each going to do five pictures for him so that over three years he would have fifteen pictures which would give him a body to work with. It was very exciting.

"The first of these that we chose was *Fail-Safe* because we felt that kind of anti-war piece had a tremendous value. Also, we felt that it really could make money because it was an enormous bestseller in America. The company needed that kind of kick-off. The book was so well known we wouldn't have to spend a lot of money on actors and so on. After that we were going to do an Arthur Miller one-acter, two originals and a fifth one we hadn't picked."

Fail-Safe is reviewed elsewhere in this issue, and his subsequent film, *The Pawnbroker*, was covered in the October 1964, issue. This latter film, produced by Ely Landau, unfortunately does still not have a distributor in Britain. It is released in America by Allied Artists, which closed its London office last December. It will be a pity if *The Pawnbroker* does not get a release in Britain because it is, after *Long Day's Journey*, Lumet's most imaginative and sympathetic work, and he has come closer to the heart and social problems of a depressed city area than any other American director.

Lumet then directed Britain's entry to the Cannes festival this year, *The Hill*. It is based on a story by Ray Rigby about an army detention camp in North Africa during the Second World War, with Sean Connery as the "busted" RSM sent there on a gruelling punishment course. The main conflict is between him, the camp's RSM (Harry Andrews) and the sadistic officer in charge (Ian Hendry) of the "exercises," who are out to break Connery mentally and physically in the course of which they cause the death of another man. *The Hill*, shot on location in Spain and at MGM's Elstree studios, was completed in forty-four days.

At the moment Lumet is working on *The Group*, based on Mary McCarthy's novel, in New York. In contrast to *The Hill*, which was an all male cast, this will be virtually an all female cast.

Long Day's Journey Into Night: An Interview with Sidney Lumet

DALE LUCIANO / 1971

Along with Les Parents terribles, *Lumet's film of the O'Neill play has gained a reputation as one of the rare truly successful examples of filmed theater: works that devote themselves fiercely to the theatrical substance of their sources, they surpass films aiming to "open up" or "adapt" plays, and somehow transcend their origins.*

DL: *How would you describe your approach and technique in making* Long Day's Journey Into Night?
SL: I'd had some dissatisfaction when I'd seen *Long Day's Journey* on the stage. I had felt O'Neill's intent had not been realized. Also, the experience with *The Iceman Cometh* had illustrated for me that there was a superb method of focusing the play through the use of the camera. This is not in any way to reduce its dimension. For me, it intensifies it by getting it specific. By pushing it very hard along one interpretive level, along one *directed* level, it assumed even greater size. *Iceman* had shown me there was an ability to take tragedy and do it on a screen that was, in that instance, a small screen. It seemed to me the chances for an artistically complete thing were even increased by doing the screen version of *Long Day's Journey Into Night.*

From *Film Quarterly.* Summer 1971:20–29. Copyright © 1971 by the Regents of the University of California. Reprinted by permission of *Film Quarterly.*

DL: *Can you be more specific about your dissatisfaction with the José Quintero production?*

SL: Primarily, it had always seemed to me, if the play was about any of the four, it was about the mother. In the Broadway production, largely because of the dominance in performance of Jason Robards and Freddy March, the play focused on the men, the father and the son . . . and the eldest son's relationship. I'm not just talking in a Freudian sense. It seemed to me the fullest, and the most moving, tragic elements lie in the relationship of Mama and Edmund. I felt the screen would really allow me a way, if I channeled *every* technical device at my command, to make a movie of what I felt the play was about.

DL: *So* Long Day's Journey *is a movie about a play?*

SL: Well, it is not, in any sense, a photographed stage play. It is a movie; the amount of technique was so prodigious, it was a technical *tour de force* in many ways. And all directed toward the one thing which I feel does make it "cinematic." It is a "movie" if those people or that situation is defined in a way it *cannot* be defined by using any other form. That more than completed itself for me in *Long Day's Journey*.

DL: *How did the O'Neill script make certain demands that required extraordinary technical means to transfer the play to the screen?*

SL: The obvious demands in terms of making a movie of it: four people, essentially one room, even though I did move the very beginning of the script outside. The technical demands were enormous. The reason by the way for the moving of the first part outside was not the usual movie thing of "breaking it out." Obviously, that would be silly. Finally, we were "stuck" with four people. I had decided in my early conferences with Boris that I wanted the greatest shift of light possible. I wanted *literally* to take a "long day's journey into night." I wanted to start with the brightest sunlight (in fact, the opening title shot is against just the sun) and wind up with the last shot of total blackness, just the lighthouse light sweeping the four people at the table. That is the reason for moving the very opening of it outside.

I also don't like tragic omens. I wanted to start it off as lightly and brightly as an Andy Hardy movie. The exterior, with its leaves, with its sunlight, provided the best opening.

There was no screenplay. As you know, I used the text of the play. Of the hundred and seventy-seven pages, we cut seventeen. The cuts were made during rehearsal when we found out what we no longer needed. Knowing by then what I'd be doing with camera, certain elements of the drama would become clearer sooner, and we could make certain cuts. I've got a good technical memory, and the complete technical breakdown developed from the rehearsal period, I carried in my head.

DL: *How much time was spent in actual preparation prior to rehearsals and actual shooting? What was the nature of such preparation?*
SL: The preparation time was enormous to me. Usually, on work that's turned out well for me, I go through a rather simple process. I know a long time in advance I'm going to do it, and then it just gestates. I read it slowly and think about it, and read and think, and read and think, and really, in a strange way, make no decisions. The actual gestation period—well, on *Long Day's Journey*, I think it was close to a year; on *Seagull*, almost two years. Then when the working time comes, that is, going into active preproduction, at work with the set designer, the cameraman, choosing locations, rehearsals, shooting—that all proceeds at white-hot heat. The actual preproduction time, not counting "thinking time," was only about six weeks.

DL: *How closely did you work with the actors during the rehearsal period prior to shooting?*
SL: The closeness in the work with the actors is the heart of the picture. Like all good working experience, I think we emerged from it totally close personally, a complete connection for all of us. That was accomplished, really, in the pre-rehearsal period in quiet conferences between ourselves. Then in rehearsal itself.

What was fascinating was that each of the actors worked very, very differently. Ralph Richardson works on what amounts to a musical basis. I finally found a shorthand with him of "Ralph, a little more bassoon, a little less violin, a little more cello, a little tympani here," literally in those terms. It was immediately picked up and translated into acting.

Dean worked very internally, needed total discussion . . . Strasbergian analysis of each moment in him, in the character.

Jason likes to think of himself as an out-and-out technician. Of course, he's not. He's a totally inspired artist. With Jason, as always when we've worked together, one doesn't talk about the most profound elements of it or the most moving. They are somehow understood between you. One deals largely on a technical level with him.

Katie was a fascinating factor. Because I'd never worked with her before, I let her go. In the first three days, she took off with that extraordinary instinct, that incredible energy of hers. On the third day of rehearsal, she panicked because, as so often happens on a great role, instinct isn't enough. It only lasts for a short while and then starts collapsing under the weight of the emotional demand. It became necessary to search for it elsewhere. Searching for it someplace else meant, at certain times, sheerly technical adjustments, on a level of "Let's get on with it. You're taking too long with this speech. Don't try to stretch the emotion. Let the words carry it," that kind of thing. Too, really profound, close, personal discussions between the two of us, *as* the two of us, of that character, of O'Neill.

DL: *What kind of moments would come out of these discussions?*
SL: For example, the moment when Edmund tells Mama that he's dying. We were, I guess, in about the eighth or ninth day of rehearsal, and I said, "Katie, I'm going to ask you to do something that's going to shock you at first. It may terrify you, you may refuse, I don't know what's going to happen. But when he says, 'Mama, I am dying,' I want you to haul off and hit him as hard as you can." The first look on her face was one of such shock. She is not a physical actress, she doesn't clutch people, she doesn't use props, she doesn't need physical sources of security. Certainly physical violence is not anything that comes easily to her.

I think we stared at each other for about two minutes, just gathering on a kind of osmosis level an understanding of why that moment called for that. We didn't say a word, but we just stood there for almost two minutes, I think, staring at each other. Then she dropped her eyes and said, "Okay, I'll try it." The first time she did it, it was so brilliant and pulled so much out of her, involved her to such a degree, we never tried it again until we did it on camera. I didn't want it to become too familiar an emotion for her.

DL: *Did the actual shooting of the film differ from customary procedures of shooting?*

SL: The actual shooting wasn't really far different from the shooting on any other film, except I did try to give them more continuity than one usually gets. This wasn't too difficult. We were on one set, and a confined one. Also, this was necessary, because when they are acting on that kind of level, they're exposing areas of themselves, conscious and unconscious. Every source of security they can have—knowing where they're at, in the character, knowing where they're going—all of these things are important if they're going to be free. Continuity, and sticking as close to continuity as possible, was the only difference from normal shooting.

DL: *What advantages and/or disadvantages were there to working on such a tightly-knit shooting schedule?*

SL: There were no disadvantages for me in the six-week shooting schedule. You always shoot very quickly anyhow. This comes, I guess, out of the television training, of, in a sense, "pre-editing" my films, and knowing what I want in advance, making the dramatic selection in advance. As a matter of fact, my guess would be that on anything like *Long Day's Journey*, a short shooting schedule is almost a necessity. The same thing happened on *The Seagull*. We did *Seagull* in twenty-nine days. I've found for myself, and I'm quite sure the same was true for the actors, there is an emotional exhaustion. You'd get home at the end of a day of shooting on *Long Day's Journey* . . . at the end of the six weeks I felt as though I'd been weeping for six weeks, and was just so tired, really spent inside. I don't think I could have shot for much longer than that. So, my guess would be on something of that level, there is an advantage to the shortest working time possible.

DL: *By what standard might one measure the manner in which you and Boris Kaufman work in creative collaboration? For example, who would evolve or devise certain shots, such as the three-hundred and sixty degree pan of Katharine Hepburn?*

SL: A question of collaboration between a director and a cameraman is always such a highly individual one. Boris and I have done, as you know, eight pictures together, and it's always a very close relationship.

The choice, the selection of a shot, I guard jealously. And that is my prerogative. The three-hundred and sixty degreer was mine, the final pullback was mine, the shooting plot of the picture was mine. But I don't in any way mean to denigrate Boris's contribution. Where he begins, and this becomes an enormously vital element, is in the lighting. In black and white, particularly, the light is one of the key ways in which one extracts the meaning of the drama. Boris's triumph, from a lighting point of view in *Long Day's Journey*, lies in the fact that if you take the same close-up of Ralph Richardson from Act One, and a close-up of Ralph Richardson from Act Four, the exact same size, and put those two faces next to each other on the screen, they will look like a different man. It'll almost be hard to think the same actor is in both shots. That is Boris's triumph, and it's a tremendous, one through the use of light.

DL: *But, still, the collaborative aspect must become an intensely fluid kind of creative relationship?*

SL: He carries out a dramatic intention so that, in a way, it's hard to say where one begins and one leaves off. I'll say, "This is the shot." In advance, we've discussed the feel of it. The gradual shift of light, for example, was predetermined before shooting even began. Boris executes that in terms of light, and this can be a great accomplishment of the camera.

There are many fine, fine cameramen in the world. Very few films come out, you know, out of focus or badly exposed. Almost everyone's competent on the technical level. Boris's mastery lies in his ability to translate a dramatic situation into the gray scale from white to black. We used no special film stock or any special process.

DL: *What other guiding factors, if any, unite the two of you in terms of a central aim or approach?*

SL: One of the things that was terribly important was that there be no sense of technique . . . that no technique ever show. The greatest art of it, it seems to me, is how Boris's art and my art is *hidden* in that movie. You don't see that it's well directed, you don't see that it's brilliantly photographed. It's just there, it arrives full-blown. We didn't want to do anything that was "spottable" by an audience.

DL: *What other individuals—for example, Art Director Richard Sylbert—were most important contributors to the success of the film? How did you work with them?*

SL: The same sort of relationship exists. We would sit and talk in advance, and I would say, "Dick, the parlor which is never used, I want it to have a really funereal feeling, just in the back of the dayroom, in the back of this summer room where they *do* live, in the back is this past thing. The past is always present with them, and the past is always death, as the future is death for them." Dick takes this and converts it into black horse-hair furniture which is right for the period and, visually, kept the parlor looking like the inside of a funeral home. The upright that he chose, the upright piano which we finally do touch in the last act, close to the ending. These levels of interplay between the director and the art director and the cameraman, the closer the better. The ideas come from every place, and like all good things, sometimes you don't know who contributed what. Also, like all good things, they are all pushing toward the same thing. One of Dick's favorite expressions is, "We're all making the same picture."

DL: *How was such an appropriate visual equivalent of the O'Neill play achieved? For example, what processes were involved in the selection of film stock, processing, and lighting?*

SL: Before, when I said it was a prodigious piece of technical work, this is no exaggeration. We used everything film would command. The camera is really a fifth actor in something like *Long Day's Journey*. As such, it has to be integrated into the domain of the other four as much as if it were a live person. A lot of these selections were made in advance of shooting—a specific lens for each character, a specific lens change for each character—for both Ralph Richardson and Jason Robards, the lenses kept growing wider as we went act by act. For both those actors, the eye level (where the camera was in relation to eye level) kept dropping. By the end of the piece, in Jason's case, literally shooting from the floor, from almost below the floor level.

The takes were even shot in the kind of eventual rhythm in which they were edited. For example, Jason and Ralph were almost always handled in short takes. (By the way, this is up to the fourth act, at which point a great many things changed.) As opposed to Hepburn who is almost always handled in very long takes. And handled that way in the editing, too. Nothing interrupted the takes. If I remember correctly, because it's many years now, there were some seven- and eight-hundred-foot takes on Kate. This was not only marvelous for performance it was right for the character. The whole editing sense of her character was to be *legato*.

With Kate, the opposite happened with eye level as the character progressed. I kept getting higher and higher on her, shooting down on her more and more. Edmund stayed as long as possible the most "objective," the fewest lens changes on him. On Katie, the lenses kept getting longer and longer, so the outside world kept disappearing more and more—the focal depth was, of course, smaller on a longer lens. Lens opening and key light were all chosen with that in mind. For Jason and Ralph, we could finally be stopped way down but using quite a lot of light so the backgrounds would be in focus . . . and, therefore, have more life to them. That mattered in terms of character.

As I said before, there were no special film stocks or processes. But, shot by shot, there was the most intense delineation on a visual level that both Boris's and my experience could make. You'll find an extraordinary thing when you study the film. It wasn't a conscious decision other than the fact that a set-up has to say something: no two set-ups with four people inside one or two rooms for over three hours . . . there was never a duplicated set-up! Yes, of course, there are instances of shooting two over-the-shoulders and, in the editing of it, as you cut back to each over-the-shoulder shot, you're cutting back to essentially the same shot. But in camera placement, in camera positioning, in lens opening, in key light, in lens used, once "Cut" was called, there was a brand new set-up for each shot in the picture.

DL: *What problems were confronted in the editing? How much of the film's success depended on the editing? Was the editing ever taken out of your hands?*

SL: The editing has to be an integral part of what's been going on. To have shot eight-minute takes on Hepburn, and then interrupt them with reaction shots, would have been a wasteful expenditure of technical energy and Hepburn's energy. If that's the way it was shot, it was shot with that intent and was to be used that way. Essentially, the rhythm of the editing followed the rhythm of the shooting which was following the rhythm of the performances which were evolved in rehearsals.

The editing, as I say, I was there, physically present every second, my own hand on the Moviola brake. It's again a very close thing. The only eventual problem that ever came up—not the editing—was after the initial release of the picture. I don't remember the final length when we opened. I'm not sure whether it was two-fifty or three hours and ten minutes. I'm not quite sure. [The original length of the film was 174 minutes. A shorter, 136-minute version was circulated for the film's general release, though the unedited version is available for rental from Audio Film Center's New York office.] Contractually, I did not have final cut. Ely Landau, who put up the money for it—his own personal money, I might add, it was not studio money in any way—Ely had final cut. When we sold the picture to Joe Levine for his release, Joe happily went along with the picture as it was and opened it. It opened under the most unfortunate circumstances, with the longest newspaper strike in New York's history. Papers were out at least fourteen weeks, so whatever good notices we had were lost. There was no chance to spread the word. The picture still ran for a long time–fourteen weeks at the Loew's Lower East. There were no Critics' Awards that year because of the strike, which ran into December.

DL: *But an unedited version of the film was eventually released?*
SL: When the picture went into general release, they found they could not release the picture at its full length. Theater owners simply would not accept it. It was then cut.

DL: *Did you have a hand in the cutting?*
SL: I don't know who physically cut it, took out the . . . I don't know whether it was twenty or forty minutes. I've never seen the cut version; I couldn't bear to. But it could not have been legally done without Ely Landau allowing it. Joe gave it its fair shake. He released it, as it was, and fought for it, advertised it well, tried to get Katie the Academy Award. She was nominated. He opened it in New York and Los Angeles and, I believe, London—I'm not sure—in its original length. And he was the one who suffered the financial loss. He paid Landau the full cost of the picture for the right to release it.

DL: *How would you explain your use of the camera as enabling you to com-*
press the actual "playing time" of the drama? What is the end result of this
approach to the use of the camera?

SL: The camera makes things clearer sooner and also makes other
reactions clearer sooner. Knowing the impact, the meaning you want
it to have on this character, even though the other character is saying
it, you are able to compress in that way. As I say, I only cut seventeen
pages. I find O'Neill a great writer. "Great" in the classic, total, historic
sense of the word. I find every word useful and needed. People are so
used to finger-tip experience and a lack of a really profound revelation.
They're impatient; they think it can come quickly. Well, in many
instances, it can't. It's so often like life, and O'Neill is like life. It has to
go around the same circle four times, but all the time it's like an awl
which is biting deeper and deeper into the wood each time it goes
around. It's not going around on the same level, it's going around on
one level deeper until, finally, something bursts within you as it bursts
within the play. For that, all those repetitions are needed. You need
them in I*ceman*, you need them in this. I think it's true of really all
great drama. The camera, by allowing me to take out, as I say,
seventeen pages of a hundred and seventy-seven mimeoed pages,
that is already an extraordinary contribution the camera can make.
Certainly, without camera, those seventeen pages would have been
vital. But as I say, they were all in the area of "You got it. You got the
point," just that much sooner, so half a page would go here, half a
page would go there . . .

DL: *You have spoken of the interaction of camera and subject, the idea that*
the camera becomes one of the actors. How do you employ this principle in a
technical, physical sense?

SL: It has to relate to each performance in such a specific way that
it is defining, revealing, and, if anything, increasing what the
performance is doing. One simply cannot record. I remember very
early in my television experience, I had a marvelous performance on a
television show, then we got off the air and turned around to everybody
in the control room, beaming and saying, "How about that performance?
Wasn't that magnificent?" Nobody knew what I was talking about.
In essence, what I had done with the camera was undermine what

the actor was doing. I had weakened the actor. When I saw the kine four weeks later, I realized that, and I've been very careful that that never happen again.

An actor saying a line, the same feeling, with the same size, if it's a close-up, the top of the frame cutting just below the chin, you can get the same size with a 25 mm lens or a 15 mm lens. It's a question of whether the camera is physically close or farther away from the actor. But there is an emotional difference in what that lens records: a 50 mm lens gives me a different feeling about a face than a 25 mm lens. A graduated scale of use of lenses is, to me, one of the contributing factors to a movie. I always make a lens plot. It seemed extremely important the right lens selection be made in relation to performance. As I say, in the most general sense, in the case of Katie, I kept going onto longer and longer lenses. In the fight between Dean and Ralph in the last act, as the fight went on, the lenses became shorter and shorter until, finally the end of the fight was shot on 18 mm lenses. Yet the introduction of them had been so gradual, the normal distortions you see with an eighteen, and which are there in the shots—they are distorted—but your eye isn't aware of them. I'd led you to them gradually, not wanting to make a point of it. But there was an increased hostility, an increased violence, an increase in the change of emotions the two characters were going through. And the lenses were changing with the emotion. It's in that sense that I talk of camera as another actor, and in something like *Long Day's Journey* where you have no relief to the eye, where you are caught in the same physical set-up shot after shot after shot, lens selection, lens opening, key versus filter, all those camera considerations become terribly important.

One of the nice things I like is that a lot of people never even realized, until they'd seen the picture a second or third time, that at the end of the first act, when Hepburn takes off on walking around the room, we went around the room four times on a three-hundred and sixty degree pan. It was so integrated into her emotion, the technical *tour de force* never occurred to the people. In the scene I was just talking about with Dean and Ralph in the fourth act, whereas I'm sure a great many people who are aware of film would spot an eighteen immediately, I doubt if they know it was used there.

DL: *What about the changes in the visual make-up of the Act Four scenes?*

SL: The way Jason was shot in the fourth act, the way Hepburn was shot, the lenses used in the last four close-ups of the four people just before the final wide shot, those lenses help make a tremendous difference in the character delineation of those faces—the eye level at which they were shot made a tremendous difference—for your information, Ralph's close-up was an 18 mm lens, Jason was an 18 mm lens, Dean was a 25 mm lens, Katie was a 100 mm lens—a total reversal in the field, again for a deliberate and dramatic purpose.

DL: *What problems have you faced in the direction of other films adapted from plays, i.e.,* The Fugitive Kind, A View From the Bridge, The Seagull, *that seem to arise repeatedly in such adaptational work?*

SL: The problems on, let's say, *The Fugitive Kind* or *View From the Bridge*, are not at all similar in the sense that they're not great plays, they're not masterpieces. In each instance I felt the movie would really get a tremendous chance to correct some of the dramatic errors in the plays. They presented no problem from a confinement point of view—you have a much greater liberty in that regard. The obligation is to keep true to the play's theme, the meaning and intent, assuming that they are what attracted you to begin with. I don't see the point of taking a masterpiece like *The Seagull*, or *Long Day's Journey*, and changing it. Number one, I'm not going to improve upon the original! Second, there is more value to extract from what *is* there. The most brilliant film sequence of Jason in the whorehouse would not have been nearly as meaningful as the way he was using it in telling it to Edmund. That's what was important, not the information of it but the emotional point he was going to get to by starting to talk to Edmund on this kind of level.

Similarly, that's why "breaking out" would be useless for *Long Day's Journey*. The same is true of *Seagull*. You are dealing with a complete piece of work. The problem is to reveal it. We could have gone to Moscow to show Trigorin and Nina's affair. Again, that's not what is important in it. When David Warner (Konstantin) tells what happens to Nina, he is being attacked and beset by the people around him. The questioning of him at that point, by making him relate that story (which is obviously of a most painful nature) is one of the steps to his suicide. It is in that way Chekhov uses the exposition of what happened to Nina and Trigorin. You can't show Nina and Trigorin and cut that speech simply because it is descriptive.

It depends on the material you're doing. When it is a masterpiece, it is a masterpiece for a reason. I don't think its structure can be tampered with. I think you can take off and do your own version of an Orestes theme or one can pick up *Romeo and Juliet* and do a completely personalized version of it. That's not what interests me.

The use of the word "adaptation" is true, but plays, of course, aren't the only source of it. Other than, I guess, a documentary, any movie is really an adaptation. It is an adaptation because it is artificially created. Again, getting back almost to the first question, it's a movie, and a creative one, if it has defined those people and that situation in a way that could not have been defined without the form you were using.

DL: *In what manner did you achieve the very specific rhythmic shifts and tones, apparent both in the delivery of the actors and the editing of the film?*
SL: The following through of what began in text and what happened in performance was to determine what would happen on camera, and from on camera into the editing. In terms of each character, it is that following through that gives the picture the very specific rhythmic feeling that it has. Knowing that, as a character, Jamie interrupts, and is interrupted, and in a way *wants* to be interrupted, wants conflict—he lives *stacatio*—that basic character element in him determines a great deal right away. Knowing that Edmund tries to play the observer but is, in actuality, the victim in many instances, determines that rhythm.

DL: *How much attention do you direct toward the over-all rhythmic structure of the work?*
SL: The word "rhythm" is fascinating. I've only worked on three great texts—*Seagull*, *Iceman*, and *Long Day's Journey*. No, no, no, wait: I once did a production of *Bourgeois Gentleman*, that's a great text. A similar experience on all four of them, you feel much more like a conductor than a director. This wasn't only in the specific instance of using musical terms with Ralph Richardson. You very often make a selection, whether it's in staging or in the tempo of the scene, very much in relation to what went before and what's about to come after. In a very rhythmic sense, if the scene in the playing developed into a scene of

slow tension and pauses and so on and so forth, you will therefore try to justify and try to find reasons for a complete reversal in tempo, much as that pattern develops from scene to scene, to act to act, so that each act takes on its own tempo.

I've mentioned before the last act of *Long Day's Journey* being so different from the other three. It not only was from a lighting point of view but also from the total rhythm of it. That is due partially, of course, to the fact that Mama's not there, she doesn't appear in the fourth act. It's left to the men, and that changed the rhythm, the tempo, the feel of it. And I felt that feeling of conducting very strongly in *Seagull*.

DL: *What do you feel is the most significant technical achievement of the film?*

SL: The fact that it took so long for people to discover that it was a marvelous technical achievement. I'm very proud of the fact that it's only really been in the past five years or so as people have seen the picture. There's been this very slow discovery that, technically, it was really brilliant. At the time of release, it was terribly irritating, because you're always tempted to show off and show people how brilliant you are. When it opened, it was referred to very heavily by many of the reviewers as a photographed stage play. You wanted to kill, because you knew any critic who would say that had no eye, did not belong in movies, should not be criticizing movies. He can't see what a lens does, he can't see what light is doing—sheer technical ignorance. Katie knew, she knows all there is to know about movie-making, Boris knew, I knew, Dick Sylbert knew. We knew that we were doing something magnificent, technically, and yet the source of pride in it was the subtlety of the achievement—the fact that when transitions were made, they were made so slowly, so gradually, you didn't see them taking place.

The technique is hidden. As soon as you can spot technique, as soon as the shot looks magnificent; as soon as you're aware of that in the first scene of a movie, I think the director has blown it.

DL: *Are there moments in the film which you would direct in a different fashion today?*

SL: I haven't seen it now in four years. I'm going to take a look at it this summer again because I miss it. Four years ago, when I guess I'd seen it

six times since I'd finished it, there's not a shot I would have changed. I
don't know if I'll feel that way today. But . . . very possibly I might feel
the same way.

DL: *Is there anything you might care to add that would clarify an understanding of either your working methods or techniques in regard to* Long Day's
Journey?
SL: The basic thing, it seems to me, is to guide the work, and somehow
keep yourself "out." To put yourself in totally, to exhaust yourself, to
expend yourself, to make it what you feel about it—and yet not let any
of that be apparent. It seems to me, and there's obvious room for argument in this, doing *Long Day's Journey*, doing *Seagull*, to try to define
those plays in terms of what they mean to you and yet not to be the
"hero" of them, not to be the savior of them, not to be anything but
the instrument through which they pass.

   I know there are other methods of work, I know one can argue. But I
wanted the best *Long Day's Journey* I could achieve, or the best *Seagull*
that I could achieve. Both pieces satisfy me profoundly. *Seagull*, I think
is my best piece of work. And *Long Day's Journey*, certainly, close to my
best piece of work. In both of them, I feel, you know O'Neill better for
having seen that film, you know Chekhov better for having seen *The
Seagull*. And you know every one of those characters better.

DL: *But something of your own personality inevitably emerges, too?*
SL: Like the technical side of *Long Day's Journey*, and the slow revelation
that that really was rather super, if you look very closely under the edges
and so on, you'll know me a lot more. It is not the "personalized movie"
in the European sense of the word. (I don't want to get into the argument because it's a spurious one.) I think as much of myself is revealed
in the way Denholm Elliott and I worked on the character of Dorn in
The Seagull. As you know, Dorn in *The Seagull* is always played as your
kindly old winemaker/doctor, sweet, cuddly, and the observer, sighing
gently at life's follies, just looking at it all objectively. I think the "objective man" is a lot of crap. I don't think any such thing exists, and I think
people who lead that kind of life—the nonparticipators—are hiding and
are bitter. We made Dorn a rather vicious, dàngerous man. That's the

way we chose to do the man, and that's just as revelatory of me as if I had included a piece of autobiographical material done *à l'auteur.*

DL: *Did your direction of* Long Day's Journey *influence your direction of other films?*

SL: One of the great pleasures of *Long Day's Journey* was that it showed me how far one could reach in terms of subtle, technical mastery of your craft. Since then, I've never done without the shooting plot . . . the lens plot. That is much more important to me than the conventional shooting plot. For example, on *The Hill*, I did that entire picture on four lenses. The first third of that picture is in 25 mm lens, the second is on an 18 mm lens, then for one quick scene between Sean Connery and Harry Andrews—a marvelous scene in the courtyard where they're battering at each other—I went to 6-inch lenses, did it with two cameras so that it was just one take. From there on in, the rest of the picture is shot on a 14 mm lens. I don't know if you've ever seen that much film on a 14 mm lens. It's an extraordinary lens, it's a very *dangerous* lens to use. Yet nobody is aware of it, because the arrival at it was so built, stylistically, through the body of the picture. But it is a unique lens and finally to be used simply within the confines of the cell itself, with close-ups and everything shot on the same lens—close-ups, long shots, it didn't matter. And yet it gave that piece a kind of emotional directness and drive that I found very impressive.

DL: *Did you later apply certain of the same techniques that were successful in the film?*

SL: It's interesting that, having chosen a picture like *Long Day's Journey*, so often called a "photographed stage play," I found because of its "uncinematic quality" this tremendous technical expansion. I've found the most extraordinary cinematic contribution to my work since then because these tools are so ripe, ready, available, alive for me that it's become second nature to me now.

Sidney Lumet: *The Offence*

SUSAN MERRILL/1973

SIDNEY LUMET'S HOME IS LIKE a page out of a *Better Homes & Garden* summer edition featuring unpainted wicker furniture puffed up with apple green and strawberry cushions. A pink Oriental softens the glossy hardwood floor. One feels that the paintings are probably original, done by illustrious artist friends for the Lumets, especially the portrait of the young woman. She presides over the room and its huge Chinese vases and gray marbled fireplace and venerable mirror with its black specks.

Sidney Lumet enters in wheat jeans, blue turtle neck and apologies for making us wait. His voice is big, warm and reassuring; his body, small, tight and restless. His hands move almost as quickly and as often as though he were using sign language. His fingers seem to be responsible for his thinning pate; they comb over it so often on their way to smoothing the abundant length of hair that reaches to his collar. His fingers also seem anxious to keep the ends of his tawny mustache from going awry.

He smokes unconsciously as though he were born with a cigarette in his mouth, and he gobbles pistachios hurriedly in the few moments when he relaxes at all. He moves and speaks like the actor he was. He's the director of such cinematic accomplishments as *12 Angry Men, View From The Bridge, Long Day's Journey Into Night, The Hill, The Pawnbroker, Fail-Safe, The Group, The Seagull,* and *The Anderson Tapes.*

Q: *You're leaving shortly for London where you'll be directing your sixteenth motion picture?*
LUMET: Maybe eighteenth. I'm not sure.

From *Films in Review*. November 1973: 523–28, 556. Reprinted by permission.

Q: *That's more than a picture a year since you left television and did your first picture, 12* Angry Men *in '57. What is this new film about?*

LUMET: This piece is called, *Something Like the Truth* (released as *The Offence.* He has now completed *The Wild and the Sweet.*) and it's about a cop who picks up a criminal. John Hopkins, the author, is most unsparing. No easy ways out. The criminal is a child molester, and during the course of the questioning, it finally becomes clear that psychologically they are simply opposite sides of the same coin but that there is a total psychological link and when the cop realizes it, it horrifies him so he just beats the criminal to death with his fists. It's your average funny movie. But that's the area that John's constantly into, and it's going to be thrilling to work on.

Q: *What made you interested in it?*

LUMET: Well, it's one of the most complex pieces I've ever read. If he's not a great writer now, Hopkins, he will be shortly. He's extraordinary. Unlike Kazantzakis, who keeps looking for what's godlike about us, John keeps looking for what's hellish about us.

Q: *How do you come upon your scripts?*

LUMET: It varies, Susan. Some are sent; some are things that I initiate or get interested in. No set pattern in it at all.

Q: *Do you sometimes have a theme in mind and go around looking for a play that will express it?*

LUMET: That goes on a great deal of the time and probably, subconsciously, that's what you pick. That's what you say yes to. I can always sort of see a pattern five pictures later.

Q: *Of your own development or thoughts?*

LUMET: Yeah, but I very rarely, in fact, never make that determination in advance because I'd be suspicious of it. I'd much rather just let the unconscious level take care of that.

Q: *How do you see your development in film?*

LUMET: I don't. I'm pleased about a lot of things. I think there has been development in the sense that the work is getting simpler and simpler and simpler. Just less attempt to let you know the director is there. I'm terribly out of fashion now because I don't like directorial style. I think the theme should provide the style.

Q: *You have been called the director of many styles.*
LUMET: It's because I like to work out of material. What I mean by the growing simplicity is, I think, for instance, *Anderson Tapes*, even though it's an absolutely nice straight caper movie, I think ten years ago I would have done it with a lot more hoke. It's actually very simply done, and that's part of why it's so much fun and so gay, and it's got life in it. It's because there's very little directorial imposition.

Q: *Why did you do that movie: it seems to me a departure from your "film of conscience"?*
LUMET: I like about every four pictures to get back to a melodrama and try to get a melodrama with a kind of thematic size about it. I did a very good picture, quite unsuccessful, called *The Deadly Affair*, many years ago. It's a good film, very unpretentious and direct and yet it's got a little weight in it. I find that every four years or so it's very important, especially for somebody who tends to work from inner sources, to break that mold and get back to . . . well, it's like getting back to a bar in dance: shoot it for story; direct it for story; cut it for story, story, story. Just as a kind of refresher in fundamentals.

Q: *You say that a melodrama is a departure from your usual films of inner resources and yet you've never written a script.*
LUMET: Right. Again, it's part of my whole out-of-fashionedness now. The whole idea of director as writer is nonsense. It arose because the directors in the twenties in silent days had to write the script so that they could budget it and so the production department could go to work. I've got just too much respect for writing. It's another talent. There are certain directors who can do both, but I don't think many. Very few directors are good writers.

Q: *There's a wonderful quote that you made to Robin Bean in an interview in '65. You said, "I am a great believer in words in films, and I think that the idea of literature being dead as far as cinema is concerned is one of those temporary little fads."*

LUMET: Yeah, and it's been born out, I think, to a large degree. I remember I used to be constantly attacked for doing plays as movies and now it's such an accepted part of movie making. Again, it came out of this same thing, people were constantly confusing cinema with scenery. If it was against a mountain, it was a movie. If it was against just a face, it wasn't a movie. Then it became a photographed stage play. Actually, the technique developments in a picture like *Long Day's Journey Into Night*, for instance or *The Seagull* has more sheer film technique in it than nine-tenths of the action/adventure dramas that you'll see.

Q: *Isn't one of your film techniques close-ups and emphasis on faces?*
LUMET: I spend an awful lot of time on them because it's what interests me most. But the basic thing has to do with the fact that the whole relationship is changing. I mean, John Hopkins, who's written this script (*The Offence*) wants to write nothing but movies. He doesn't want to be a novelist. And this is something I find very prevalent, a tremendous shift in the writer's attitudes. Instead of just taking the money and running, they do want really to write for movies. If I've helped in any little way at all in movies, it's been to keep insisting that there is a place for the word in it. It's not the only kind of movie. That would be silly, but it certainly is a kind of movie and the fact that it used to be dismissed automatically is no longer happening. The writers themselves are changing. A great many serious, quote, unquote, serious writers just want to write now for movies.

Q: *Do you anticipate any new film techniques in this picture?*
LUMET: I never try to come up with a technique. The sort of cutting style of the *Pawnbroker*, which is now banal because it's just been imitated so. As far as I know it was the first time it was used and it came out of the precise way my own memory works. I literally, if I'm trying to block something out, find it cropping up in little tiny bursts, little tiny flashes. But I'm not really even very concerned with being original. I don't think it's very important in work because it's a pursuit of form rather than content.

Q: *Who are the actors in this film?*
LUMET: Sean Connery, Trevor Howard, Vivien Merchant and Ian Bannen.

Q: *How do you choose actors for a script? Does the script just bring people to mind immediately?*
LUMET: Very often. I know so many just out of the whole television training that I usually find casting quite easy. In this one the acting demands are so extraordinary that I had to start, literally with just the size of the talent first and then wonder about the rightness of the part. It's because the last three scenes of the picture are three, twenty-minute scenes of just two people each and that's all. So they're going to have to carry quite a load. There's no help. There's nothing to lean on. There's no safety in it. If the performances don't make it, there won't be anything there.

Q: *In everything I've read about you the one thing that stands out most is how great you are with actors and how they respond to you so well. What is this quality you have with actors?*
LUMET: I think it's just that I'm really genuinely interested in them. Again, that's not fashionable. As you know, many of the European directors won't allow the actors to even read the script. I started rehearsing for my first picture, and I've rehearsed every picture I've ever made. And long rehearsals so that the actors know precisely where they are in terms of the character and development and the relationship to the whole piece. That in itself would be enough to endear one to most actors because they usually come on set and I mean, literally, the classic story is Hank Fonda coming on to—I've forgotton what picture, I think it was for Leone—coming on the set in Rome and Leone saying, "Mr. Fonda, this is Miss Cardinale," and they said, "How do you do," and took off their bathrobes and got into bed. And that was the first shot the first day of shooting.

Q: *How does an actor feel?*
LUMET: He feels awful.

Q: *He's not that callous?*
LUMET: No, he feels awful. He feels like a fool. The performance is going to be stilted. Nothing about it is really going to work, and he knows it,

and he just feels foolish and in the instances where he can control the situation somewhat, he'll usually demand quite a bit more.

Q: *After your actors read the script, do you have sessions with them?*
LUMET: Oh, enormous, enormous. Sometimes individually, sometimes in a group. On *Seagull* we were meeting individually for a year before we went into rehearsal, just short, four-hour sessions kind of thing.

Q: *What about color in this film? One of the things that seems important to you is color or the lack of it. Did you not once say, "You just can't do tragedy in color. In the movies black and white is more realistic than color."?*
LUMET: I did and I'm wrong. What it really amounted to is, I think, those of us who had been brought up in black and white, number one, had a terrific emotional attachment to it simply because that was the way we had seen movies. Then when color came in it was so horrendous and used so horrendously, the quality itself was so dreadful that it wasn't until well after the war when the Japanese came over and worked up at Rochester for a little while and then went back to Japan and broke all the rules that color could be good. That marvellous shot in *Gates of Hell* where you were never supposed to use white and especially not white in the sunshine and the first shot of the picture, if I remember correctly, were a hundred white robed priests sitting on a balcony in the brilliant sunlight. I think from most of us older ones what happened was that having been brought up that way, we resisted color. For example, Freddie Young and I did something very very interesting on a picture called *The Deadly Affair* . . .

Q: *You called it "colorless color"?*
LUMET: Yeah and it was terrific, and it's nice to know that you can do it because I got that gray picture I wanted. That London middle-class dreariness, those miserable London apartments that Mason lived in and Signoret lived in. They had a specific kind of light. But the thing is that I think where I was remiss, and where a great many other directors were too, is that we were treating the color as if it couldn't possibly be a contributive thing to the movie. Somehow it was as if the movie and I were being compromised in being commercial by being in color. I felt that I was making it an extravaganza, blowing it up too big.

Q: *That it lost intimacy?*
LUMET: Right, that it lost intimacy and reality. Well, it's obviously not true that it loses reality. The question is how to capture the reality and *The Deadly Affair* was one attempt. Since then I've really abandoned any attempt to mute the color at all. What I'm trying to do now is just use it exceedingly, exceedingly well for dramatic effect and emotional result. Now all I'm trying to do is just simply find either through the locations or the use of the art director as well as filtering and my work with the cameraman, to make the color work full story. Not to try to hide the color, in fact, to try to use it more.

Q: *Getting back to rehearsals, you have long ones but very short shooting schedules, right?*
LUMET: Yes, I'm very lucky, again, from the television training. The organization always functions well. I never shoot a chaotic picture.

Q: *Why do you shoot so fast?*
LUMET: It's really just a question of my own energy level, my own tempo. I can't work slowly.

Q: *Is it true that you once said that you work quickly because you can catch mood and spontaneity better that way?*
LUMET: I don't know, but I've always gotten what I wanted on a movie in terms of performance and so on. Most good actors I find work better working quickly.

Q: *Why, because they get primed?*
LUMET: Yes, their motors are going and if you put them through extended lengths of time working on something, you can kill something as well.

Q: *Is there a certain pace and a climax that the actors reach in relation to their parts during the shooting?*
LUMET: Sure, sure. I always call it the "hot take." Sometimes it's not technically the best take. Something goes wrong with the sound or the camera move wasn't perfect. Then you've got a choice, if you

think you can get it again, to go for it again but that usually is a
very long drawn-out process, a good twelve or fourteen takes before
you get it again because usually what happens is that the actor
has really emptied out on it and has to be filled up again and
that's slow.

Q: *Do you feel that you've actually communicated any kind of idea
in your films, any view of mankind or of the psyche that you've wanted
to explore?*
LUMET: I'd be terrified to get into it. I think there is too much
articulation about the meaning of movies today.

Q: *Is it safe to say that you pick scripts that show a kind of conflict in your
characters between their past and their present?*
LUMET: Yes, I think that's very true. It's not that I don't see a common
line in it. If one's forced to say it, I just want to say it as simply as
possible. I think most of the pictures were about a conflict in what you
are. What you are is no longer working for this moment and the hell
that that causes.

Q: *Do you look to any young writers for scripts in the future?*
LUMET: Well, I can't wait (I hope racially things cool off enough in
that some cooperation is possible) until the black writers start writing
for movies. Ed Bullins and Charles Gordone and so on because
certainly in terms of the theatre, it's the most alive theatre. It's the
only theatre I go to anymore.

Outside of the blacks, Hopkins is extraordinary to me. The funny
thing is I've read more good scripts in the past year than I've ever
read. That's because a great many writers, since the collapse of
Hollywood and since nobody is any longer a $250,000 a picture-writer
and since a lot more things have to be done on spec and on what we
call step deals in which the company can stop production of a film
anywhere along the way, a lot of writers have been writing things
that are a lot closer to them. They haven't been looking for the sure
fire thing because, number one, there is no more sure fire thing and,
second of all, as long as they are writing on spec at a smaller salary
they might as well write what they care about. So I've read some

enormously talented scripts from young American writers, none of which I've seen done.

But in terms of genuine movement, in terms of everything I was saying before, if a new form is going to come out of anything, it's going to come out of a new idea and I think the black writers are the only ones dealing with any sort of a new idea at all. As for myself, I'll stay in my old investigative bag of my own brain and my own life.

What's Real? What's True?

GORDON GOW/1975

THERE IS A FACTUAL BASIS to the new Sidney Lumet film *Dog Day Afternoon* as there was to *Serpico*. There is also the same star, Al Pacino. But between these two dramatisations of life, Lumet has varied his range with a Western excursion, *Lovin' Molly*, and the resplendently merry triumph of *Murder on the Orient Express*. His kind of cinema grows increasingly eclectic.

Of the latest work, *Dog Day Afternoon*, Lumet speaks with an enthusiasm that rings truer by far than the average show-biz sell. "It's an extraordinary story. In 1972 there was a bank robbery in New York which was a total mess. Two men who were amateurs, and had never done anything like this before, got stuck with twelve hostages without wanting them. And the reason for the robbery is that one of these two men needed the money for his boyfriend to have a transexual operation. He was leading a double life: he had a wife and two children but was living with a transvestite at the same time.

"True story. Insanely funny, terribly sad. What I hope it will be is a serious treatment of an area of our population which has been so far exploited and used for sensationalism or camp. Mind you, I think that *The Boys in the Band* was terrific, precisely because it presented homosexual life on a human level. Their world, though, was far more rarified. They were people who listened to records and read books. The leading character in *Dog Day Afternoon* is a 'dese-dem-and-doser'—a punk with no intellectual pretensions and the most ordinary kind of life. He lived

From *Films and Filming*. May 1975: 10–16.

off welfare. He led this totally self-destructive life which finally caught up with him. His partner in the robbery, who was not homosexual, was killed in the attempted escape. The survivor, the man played by Al Pacino, is in jail now for twenty-five years. And this sad waste is only funny as well because of the bizarre nature of the robbery and the insane things that happened. It went on for fourteen hours; a crowd of thousands assembled. The bank didn't even have much money in it. He fixed the robbery for Friday afternoon, but he didn't realise that then most of the money would already have been taken out of the bank. Well, there was only something like five thousand dollars left. And in anger he took it and threw it into the crowd which started fighting for it, and the police started picking up the money."

The mixture of the compulsively comedic and the macabre has a certain affinity with Lumet's *Bye, Bye Braverman*. "Only here the level is much more naturalistic. One of the loveliest things in *Bye, Bye Braverman* is George Segal's speech in the graveyard, where he's trying to tell the dead people what's been happening since they died. Totally unreal and one of my favourite moments in that film. The pathetic quality in *Dog Day Afternoon* resides primarily in the fact that the central man, being homosexual, doesn't want his boyfriend to have the transexual operation but at the same times he loves him so much that he's prepared to give him anything he asks for, even if it means stealing to provide it. Pathetic. And when he did the whole thing and had gotten a jet waiting at Kennedy Airport, the transvestite was to be brought there from the hospital where he had been taken because he had tried suicide. But at the crucial moment, he wouldn't go to the airport. He said he hated the bank robber and wouldn't touch him. So there was this inept thief abandoned even by the person he'd done it for."

Here is a contrast indeed to *Murder on the Orient Express*, which in itself marked a beautifully bright departure from anything its director had done before: the gloss so deliberate, the stylisation of the train's departure from Istanbul so blithe and the characterisations so chirpily idiosyncratic.

"The idea of having a cast full of stars was mine. This wasn't a thriller; it was a whodunnit and therefore old-fashioned. I was dealing in nostalgia, not only for the whodunnit but for the train films like *Shanghai Express* and *The Lady Vanishes*. Then there is the affectionate memory of trains themselves. I'm a train freak myself. I've had some of the most glorious times of my life travelling in trains. I love sleepers. The first time I went from Paris to Rome, I just couldn't believe it. So all of this affection seemed to me to determine what kind of a movie it had to be: glamorous, incredibly attractive, and it's more charming to watch Sean Connery as a pukka colonel and Ingrid Bergman as a Swedish maid than to put the best supporting character players in the world into those parts. It needed stars. The byword became, 'Let's do a thirties movie, but if reality ever gets in the way, then to hell with reality'. The star casting didn't have to do with making it commercially viable. It had to do with style. And bless the backers for going along with it and taking what was really a risk. It wasn't the kind of operation on which you could ask anybody to take a salary cut.

"As always, these things begin selfishly. I've had a big problem that I've been aware of for years in my own work: a certain lack of charm. There's a kind of lightness that's extremely difficult to achieve. In the theatre it is best exemplified by high comedy—like *The Importance of Being Earnest*. Of course, I'm primarily a dramatic director and I think I'll always remain so, but what I'm talking about is a degree of colour that is terribly necessary just to have as a way of, among other things, offsetting drama. So immediately I read Paul Dehn's script for *Murder on the Orient Express* I knew that from a style point of view it was something I'd been trying desperately to achieve. I mean when I did *Bye, Bye Braverman* I really messed it up."

Not everybody would agree. The elusive *Bye, Bye Braverman*, made in 1968, drew a packed and attentive house when it was screened in the undeniably small auditorium of London NFT2. And opinions overheard on the way out were conflicting, to be sure, but there were those who reacted most favourably, myself included. The film was in the black comedy genre: an essay in character study allied to a meandering journey to a funeral. It toyed on the brink of tastelessness but maintained its equilibrium. Yet Lumet remains dissatisfied with it.

"Let me put it this way: I think it was one of the best scripts I've ever received, but I felt that my own work didn't match it. My control wasn't firm enough, I wasn't really in command, and I edited it badly. Its meanderings really seemed like meanderings, rather than making points. At the same time I love it, and I know that a lot of people do, and yet I know in my heart of hearts that there was more to be gotten out of that material."

In any case, *Bye, Bye Braverman* could never have attained the high comedy that Lumet speaks about, because it was weighted quite strongly with its inherent blackness, and it arrived at a realistically unhappy conclusion. But when I pointed this out to him, he said I was actually providing a perfect example of what he felt was wrong in his direction of it.

"If my control had been total, it would have been a far more hilarious film, and therefore, when it switched at the end, it would have been far more moving. I missed also with *The Group*, which again had something finally serious to say and yet didn't have enough command in its lightness of style to offset the final point, which should have been stronger by contrast with what had gone before."

The Group, from Mary McCarthy's novel, concerned the high hopes of college girls and their later adjustments and compromises as life failed, in its well-known way, to meet their earlier and dewy-eyed expectations. Maybe it simply wasn't Lumet's meat.

One associates him first with pretty stern stuff, partly because he came on so strongly in 1957 with his initial cinema work, *12 Angry Men*.

He was born in Philadelphia in 1925 but raised from the age of four in New York. His father was a Yiddish actor, and the son followed his dad's precepts for a time, graduating in 1950 to the production side of television. That was the "golden age" of live American TV, from all accounts a soul-wracking but mind-expanding sphere in which a tyro director had to operate in a catch-as-catch-can fashion. The period threw up some notable names, of course, all leaping out of where they were and into the cinema studio at the least enticement. Lumet was prominent among them. But he made his first impact not by seizing upon the expansiveness of the big-screen medium, but by contrast to its usual processes. *12 Angry Men* was set claustrophobically in a jury room filled with hot argument (Lumet himself, incidentally, has more than once been enthralled when called up for jury service), and there was none of the cinema's customary out.

"The point was to use the confinement and not to expand the original TV script—or to open it up. What we did was to restrict it more and more from a visual point of view. As the film went on, I used longer and longer lenses so that the ceiling became closer to the heads, the walls became closer to the chair. I kept putting it into a smaller and smaller box to increase the claustrophobic feeling of it. It took a great deal of technique. The cinematographer Boris Kaufman and I worked out a lighting pattern. We talked about how at the beginning of the movie we'd separate the people from the walls, but then as the piece progressed we'd bring those walls closer and closer until finally it would look as if the walls were only two inches behind the jurors. This was all achieved between the choice of lenses and the lighting.

"The audience, thank God, was not aware of those things. I hate to do technical things that one sees. But slowly over the whole film that room keeps getting smaller and smaller."

For all that, Lumet certainly had a technical effect that could be very clearly seen in *The Fugitive Kind*, which was adapted from the Tennessee Williams play *Orpheus Descending*. For a moment, reminiscent of the upside-down disorientation on the battlefield in Grigori Chukrai's *Ballad of a Soldier*, Lumet had his camera on a balcony taking an upside-down view of Anna Magnani as she ran into the space below at an extremely agitated crisis in the plot. Lumet hadn't seen *Ballad of a Soldier*, which was possibly made no earlier than *The Fugitive Kind*. He cannot tell what prompted his upside-down shot.

"You never know where these things come from. I remember in my early television days I had done a scene where a man is waiting at a police sergeant's desk and they were about to put him through it, and the police sergeant never looked up at him but just kept scribbling away in the entry book. There was the sound of the scratch of the pen, and the waiting man was sweating, and this went on for two minutes. And I thought, 'Oh boy, Sidney, that's terrific—what a good idea'. And, of course, five years later, seeing *The Informer* for the umpteenth time, it suddenly dawned on me that John Ford had done it first, and brilliantly, when they brought McLaglen as Gypo in to be questioned. You know, you're part and parcel of everything you've seen and felt and done.

"I'm never really concerned about the originality of something. All I think about is whether it's necessary."

Quite often, without relinquishing any realism, he has worked with very high-powered and individual stars. When they are as distinctive as Brando, who took the lead in *The Fugitive Kind*, Lumet is exultant.

"It's terrific. There's no great secret about directing. The job is to get the best out of every element of the production. So the better the elements are, hopefully the results are going to be that much fuller. Take Marlon—when that motor kicks over and he takes off, it's extraordinary to watch. And it's interesting to talk to him and to find ways of releasing that."

Is he the kind of actor, I wondered, who looks much to a director for guidance? "Oh yes," said Lumet at once. "He's very knowledgeable about his own instrument. And like all people who are, he therefore knows that his talent and ability have to be put into place. Marlon works in a fascinating way, by a process of elimination, constantly questioning why a point couldn't be made this way or that way. Primarily what he's doing is eliminating any other possibility of how to commit himself. It's thrilling to watch it. And it's thrilling also to argue with him and thereby to help him channel that extraordinary motor into the place that the script demands."

For Anna Magnani, though, *The Fugitive Kind* seemed a difficult assignment. "I think she hated acting in English. Of course, Tennessee had written it for her, and she was a great friend of his. But what happens is that when you get down to an emotion, you revert. Under certain emotional conditions, the accent would become stronger and stronger and stronger, until she was finally incomprehensible. So after the shooting she had to come back and loop about 50 percent of her lines."

An earlier Lumet film, *Stage Struck*, seems now like a variation upon *All About Eve*, only gentler, dealing as it does with a girl whose ambition to build a New York stage career for herself assumed compulsive proportions and a trace of ruthlessness. Her impromptu Shakespearean audition at a theatrical party, aided by champagne on an empty stomach, was a testing exercise for Susan Strasberg whose father Lee was a drama teacher much esteemed by members of his Actors Studio. Not only did his daughter have this to live up to, but *Stage Struck* was dangerously inviting comparison with a Katharine Hepburn classic. Because, long before *Eve*, Hepburn had won an Academy Award for her interpretation of the very same subject in 1933, when it was known as *Morning Glory*— a film which Lumet had never seen.

"I didn't dare take a look at it. I'd loved Katie Hepburn's work all my life, and I didn't want to be unfair to Susan by trying to get her to act like Kate. But I have seen it since I finished *Stage Struck*. It's old-fashioned by now, of course, but all the same I love it."

Certain moments were deleted in *Stage Struck*. There was no duplication of Hepburn's brave face as she sipped the cup of coffee which was the only nourishment she could afford, and upon being discovered in her solitude explained that it was "after dinner coffee"—this memory survives the years and revives superbly, and somebody was wise not to attempt an echo of it in the remake.

Of *Stage Struck* as a whole, Lumet feels that "it was not as good as it could have been. One of the reasons I wanted to do it so badly was that I love the theatre. I came from the theatre. And this was a sort of Valentine to the theatre, with its fairy tale of the understudy going on, which I'm very moved by. I wanted to make it a lovely light soufflé of a movie, but I'm afraid I came up with a bit of a pancake.

"I acted on the stage, you know, in my childhood, and later as well." He has directed for the stage too and, of course, quite a number of his films, *Stage Struck* included, have had their origins on the boards.

But in 1959 with *That Kind of Woman*, Lumet seemed at least momentarily to be sinking into a Hollywood quagmire. Tab Hunter as a clean-cut sailor fell for Sophia Loren as the kept plaything of a well-heeled type played by George Sanders. "Pretty crummy," Lumet concedes, "although I still think the first forty-five minutes are absolutely terrific. The sequence when they're on the train is marvellous. And Sophia is wonderful: I love working with her. A really talented lady."

And what about Tab Hunter? "Also talented but primarily a character actor—yet always used as a leading man because he's so pretty. I've seen him do character parts in which he's really great. But as a leading man he tightens up. Mostly he turned to character work in American television when his Hollywood career started going sour. Then he played the roles of psychotic killers and so forth, and his talent became clear."

In 1962 Lumet made *Long Day's Journey Into Night*, which was exceptional among film versions of stage plays, in that it employed close-ups and angling and cutting to tremendous advantage, but scarcely extended its acting area beyond the single setting of the Eugene O'Neill original, nor did it enlarge upon his cast of four characters. Lumet was on not dissimilar territory, in cinematic terms, to the confined space of *12 Angry Men*. His players, of course, were exceptional too: Katharine

Hepburn, Ralph Richardson, Jason Robards, and Dean Stockwell, the latter in the role that O'Neill based on himself when younger.

Among these, Richardson, that superb creature of the stage who graces the cinema not infrequently, was put to perhaps his most exacting filmic test. Lumet says, "There's no secret about the fact that Ralph is terrified of the camera. But at the same time he is unquestionably a great actor. Yet he looks to a director, too. A piece like *Long Day's Journey Into Night* has to be more rigidly controlled than almost any other kind of film—because there are only four people. We used almost the total text of the play. There was no screenplay. I cut ten of O'Neill's 177 pages, but in small trims; I never cut a scene out or anything like that. The only reason I could cut it at all was that the use of close-up will make a point clearer sooner than words.

"But now we're into an old argument of mine. I think one of the misdirections that films went into was a confusion of cinema with scenery. If a scene took place against a mountain, it was a 'movie'—but if it took place in a wallpapered room, it wasn't. Well, that's nonsense to me. Movie technique, to me, means using a camera and lighting, in addition to the script and the acting, to reveal more about human behaviour. The technique is making a contribution that no other means of doing it *could* make.

"I think now that *Long Day's Journey Into Night*, although it was a commercial failure, is one of the best films I've ever seen. I say that because, you know, you get away from your own work after a while, so that you can look at it fairly objectively. And it's an extraordinary movie."

The employment of close-ups for dramatic value as well as for character observation was again most fruitful in *Fail-Safe*, with Henry Fonda poised tensely at the telephone in a story destined to be regarded eventually as a straight-faced treatment of the kind of U.S.-Russian nuclear threat which Kubrick handled satirically in *Dr. Strangelove*. The thematic similarity of the two films came as surprise to Lumet.

"I didn't know anything about it until we'd finished shooting and were sued. I'd never read Peter George's novel *Red Alert*, on which *Dr. Strangelove* was based. I knew we were dead as a movie as soon as Columbia bought us, because I knew they had done that to hold us off until *Dr. Strangelove* was released. But funnily enough I think they made a mistake. Because although *Dr. Strangelove* did so well, I think it would have done even better coming out after us, rather than the other way around. The wry comment would have worked more effectively after the serious one."

Lumet's next film is still considered by many to be his very best: *The Pawnbroker*, based on a novel by Edward Lewis Wallant, with Rod Steiger in one of his finest performances as a Jew whose mind is perpetually disturbed by recollections of his time in a concentration camp. For this, Lumet was a pioneer in the use of near-subliminal memory flashes. While racketeering provided a flurry of action, the chief thread was earnest and relentless, the Brooklyn setting imbued with doom, and the drama as fervent as it was tough to take. Critics enthused and so did a healthy proportion of the public.

"It was one of the surprises of my life that *The Pawnbroker* turned out to be such an enormous commercial success. Because, of course, I just don't know what makes a commercial success, but it was my first really big grosser. We all did it for practically no money—I took a much smaller fee than I was worth on the commercial market at that time, plus a percentage of the profits. It was privately financed, not studio financed. It had a tremendous run in America and did very well in Italy and France. Maybe the public was attracted, as I certainly was myself, by that extraordinary story."

Overtly tougher than Lumet's norm, especially in physical terms, was *The Hill*. Packing an even more violent punch than *The Pawnbroker* and persuasively opened out by Ray Rigby from a play he had written in collaboration with R. S. Allen, it was set in a North African prison camp of the Second World War, where a sadistic British sergeant-major, played by Harry Andrews, took delight in making his victims climb a hill carrying heavy burdens in blistering heat. For its day, 1965, it used uncommonly forthright serviceman's language. And it drew rather elementary yet persuasive he-man performances from Sean Connery and others.

"It was something very personal to Rigby. This had happened to him. And therefore one felt that extra obligation of not exploiting it, not over-dramatising it, of not cooking it in any way. For example, it had no music score. It was not a film in which crashing cymbals could be heard at the denouement. It was a question of trying to do it as honestly and as close to reality as possible, and I think that's what made it good."

Location shooting under a hot sun gave *The Hill* an especially cinematic quality. But Lumet's enthusiasm for theatre was affirmed once
more in the centrepiece of his fairly persuasive spy melodrama, *The
Deadly Affair.* Realism in muted colour pervaded. Yet at the heart of it
was a jab of melodrama when a theatre audience rose to leave the stalls
after witnessing the brutal murder of the title figure in Marlowe's
Edward II, but just one person remained in her seat: the woman portrayed by Simone Signoret, who had been stealthily done to death by
the man sitting next to her during the performance. The *frisson*—to be
equated, of course, with famous bits of Hitchcock, such as the
Palladium pandemonium in *The 39 Steps* and the bun-rush at the ballet
in *Torn Curtain*—springs from the fact that more drama is being generated in the audience than upon the stage. The killing in the stalls in
The Deadly Affair was witnessed by secret agents installed inquisitively
but rather helplessly in the front row of the balcony.

"The thing about that," says Lumet, "is that, of course, it's not *real*,
and yet in the final analysis it is *true*. There's a difference between reality and truth. The strongest point to be made is that these are seedy
people doing seedy things which are actually of a significance far
greater than they, in their petty little lives, know about. The cost is so
much greater than the quality of the people involved. But the problem
in that sequence of the death of Simone Signoret was how to make
something believable for the moment of watching it, even though it's
almost impossible.

"The murder scene on the stage—the play within the film, in which
the king is killed with a red-hot poker—was chosen by Paul Dehn, who
wrote the screenplay which was based on John le Carré's novel *Call for
the Dead.* And I was absolutely thrilled by Paul's choice. It was a matter
of trying to find a really outrageous drama that could be going on
while, in our terms, a far more realistic drama was being played out in
the audience. So therefore the heightened theatrical nature of *Edward II*
helped to offset the problem we faced of making that moment believable. Of course, there's nothing like that sense of gore the Elizabethan
dramatists had—it can really make you feel humble in the theatre."

It is, of course, a sensationally horrendous death scene (the heated
poker is thrust deep into Edward's anus, and the occasion has since
been engraved upon the minds of many playgoers by the distinguished

Prospect Theatre production in which Ian McKellen played Edward): "And they talk about the violence of today's movies!" says Lumet. For the film, Peter Hall directed actors from the Royal Shakespeare Company in the Marlowe excerpt, and censorship was not so relaxed at the time (it was 1966) that Lumet could show the vital incident as graphically as might be possible today.

"I wanted a *pure* theatrical performance. So Peter gave us that complete, and I looked at it once and decided right away how to shoot it. You got the *idea*. Which was quite enough for the purpose. And although I could be more explicit now if I chose, in a case like that I wouldn't choose. I feel that a lot of people now are releasing a lot of behaviour on the screen, not because they are at last allowed to, but simply because they think it will sell well."

A Lumet film of 1969 has been virtually "lost": *Blood Kin*, derived from a Tennessee Williams play, with Lynn Redgrave and James Coburn. "It was an extraordinary story about two half-brothers in Louisiana, one black and the other white. The white one married a dopey car-hop waitress, so that the old family mansion would not fall into the hands of his black brother. It wasn't a success. But my feelings are that I would rather do incomplete Tennessee Williams than complete-any-body-else. It was lovely to work on, and I'm sorry I couldn't solve it."*

The Anderson Tapes, a crime thriller with electronic spying connotations, proved another beneficial working partnership between Lumet and his *Hill* star Sean Connery: a liaison that bore still more interesting results in *The Offence*, adapted from the John Hopkins play *This Story of Yours*, and once more proving Lumet's ability to wrest filmic virtues from restricted settings. The claustrophobia, indeed, was as aptly subjective for Ian Bannen as a brutally assaulted suspect as it was for the pressurised mind of the psychotic policeman played by Connery. Here the crime of molesting minors was skilfully used as a trigger for the lawman's obsessive behaviour. Pains were taken to indicate that the policeman's case was an exception rather than the norm, but for a film made in

---

* Editor's Note: This film was retitled *Last of the Mobile Hot-Shots*.

Britain *The Offence* was uncommonly pungent in areas more frequently broached by the American cinema.

I asked Lumet which he found more difficult, the confined drama or the wide-ranging realism of *Serpico* with its many changes of scene and its 107 different locations.

"As a matter of fact both are equally hard. *Serpico*, just physically and in terms of logistics, gives you the problem of keeping your emotional themework in perspective. You have to continually ask yourself not only 'Where am I physically?' but 'Where am I emotionally?' I think I was more tired after finishing *Serpico* than almost any movie I've ever done. There was also the obligation to the real Frank Serpico—to be honest with his life and not exploit it.

"Both that and *The Offence* dealt in police corruption: *The Offence* with corruption of the spirit, and *Serpico* with the external corruption.

"And it comes back in a sense to the point of *12 Angry Men*: those who are bearing the legal responsibility of our lives are therefore in a way bearing the moral responsibility as well. And what are they like? Who are they?"

The questions hover importantly. They loom more consequentially than Lumet's desire to be occasionally lighter in style. And from what does this seriousness of purpose—this intense concern of director for them—evolve? "Just from having been a good, solid poor Jewish boy. That gets you into it. I was brought up in an essentially orthodox household. The Jewish ethic is stern, unforgiving, preaching, moralistic. And I guess it starts you thinking like that at an early age. Just like being a good Jesuit."

Sidney Lumet: Letting It Happen

MORT SHEINMAN / 1975

NEW YORK—When the gun blasts exploded in the mid-morning air of Spanish Harlem, things didn't happen exactly the way Sidney Lumet figured they would. Even before the boy crawled out of the pawnshop and onto the sidewalk, his body contorted in pain, all the people disappeared. They simply vanished. Lumet did not expect that, but he was delighted. It was just what he needed to make the scene work.

Sidney Lumet makes movies. He has been making them for eighteen years, and he has made some memorable ones. This one, back in the early winter of 1963, was called *The Pawnbroker* and, like several other films he has done, was shot in New York. Unlike a lot of other movies made in this city by men who do not really understand New York, it captured perfectly the pace and actions and reactions of the people who live here.

One reason why is Lumet's ability to let things happen instead of trying to choreograph them.

"For that scene," he recalled the other day, "we had three hidden cameras outside the shop. When the shots went off inside the pawnshop, neighborhood people were walking by. They were unaware a movie was being made. We just decided to fire the gun and let it happen. Whether it's through my own knowledge of the city or something else I can't explain. I had the confidence to know something extraordinary would happen—and it did.

From *Women's Wear Daily*. October 1975-12. Reprinted with permission of *Women's Wear Daily*.

"As soon as the shots went off, everybody disappeared—which, of course, is perfectly logical in that neighborhood. I had a police car standing by, we cued it, and as soon as it came in, so did the people. They knew if they showed up after the police, they wouldn't be called as witnesses. We were able to get the entire sequence in one take."

Lumet is a small, spare, neat-looking man who was born in Philadelphia fifty-one years ago, but who moved to New York when he was two. He has lived here ever since. He is not certain why the films he makes here come off so well, but it has to do, he says, with a sense of security.

"I've never really thought too much about it," he said. "I'm sure part of the energy of the city rubs off, but it's something I've assumed for so long and never really pinpointed. It's like knowing where a certain house is but not knowing the address. I have fun shooting all over the world, but working in New York has to do with the pleasure of shooting in an area that has no mysteries."

One of the parts of the city Lumet has lived in is Brooklyn and that is where his latest film, *Dog Day Afternoon*, was shot earlier this year. The true story of one of the strangest bank robberies ever attempted, it was shot over a six-week period in the Park Slope section of Brooklyn, came in $400,000 under budget and reaped rave reviews.

"Shooting there was like working on a back lot," said Lumet. "It was terrific. The Beame administration was a little less organized than the Lindsay administration in terms of making a movie here, but it was totally helpful. They even changed a bus route for us, because the buses would have killed us on sound."

Most of the action in *Dog Day Afternoon* takes place inside the bank, where two gunmen hold eight employees as hostages, and on the sidewalk outside, where police, FBI agents, reporters and neighborhood people wait to see what happens.

"We had about four-hundred to five-hundred extras for that film," said Lumet, "but by nightfall, when everybody was home from work, the whole neighborhood would be there. They got right into it. They loved it."

So, apparently, did Lumet. There are several reasons for this, but perhaps the biggest is Al Pacino, who stars as the homosexual bank robber out to get money so his male "wife" can have a sex-change operation.

"It's so boring for me to talk about Al," said Lumet. "Boring for other people, I mean. He is very possibly a great actor—and I'm not using the word 'great' in the *Variety* sense. His talent is just blinding. There are no difficulties. The difficulties are only in getting the satisfaction. Al is a perfectionist. I guess I'm pretty tough that way too. I'm a perfectionist on an emotional level. On *Dog Day*, the first thing we had to do was convince you that it really happened."

Pacino and Lumet worked together once before, on another film based on real events. That was *Serpico*, with Pacino playing the part of Frank Serpico, the idealistic New York City cop who tried to uncover corruption in the police department and got shot in the face for his troubles. He recovered, but now lives in Europe.

"I saw Frank about fourteen or fifteen months ago," said Lumet. "I think he's living in Holland now. You know, he's a guy who really wanted nothing but to be a cop. I hope he has some kind of life left. I don't want to sound presumptuous, but I don't think Europe is the answer for him. He seems to be such a native American. If there were only some way he could channel his talents . . ."

The thought seemed to remind Lumet of John (Sonny) Wojtowicz, the character played by Pacino in *Dog Day Afternoon*. Wojtowicz is still in jail as a result of that day's activity.

"Oddly enough," Lumet said, "I feel the same way about Sonny. He's enormously talented, but he had no place to put it. I mean, the way he manipulated the cops, the way he manipulated the crowds, the way he reacted to a situation for which he was totally unprepared. He was the last one in the world who wanted hostages. He has tremendous energy and imagination and—I know it sounds funny to use this word about Sonny—but, like Frank, he has dedication. He keeps going for results."

In one of the oddest bits of casting for *Dog Day Afternoon*, Lumet came up with Judith Malina of the Living Theater to play the role of Pacino's mother. The mention of her name brought a broad smile to Lumet's face.

"She was Al's idea," he said. "We were going crazy trying to cast the mother and Al said, 'How about Judith Malina?' (It was also Pacino, it will be recalled, who suggested Lee Strasberg for a key role in *Godfather II*.) Well, I hadn't seen her since the Living Theater did *Medea* about eleven years ago and the hardest part was trying to track her down.

"We had a phone number, but the line had been disconnected. Finally, I sent a kid to the last-known address of the Living Theater in Brooklyn. He found some old man there who was able to come up with a number in Vermont and that's where we found her. I had no idea of what to expect. I didn't even know whether she'd want to do a 'commercial' film.

"Well, let me tell you, she is an actress. Totally professional. She also had no money and we had to pay her fare from Vermont, but she walked in and was perfect. Now she's back with the Living Theater, working in Pittsburgh, and part of her fee was a donation to the company."

With two major films scheduled for next year, Lumet has plenty to look forward to. On Jan. 5, he begins shooting *Network* in New York. It has been written by Paddy Chayefsky, his first script since *Hospital* and Lumet hopes *Network* will do to the television giants what *Hospital* did to hospitals—shake them up. Faye Dunaway and William Holden will co-star, and there are two more big parts still to be cast.

One, said Lumet, is "America's most beloved news commentator." He does not know whether he will get a real TV personality for the role.

"Walter Cronkite's a good friend of mine and John Chancellor is a good friend of Paddy's, but their news departments may not think a movie like this is 'dignified' enough," grinned Lumet.

After *Network*, Lumet faces what he feels will be one of his biggest challenges as a director. He will go to London to film *Equus*, the prize-winning stage play. The script will be written by Peter Shaffer, who wrote the play, and the star will be Peter Firth, who starred in it.

"It will be a very difficult film," said Lumet. "I think I know how to do it, but I'm still exploring a lot of possibilities."

Chances are he will simply "let it happen."

Lumet: Endlessly Energetic

DAVID STERRITT/1977

WHEN YOUR NAME IS SIDNEY LUMET, hits flow from
your camera as if there were no other kind of movie. So I ask the obvious question: "What's the secret?"

Mr. Lumet smiles, thinks for about two seconds, and answers: "I
haven't the remotest idea. I'm the worst guesser in the world—I sometimes think the picture won't make a dime—and I can't figure it out. If
I could, I'd have hits all the time!"

Of course, Lumet does have hits all the time. Right now it's *Network*.
A few months ago it was *Dog Day Afternoon*. Before that it was *Murder on
the Orient Express* and before that *Serpico*. A few flops have peppered his
career a well, but other milestones include *The Pawnbroker*, *12 Angry
Men*, *Long Day's Journey Into Night*, and *The Sea Gull*.

Explains the director, "I just go with whatever interests me. Of course
you want a hit, because it gives you muscle. And money never hurt
anyone. . . ."

Mr. Lumet's latest "interest" is *Equus* which he shot in Toronto with
Richard Burton, Joan Plowright and Peter Firth. The filmmaker calls it
"an emotionally exhausting piece," and admits to having questioned
"whether it should ever be a movie, since it was such a singular theatrical experience [on Broadway] and we had to throw out that stylized
approach, which would have seemed like copping-out on screen."

Describing the Peter Shaffer work as "the drama of a man in doubt about the efficacy of his life," Mr. Lumet acknowledges the pitfalls of spelling out the story of a psychiatrist aiding a boy who has committed a violent crime against a stable-full of horses. Yet he defends his approach to the subject, and compares the script to works of Eugene O'Neill—"It stirs up a lot of mud that you thought was just lying there."

Though Mr. Lumet's work has not pleased everyone over the years, even one of his harsher critics—film commentator Andrew Sarris—has remarked on the "innate good taste" that salvages most of his pictures from "mediocrity" and helps compensate for "the middle-brow aspirations of his projects." Mr. Lumet himself doesn't read reviews and wouldn't care much about all this. He sees films as galumphing adventures in form and content and delights in learning a new style the way a child enjoys mastering a larger bicycle.

Take the immensely popular *Murder on the Orient Express*, based on Agatha Christie's whodunit (or, more accurately, who-didn't-do-it). "That was a tremendous effort," says the small, endlessly energetic director. "I'd never been able to do that style before, and I'd ruined three pictures trying. But I knew that one can learn styles, and I did. Making this light-in-spirit film, I was the most intense person you ever saw—though it didn't stir up the profundity of emotion of *Equus*, with the four a.m. wakeups and all."

Happily, Mr. Lumet agreed with the general public in being "thrilled" at the result. "And learning that light style has been a great help to my dramatic work. I'd always felt there were a couple of arrows missing from the quiver." Next the versatile craftsman would like to try a musical. "I got fired from *Funny Girl* after six months of work," he recalls. "But I think I have a feel for that, and I'd like to get my feet wet."

In *Network* Mr. Lumet collaborated with celebrated writer Paddy Chayefsky, another veteran of the "golden" TV years that began more than two-and-a-half decades ago. Together they fashioned a scathing portrait of the United States as reflected in mindless prime-time entertainment.

"Paddy found the perfect image for talking about America," the director comments. "The television medium says more about this country than anything else, even the automobile!" Moreover, "Paddy and I feel the same way about TV. We didn't leave it—it left us." Mr. Lumet laments that TV often avoids the "realism" of videotape because it reduces earnings (by precluding foreign theatrical releases of TV dramas). He complains that TV frequently refuses to deal with meaningful material. "They call it depressing or something."

Like *The Front*, which was released slightly earlier, *Network* has been accused of self-righteousness in attacking a medium no more corrupt than the movies themselves. Mr. Lumet disagrees. "Whatever crimes the movies have been guilty of—and heaven knows they have been— movies are still voluntary. The audience pays to get in.

"And nobody ever sat a screaming two-and-a-half-year-old in the first row of a theater to quiet him. TV is used as a babysitter and a pacifier. It is in the home, unrestricted. And this is where it begins to dovetail with American behavior. It is a perfect excuse for the lack of personal responsibility. And this is what our picture is about."

So Mr. Lumet supports Chayefsky's criticisms of the tube. "Like all real ragers, that's what Paddy's about—the sane man yelling in an insane world." But the director retains a wistful fondness for television. "I'm very caught up in life and involved, and I love TV's immediacy." He doesn't even mind its evanescent nature. "Too much is permanent. A lot of things shouldn't be. We're getting drowned in garbage."

Speaking of garbage, Mr. Lumet is keenly aware of the proliferation of meaningless violence and sex in today's films. He places the responsibility, and the solution, on the shoulders of moviemakers themselves. "There are the exploiters who could make Shirley Temple's first kiss with John Agar seem dirty. And there are the nonexploiters. Simple as that. Exploiting means it wasn't necessary to the story, or was put there for shock effect or to get attention or pick up the pace.

"In the old TV days I did a melodrama series called *Danger* that was always accused of violence. Actually we had less violence than the other shows—they were blowing up bodies and all, but you never believed them. We had better scripts that were better directed, so just a slap in the face seem real. . . .

"When you have a work of art, it has the responsibility of being so well-done and generic to its thematic line that there's no possibility of being too violent or pornographic. Otherwise it's not art. The only germane question is, is he an honest moviemaker? This leads to anarchy in terms of opinion, because my idea of an honest moviemaker might not be somebody else's. But over the long run there's not much doubt about where creative people migrate to."

Mr. Lumet says his daughter, recently turned twelve, is now old enough to be taken to *Serpico*, but not yet to *Dog Day Afternoon*—even though he used "self-censorship" in the latter so the film would have fewer sexual overtones than the real-life bank-robbery incident on which it was based.

"My kids are going to learn about values from my wife and myself," he concludes. "I'm her parent. It's not her church or TV or school that's responsible—it's me!"

Colour and Concepts

RALPH APPLEBAUM / 1978

THE STAGE PLAY AND MOTION PICTURE are worlds apart
and when one tries to transform the play into cinema terms, he often
finds that the theatrical conventions—monologues, expositions, and so
on, just prohibit a faithful adaptation. The far easiest play, of course, to
adapt to another medium, especially one as visual as film, is that comedy or drama whose scenery and level of performance remain on a naturalistic plane. But Peter Shaffer's *Equus* was enigmatic, because although
the play was rooted in realism, it nonetheless went a few degrees past
the norm by employing actors to mime horses. And to enhance their
performances, they wore brown leotards and large skeletal horses' heads
and silver-wire hoofs. The audience was so enthralled by the sheer
brilliance of John Dexter's staging and the high calibre of the acting—
especially by Peter Firth—that the play about a psychiatrist's attempt to
treat a young boy who inexplicably blinded six horses became a huge
success on both the London and Broadway stages.

The monumental task of transferring this complex and gripping tale
to the screen fell into the lap of Sidney Lumet, a director of immense
stature and intelligence who has directed versions of Tennessee
Williams's play *Orpheus Descending* (known on film as *The Fugitive Kind)*,
Arthur Miller's *A View From the Bridge,* and Eugene O'Neill's *Long Day's
Journey Into Night* for the big screen in addition to such fine entertain-
ments as *Network, Dog Day Afternoon, Murder on The Orient Express, The
Pawnbroker* and *Fail-Safe.* Lumet has also directed Camus's *Caligula* for
the New York stage, and his live television version of O'Neill's *The*

From *Films and Filming.* May 1978: 13–18. Reprinted by permission of the author.

Iceman Cometh won an Emmy Award from the Academy of Television Arts and Sciences.

When *Equus* was released, the critics were respectful, and the picture did get some fine notices, but that adulation did not extend to the big money critics, those whose every word can sprinkle a hard-sell picture with box-office action. When I spoke with Mr. Lumet briefly at *The Wiz* cutting room (his all-black musical is in the midst of post-production), he was eager to express his feelings on *Equus* and, of course, *The Wiz.*

"I think *Equus* was very vulnerable to attack," says Lumet. "I think you can ask a very legitimate question, and that is, when it's so perfect a theatre piece, why do it as a movie at all? I saw the original London production, I saw it with Tony Perkins, who is marvellous, and I saw it with Richard. And in none of those three did I feel that the kernel of the play was evident. And that is Dysart's (the doctor's) conflict, which is also Peter Shaffer's conflict. So I thought as a movie we could find a new way of looking at it. But I think the critics were exposed to a much more multi-levelled experience in the movie because of the realism, because of the stylisation, because of the shift in Richard, and for some of the people it was overcomplicating it or exposing the play from the wrong point of view. For other people it was a greater experience than the play. We actually got some extraordinary reviews, but not from the 'important critics'. But I've no idea of what's going to be the reception to a given picture in advance."

What Lumet does realise is the importance of good reviews. "The fact is that an awful lot of my pictures are not your normal commercial fare, and unless it's something like *Murder on the Orient Express,* good reviews are necessary to launch them. Even the fact that you have stars in a film today doesn't help. *Bobby Deerfield* had Al Pacino in it and still it went to the shit house. So I care about reviews only from the point of view that it can help the picture get started. And except for the *New York Times* and the *Daily News,* which I get with my morning coffee, I haven't read a review since 1968."

Equus, as most would agree, was a play of great beauty and imagination. But it was highly stylised, and Lumet realised almost immediately the idea of men acting as horses would not work on screen. "We did not want to make a stylised version as a movie. The problem was if you start with Dysart's reality and move that into film terms, then the boy's character and everything that happened to him in the stable had to be realistic, because the reality he was being watched in was going to create the dilemma within him. So it became quite clear to us that we had to treat the boy and the horses realistically.

"It is not, however, a naturalistic piece. *Equus* does not fall into the category of films like *Dog Day Afternoon, Serpico* and *All the President's Men,* where the first obligation directorially is to convince an audience that this really happened. From Peter Shaffer's point of view it's much more of a poetic vision, because the basic dilemma that he finds in life, and one sees this in all his work, whether it's in *Equus* or *Royal Hunt in the Sun,* is the struggle between the Apollonian and Dionysian man. And that duality in people is what I think Peter is primarily interested in. So, in a sense, we wanted to make *Equus* about that, about the conflict between the Apollonian and Dionysian approach to life, and that tremendous, if not impossibility, of uniting the two in any one person because that just doesn't seem to happen. We wanted to get the Dionysian side on a more realistic level, so that it could be presented squarely in both its horror and its magnificence. For example, and now I'm talking techniques, which I don't like to do, in a way the horse ride of the boy and the stabbing of the horses are done in an almost identical light pattern. They both start in natural light and as the scene continues the light changes until it becomes a totally unrealistic visual effect. And that's more or less the pattern in the entire movie. Starting with reality but never letting reality become the overriding thing, always being free to move away from it."

Lumet calls his early years as a director the "good old days" because the pictures were filmed in black-and-white which he says was capable of showing genuine tragedy. "There is something about the nature of colour itself," says Lumet, "that is so unreal that it prevents you from going through a major tragic experience." For *Equus* he worked out a very elaborate colour scheme with his cinematographer, Osward Morris, and production and costume designer, Tony Walton.

"We decided on certain tonal values to run through the entire piece. Some are constant and others were used only for specific scenes and instances. For example, if I'm not mistaken, the colour red never appears except as light. The colour blue never appears. None of the simple colours that you could easily define and say, that's red, that's blue, that's yellow, were in it. Because we were dealing constantly with duality, from both the lighting, costuming and scenic points of view, every colour had mixtures in it. The only scene in which we did have pure colours, and that was deliberate, was when Richard and Joan Plowright fight at the hospital. And against their background are these distorted children's drawings."

On stage, the blinding scene was rather lame, since it was done in mime, with the boy raising the spike up to the actor's eyes, who would then react accordingly. But when it occurs on screen it is a paroxysm of fury, heightened by a series of quick cuts—the boy raising the scythe, blood spraying on his face, the startled horses, their burnt out eye sockets, a Balinese dagger with the skeleton of a horse's head. Lumet has been attacked for that scene's realism, but he defends it on the basis that it was an integral part of the story.

"If you're going to show the boy's magnificence and Dysart's envy of him, you've got to get into the area of his horror also. A boy who blinds six horses is not your average hero. So we always knew it had to be depicted. There was, however, some doubt as to how it would be done. I shot a lot of footage in which the animals began to turn into other kinds of angers, faces of Christ, faces of the boy's mother, faces of his father. But I later felt that was too psychologically explicit and eliminated it, just leaving in the shot of the ancient Balinese dagger to relegate the stabbing to a much older impulse—that over and above the psychosis of the boy, that violence, or whatever you want to call it, is in all of us."

Lumet is a stickler for preparation, and he and Peter Shaffer worked on *Equus* for over a year before the cameras commenced rolling. "I know the visual style of a particular film well before rehearsal, but I use the rehearsal time to see how I'm going to achieve it. And I don't lay out the actual camera angles until either the last two days of rehearsals or when we begin to shoot. Usually, the night before I'm going to shoot a scene, I'll re-read it, block it in my mind, and mark my script with notes on the shots I want to get."

Rehearsal time on *Equus* was particularly valuable because "it seemed to me in the play there was no Dysart; it was just Burton reciting rather than really acting. And there are reasons for that, the main one being that he took over the part quickly and didn't have much time to work with John Dexter, who was working at the Met. I didn't feel Burton understood Dysart, who, by the way, this story is about. I have always felt that the drama belongs to who is going through the character transitions. When we begin with Dysart he is already in doubt about the efficacy of his profession, and here comes the one case which absolutely destroys his confidence. So Burton was very co-operative, and we worked on his character. Peter Firth, on the other hand, I did very little work with. He was almost the perfect actor." The Academy of Motion Picture Arts and Sciences must agree with Lumet, because both Burton and Firth were nominated for Oscars.

One scene called for Firth to regress in time to age five, to relive the memory of seeing his first horse. And Lumet has only praise for him. "Because he is such a remarkable actor, I felt he could carry it in attitude and that we would not need a five-year-old Alan Strang. And we also felt that was justified because in a sense we were not treating his character in realistic terms at all. Most of the lighting and shooting style is stylised because of his character. The reality that he represents is to Dysart, and so it almost becomes Dysart's subjected view of Alan's life. It reflects Dysart's feelings about him."

Because the film required some very complex camera angles, scenes in the double level section of the stable and the boy's room were filmed at the Toronto International Film Studio in Kleinburg. I asked Lumet about his stunning pan from the boy and the horse in the field to Burton addressing the audience in his office.

"I never tell movie secrets. It's like the magician telling you how he sawed the lady in half. I really do feel that way. On *The Wiz* we have quite literally a number of magical things happening and when I was working on one of these moments, the stills photographer came over and started snapping away. I just blew up at him, ripped the film out of his camera and exposed it. I am not one to expose techniques unless it's something like *Star Wars,* where the technique is important to the future of movies."

Does he feel that a literal adaptation can be made from stage play to movie?

"Oh, yes. In fact, for *Long Day's Journey Into Night* there never was a screenplay. I used the play as text. It really just lies in can, and I say what I feel about it through the process of making it a movie. Can a camera say it and define it in a way that hasn't been said or defined before? And that's my criterion for any adaptation material, whether it's a book or even a newspaper story, for that matter. The rules are the same. About a third of my pictures come from theatrical sources, and that is because of background. As to whether I choose a particular project, I leave that to instinct. Usually I will make my decision on the first reading, because the projects I've done on the basis of a second reading have always never worked out."

Lumet, when queried about his new picture, *The Wiz*, is exuberant, feeling that the picture will be "an absolutely unique experience that nobody has ever witnessed before." And he credits Frank L. Baum's *The Wizard of Oz* for providing him with the inspiration to do the picture. "The original book is quite a masterpiece," he says. "There's a reason for the cult around it. It's about finding home—home being inside of yourself rather than a place to live. And this statement becomes doubly important when thought of in terms of the black experience. Everything about the movie is dedicated to that. In fact, one of the characters tells Dorothy in the film, 'Home isn't just where you eat and sleep, home is inside you.'"

Since Baum's story was the basis for both the 1938 MGM classic and Lumet's version, there are certain understandable similarities, one being the characters—Dorothy (Diana Ross), the Scarecrow (Michael Jackson), the Cowardly Lion (Ted Ross), the Tin Man (Nipsey Russell) and the Wiz (Richard Pryor) among others. But Lumet says the resemblance stops there. "There was nothing to be gained from the original film other than to make certain we didn't use anything from it. They made a brilliant movie, and even though our concept is different—they're Kansas, we're New York; they're white, we're black and the score and book are totally different—we wanted to make sure that we never overlapped in any area."

Lumet feels that his film has universal appeal, but obviously Twentieth Century-Fox thought differently, because although they were one of the backers of the stage play, they exercised their first refusal rights on the film, thus allowing Universal to enter the picture. And Universal became so enthusiastic that they didn't even set a budget. "Because of various legal reasons which are too boring to go into, we had to start production by October 21, 1977, and so there was no time to draw up a budget for what was an enormous production. We have twenty-one musical numbers in the picture as opposed to the normal musical which has only sixteen, and five of them have a minimum of eighty dancers. Another two have two hundred and forty dancers and a hundred dancers respectively. So it was a fantastic scale, and when we went in we were in unchartered waters, trying something that has never been done before, and Universal just had faith and gave us the money we needed.

"And we had tremendous problems because we wanted to create the urban-musical-fantasy, on location, with realism as the recognisable factor, but then moving everything realistic into fantasy. So photographically, musically and scenically, it was different than anything ever done. For example, there was no such thing as going out and renting a wheelchair. We didn't use wheelchairs. Every chair was made by us, and it had its own shape. There were no real clocks. A cane was designed and painted by us, a hat was designed and painted by us, because everything had to visually conform to the urban-realistic-fantasy we wanted."

On the way to the mystical, rarely seen in Emerald City, Dorothy and her companions travel on the yellow brick road, which meant that Lumet and his crew had to lay twenty-five miles of linoleum across the streets, bridges and subways of New York. This Lumet feels was relatively easy compared to the Emerald City sequence filmed downtown at the luxurious World Trade Center. "We treated it as a giant jewel case. We lit the place with thirty-six thousand lamps. So physically that was the hardest. A great deal of concentration, however, went into exploring what level of performance, what level of reality, what level of unreality a scene should have."

Lumet also worked very hard with composer Quincy Jones, whom he considers the best in the world. Together they filled twenty-three hours of cassette tapes talking about the movie. "From a character point of view," says Lumet, "we would discuss the music and how it relates to the story. We also made selections of certain types of Black music— gospel, New Orleans, The Supremes' sound." Adds Lumet: "The reason Diana Ross turned out so thrilling is because this is the first time she really acts out her songs. There was nothing wrong with the old Diana Ross, but wait until you see the new one."

The Wiz took sixty-two days to shoot, and Lumet did 868 set-ups, making it, he says, his most difficult picture. Now, because of the volume of material that has been assembled, the post-production will take nine months. And Lumet still has to decide on what Emerald City and Munchkin-land sound like before he can lay in the background noises.

He says making *The Wiz* was a unique learning experience. "It's the first time I've ever worked with matte specialists. And Albert Whitlock, the best matte man in the world, is doing all of those for us. We also used something called the Lightflex, which is a new system that's never been used before. It reflects light back into the lens and tints every scene in whatever colour you choose without changing skin tone. And it's the first time I used a blue screen process."

Why does he stay based in New York and will he ever direct for the stage again?

"Well, I don't like company towns, and Hollywood is a company town. I think that I'm a better director because I saw Jerome Robbins new ballet recently. And I want other good works of art. I want good theatre, and I want SoHo where your best painting in the world is done. It's a thrilling city.

"As for directing theatre again, it doesn't interest me. Maybe when I'm old and don't want to move around any more I'll do it. I prefer movies to theatre because I have a much stronger control over what's going to come out of making the point of view clear. The camera is the greatest instrument for that in the world."

A Conversation with Sidney Lumet

MICHEL CIMENT/1982

TWENTY-NINE FILMS in twenty-five years, a career in show business that goes back more than fifty years—as an actor and a director—
with regular contributions to the theater, television and film: that sounds
like more than enough to give Sidney Lumet a turn at the microphone.
We discussed his films, noting each time how different they all were
from each other, the good along with the bad, without any unity of
style or even a discernable sensibility. Some directors hit their stride
gradually; others peak and then quickly decline and still others establish themselves solidly. None of that is evident in Lumet's itinerary
whose evolution is more jagged-edged. Ten or so films never released in
France but that we were able to see, thanks to the retrospective recently
organized by the *Cinématèque Française*, these films do not change one's
already formulated opinion regarding his work. Lumet himself will be
the first to admit that he is first and foremost a director, and the first to
point out the disparities and the flaws in his films. Ten or so are remarkable, testifying to the art of adapting plays to the screen (*A Long Day's
Journey Into Night, The Seagull*) or to the study of social groups (*12 Angry
Men, Fail-Safe, The Group, The Anderson Tapes*) or the relationship
between the law and delinquency (*Dog Day Afternoon, Serpico, Prince of
the City*). Even if this variety of themes reveals certain personal concerns that often are best expressed in the realist vein, Lumet's works are
of interest first and foremost for their sheer multiplicity and the energy
they release. Furthermore, his works attest to the various ways that they

From *Positif*. February 1982: 5–24. Copyright © 1982 by Michel Ciment. Translated from
French by Annabelle Cone. Reprinted by permission.

attempt to resolve the problems encountered by an American filmmaker working independently from Hollywood, the conditions in
which he works, and the question of one's social and political integration into American society. Finally, they put forward esthetic and technical questions. Similar to Robert Mulligan, whose sensibility is more
homogenous, and John Frankenheimer, so disappointing in the 1970s
but whose big successes in the 1960s are far more impressive, Lumet
belongs to a generation of "serious" artists to emerge from television,
much too touted by the American critics in their early years, much disliked by the French critics yet deserving their attention. In these gadget-
obsessed times of ready-to-wear and "ready-to-eat"—as in consuming
without thinking—so typical of Hollywood cinema, Lumet's films are
uncharacteristically laden with contradiction and the weight of history
and humanity and should not be disdained. *Prince of the City*, his most
recent film to date, attests to this.

MC: *In* Prince of the City *you return once again to a depiction of New
York, and more specifically, as in* Serpico, *but from another angle, to the life
of police officers. What attracted you to Bob Daley's novel?*
SL: The principal factor that made me decide to adapt it lies in the paradox that is central to the novel: appearances are deceiving. The most
vicious gangster can suddenly perform the most generous and noble
action. As in the character of Rocky Gazzo, the Mafioso killer who offers
sixty-five thousand dollars to someone so that this person can go to
Kennedy Airport and avoid becoming an informer, then offers him the
same amount of money to start a new life in another country, all the
characters are filled with contradiction. Also for example the prosecutors
who accomplish legitimate and important work but who nevertheless
sometimes do dishonest things and also exploit people. There is not a single character in this film whose behavior does not surprise us in the end.
That is what made me so enthusiastic for this project, not to mention
the basic idea, worthy of a Greek tragedy, whereby a man finds himself
in a situation that he cannot control; rather, the situation controls him.

MC: *That's what happened to the characters in* Fail-Safe.
SL: Yes, the only difference being that here, everything is authentic,
everything happened exactly the way we show it. It reminds me of the

old cliché—perfectly correct I might add—that the truth found in everyday facts is far richer than the wildest of fantasies. The difference with *Serpico* was that we wanted to study a character in depth, Frank Serpico, the hippie dressed as a cop. If he hadn't been able to protest against corruption, he would have found a reason to protest about the color of his uniform. Protesting is what mattered. And I knew, having made this choice of dramatic approach, that I would cast the other cops in two-dimensional roles, simple silhouettes against which Serpico would stand out. And I felt a little guilty because I know how cops live, and I know that these people are not simple. When I read Daley's book, I felt that this was my chance to show the complexity of their lives.

MC: *The story of* Serpico *was also more conventional. His character was simpler, having all the traits of a "hero," whereas in* Prince of the City, *the mosaic plot reminds me of non-fiction novels like Truman Capote's* In Cold Blood *or Norman Mailer's* The Executioner's Song.

SL: It is more like Norman Mailer. It's a news story that becomes fiction in the sense that the dramatic situations are so strong. But nothing in the book is made up. And all we did in the film was condense certain events and certain characters. But the narration is fragmented and there is no dramatic progression in the classical sense of the term. When a story asks questions rather than provides answers, the narrative structure has to change. To push a story to its narrative climax implies by its very nature that its conclusion contains a moral. *Prince of the City* has no conclusion.

MC: *How was it working with Jay Presson Allen on the adaptation of her novel, which is so long and dense?*

SL: Yes, it's an epic saga. What happened was that Jay still had three more weeks of work on another script when we decided to adapt her novel. So I cut the book up into sections, starting with the ending. For me the three critical moments in the life of the character are the day when he decides to reveal the names to his partner, the week when the judges meet in a room to figure out whether they should indict him for giving false testimony, and finally, the debate over whether to retry the most important case in which he ever had to testify. Once again, no fiction author could have imagined that both decisions would be made on the same day because it would have seemed too perfect from the dramatic standpoint. By using these three strong moments as points of departure, I was able to align the facts, the incidents that led me to them, so I made my way backwards. Just like in grade school, I wrote an outline with three sections, but I stopped at the beginning of the last third of the novel. Then I skipped to the first third of the book because, knowing where I was heading, I had to establish the basis for the narrative and link the first and third sections. This took me about two-and-a-half weeks. When Jay came back, I showed her the synopsis and the scenes that I had written. I saw her again two days later; she was very pleased. We had to get started quickly because we were in the middle of October of 1979, and I wanted to begin filming in March of 1980. I needed three seasons in fact: winter, spring and summer. The story of this man spans a ten-year period, and I wanted a different light for each season. Jay and I each took half the scenes that needed writing (I took the ones that I thought would be the easiest to write!), and three weeks later we reassembled our files like a pack of cards.

MC: *How did you find all those unknown faces that play the secondary roles and that give the film so much authenticity?*
SL: It came from my initial concept for the film. At the beginning of the project, I told Orion Pictures, the production company, and Warner Bros., in charge of distribution, that I would make the film on three conditions: there would be no "star" actor, that it would not be a thriller, and that it would be three hours long. They went along with it, knowing that there would be one hundred and twenty-six roles, that all the names would be Italian, making it impossible to identify a person by name. So the faces needed to be very striking, not only to make it easier to identify them, but also to make time go by faster. In the structure of the story, everything depends on the changes, the transitions: from one place to another, from one character to another, from one time of day to another. So a great deal of visual energy and variety was needed!

When the first version of the script was finished, Jay began the smoothing out process while I took care of casting the parts. In the past I had almost never used actors with little or no acting experience. But this time I really wanted to meet as many non-professional actors as I could, and so, between November and January, I auditioned almost five thousand people! If a face looked interesting, I gave the person a second interview, and I let the person try out whatever they wanted for three minutes: a passage from Shakespeare, a television ad, whatever they wanted. If I liked what they did, I would then ask them to play the role I had in mind for them. So preparing for this film required meticulous work. In the film there are five real cops and five real Mafiosi, but they really could play any role; they are that interchangeable!

MC: *The theme of informing against someone—the problem of knowing if one can or cannot "talk" and in what context, was this influenced by your own experience, since you were a witness and a contemporary of the McCarthy hearings working in the American entertainment industry?*
SL: Emotionally this became the hardest element for me because I didn't know myself what I thought of the issue. And maybe my own feelings of ambiguity were beneficial to the film. I had no definite opinion about Bob Leuci (Daniel Ciello in the film) and what he had done before seeing the first cut. I slowly realized that I had lived through this type of situation myself, and it became painful for me. In fact, at the beginning of the 1950s, when I was working in television, it was by sheer luck that I escaped being blacklisted. While I was working at the editing table, observing the main character, slowly I arrived at some conclusions. First of all, there is a difference between informing against someone in a criminal case versus a political one. For me, having been raised in a working-class environment, my family was poor, my attitude toward a stool pigeon was automatic, going beyond any logical distinction between the criminal and the political. An informer was an informer; it was that simple. I needed to make this film in order for my attitude to change, however. But squealing on someone for political reasons is a betrayal of democracy. On the other hand, I do think that drugs are responsible for the personal destruction of a whole generation of creative artists in this country, not to mention a large segment of the black population and of young people.

MC: *You have a special relationship with your city, New York. Two-thirds of your films were shot there (the rest were shot in Europe). How do you find locations for films like* Prince of the City, Serpico, *and* Dog Day Afternoon?

SL: First of all, I know New York very well; I've lived here all my life. Each film requires a different individual visual approach. This city has an infinity of neighborhoods; it's impossible to exhaust them all. There are entire neighborhoods that I am holding in reserve for future films. For example, I used the docks in *A View from the Bridge*, but there weren't really enough exterior shots to explore them in depth. Yet they're a fascinating place, an incredible place, even if the boat traffic is no longer what it used to be. I would also like to film the middle-class neighborhoods of Brooklyn and Queens. And I could tell you about fifty other locations that are just as interesting. If I shoot a movie in Russia, and I am pressed for time, so I need to skip a take, I know that there is a place in Brooklyn that resembles Moscow where I can shoot it when I'm back there. Same thing goes for Paris and London. Furthermore, New York is a city that is perpetually changing, that is constantly being demolished and rebuilt. For *Prince of the City* we shot all over the city. Ciello lives on Long Island, the drug addicts live in the Bronx, the lawyers and judges have their offices in lower Manhattan, and some courthouses are in Brooklyn. All together, we had one hundred and thirty-one film locations. We were always on the move, like an army with fifty-four trucks. The logistical maneuvers were worthy of World War II combat strategy. We had to know the one-way streets, the traffic flows, the various routes we could take to save time. We had planned a shooting schedule of seventy days, and we finished in fifty-nine days with two set changes per day.

MC: *Where was* Dog Day Afternoon *shot?*
SL: Aside from the scene at Kennedy Airport, everything else was shot in one location in Brooklyn. I had found it just a few blocks from where the real action had taken place. We needed a quiet street because we were going to be there for six weeks. There were two-story buildings, including one that we rented and turned into a bank. For *Serpico* on the other hand, we built his apartment in the studio. But all the other locations we found in Manhattan.

MC: *You are probably the only "commercial" filmmaker never to have shot a film in Hollywood, in all your twenty-five years of work. Why is that?*
SL: Initially it was deliberate. When I first began making films, the old studio system still existed. There were departments for each stage of the

filmmaking process: a photo department, a set making department, an editing department, etc . . . And there was someone at the very top that could give orders to the director of photography, to the set decorator, even if this person at the top had nothing to do with the film. And if you did something that he didn't like, he could easily sabotage your work. It's for that reason that I stayed away from all that. It would be ridiculous to say that Hollywood has never produced a single good or even great film—countless examples prove the contrary—but I was convinced that the musicians, the screenwriters, the directors, have rarely given the best of themselves at the end of their careers. Rather, they tend to do their very best work at the beginning or in the middle of their film careers, and this is true of great talents, much greater than my own. Hollywood has worn them down. And I told myself that if they had not figured out how to win that battle, it was no use for me even to try. I have never lived in Hollywood, but I am certain that something happens to the creative people living there. Hollywood resembles those nineteenth-century cities like Bethlehem in Pennsylvania whose sole activity depends on the steel mill that owns everything. A city that relies on just one industry can lead to catastrophe. A utopian city where artists have to create I find ridiculous. One needs to rub oneself against something real in order to create. The history of art is the history of great cities where the artist is not important, where everything is not created around him. I think that I am a good film director because in New York I can go to the ballet tonight; this afternoon I saw lots of activity in the street, and I am in permanent contact with a multitude of people and their trades. That's why I remained in New York really from the beginning. Then, in the early 1960s, when the studio system began to fall apart, I had even less of a reason to go work in California because I felt more at ease than most of my fellow filmmakers out on the West Coast. Little by little we had improved our production facilities in New York; our technicians were just as good as their West Coast counterparts. Ultimately it just became simpler to film here in New York.

MC: *You have been the producer of some of your films.*
SL: Yes, but only when it was really necessary. Producing is not something that I enjoy doing. The problem is that there are very few good

producers. When they are good, that's when you realize how important they are and how they can really help the director. In my entire career, I think I have only met five who were worth anything. So that's why I prefer to put in the extra effort, work a few extra weeks and take on the role of producer. For *Prince of the City*, that wasn't necessary because Burtt Harris is wonderful. He started out by serving us coffee on the set of *The Pawnbroker*, then he became my first assistant for ten films, then director of production, then associate producer, and then finally producer. In the case of *The Seagull,* for example, I produced the film myself because the tiny budget—seven hundred and fifty thousand dollars—made it impossible to pay for a producer. In many of my more recent films, Jay Presson Allen and I have shared the production burden. It avoids many discussions and saves a lot of time. Often the producer doesn't know much about films. Some have a perfectly viable opinion, but it is just one opinion among many, and it must never impose on the wishes of the director. For better or for worse, that's how I work. I am too involved in what I do to be helped by someone who points his finger in a direction that he thinks I should take.

MC: *You said that you have been a New Yorker all your life. In what neighborhood were you born?*

SL: In fact I was born in Philadelphia, but my parents moved to New York when I was two years old. They moved to the Lower East Side. It was during the Depression, and people were moving constantly. Landlords were desperately seeking tenants, and they would give you a one-year lease with free rent for a month. Since moving cost only about fifteen dollars and a four-room apartment cost thirty dollars a month, we were better off moving out each year in order to save fifteen dollars. That's why I lived in four different places on the Lower East Side then two places in Brooklyn and one in Queens.

MC: Bye, Bye Braverman *is closely linked to your childhood.*

SL: It was made from my personal memories. It takes place entirely in Brooklyn. It's an extraordinary neighborhood from a visual point of view, with some of the oldest landmarks in the city. It's also where the middle-class originally lived, and there are many detached single-family houses. From an ethnic standpoint, there were clear, separate neighborhoods: the Italians lived on the docks, the Irish lived near Queens, and the Jews lived right in the center of the borough and toward Coney Island. Today, half the borough is black. It was also called the borough of churches because there are so many, synagogues included. In the film, these four Jewish friends have a fifth friend, Braverman, who just died. They're all in their forties, and he is the first one to die. But they can't find the place where he is going to be buried because, unlike Manhattan, Brooklyn is a place where you can easily get lost. They go from one church to the next. I wanted to incorporate some humor, some warmth, and some tenderness. I would have liked to do that better. It's the only one of my films that I would like to do again because the script was so good and I did not fulfill its potential.

MC: *Daniel Ciello in* Prince of the City *belongs to an ethnic minority, which explains why he wants to be integrated, to be accepted into society.*
SL: I have always had an opposite attitude as far as I'm concerned. I like to be different. I often spoke Yiddish and was often accused of taking special delight in making myself stand out, which is probably true. White bread in America was created for the immigrants. They were used to eating dark bread, so they considered white bread a luxury that they wanted to offer themselves. My father would tell me this story about how, when he first arrived in the United States, he would make himself a sandwich by putting a slice of white bread between two slices of dark bread! Now it's the opposite. It's more high class to eat rough peasant bread. As for me, I have always preferred that kind of bread!

MC: *Where did your father come from originally?*
SL: He was born in Poland, in Warsaw. I will soon be returning to my roots because the State Department is sending me on a tour on October 12 with five of my films[1] in four East European capitals: Budapest, Belgrade, East Berlin and Warsaw, which I don't know at all.

MC: *In most of your films, you are attached to a certain form of realism. What books or films have influenced you in that regard?*
SL: It's very complicated. First of all, like my father before me, I come from the theater. Like him, I was an actor. At the time, on Broadway, there

---

1. The five films chosen by Lumet are *Prince of the City, Dog Day Afternoon, Network, The Wiz* and and *The Fugitive Kind.*

was a very snobby attitude regarding Hollywood. That was where you went to make money. So I wasn't going to let those films influence me. But I remember that French directors like Renoir, Vigo and Carné made a tremendous impression on me. The same goes with post-war Italian neo-realist cinema. And also people like Eisenstein and Dreyer. They all demonstrated to me the extraordinary diversity of cinema, from Dreyer's highly stylized productions to Eisenstein's surrealism, not to mention the simplicity in Renoir's films. I did not see that spectrum in Hollywood productions. Not that Hollywood was completely lacking in worthwhile films, but it did not have nearly as much variety as European film. Furthermore, like any typical New York Jew, I was fed on a variety of cultural offerings, from ballet to live music with everything in between.

MC: *Taking two of your most realist films,* The Pawnbroker *and* Prince of the City, *the former is far more high-flown, artificial, and exaggerated than the latter. Do you feel an evolution in your work?*

SL: Yes, in *The Pawnbroker*, many things were emphasized. I hope never to fall back into this type of hysteria, which is not necessary to the drama. One doesn't need to scream in order to convey emotion. When you are young, you want everybody to know what you are feeling so you tend to scream. Then later on, you realize that the truth is enough of an objective and that it does not need to be embellished. I think that this change came from an interior calm that I acquired. It also came from a certain awareness of the flaws that I discovered in my films. I ended up having doubts about myself, not out of complacency, or out of a juvenile desire to "express myself," but rather, I realized that some-times I could just be plain stupid. Maybe Chekhov had an influence on me. I'm talking about preparing for and filming *The Seagull*. Chekhov teaches you the sense of the ridiculous in some of our aspirations, of our illusions. His characters are always making mistakes, falling in love at the wrong time with the wrong person. Directing that film provided me with some of the strongest emotions I ever felt in my life.

MC: *What's curious is that some of your more dramatic films are spoiled by a certain theatricality, while your play adaptations, like* The Seagull *and*

Long Day's Journey Into Night, *resolve the problem of the adaptation. Your*
relationship to the theater is old and profound.

SL: My father played in the Yiddish theater back in Poland. From the
age of eighteen, he belonged to the Vilna troupe. He arrived here in
1922 at the age of twenty-four. He put me on the stage when I was too
young to realize it! As a child, I played in the Yiddish theater for six
years, then six more years on Broadway. I remember it with fond memories and gratitude. It wasn't horrible at all. Rather it was marvelous, so
early on to be in such a creative environment. I was thirteen when I
worked with Max Reinhardt on *The Eternal Road*, a play by Franz Werfel,
with music by Kurt Weill.[2] The following year, I played in *Sunup to*
Sundown directed by Joseph Losey, a very nice, very concerned, and very
talented man but also as pompous then as he is now. My years on
Broadway were the most enriching, because the golden age of Yiddish
theater was over when I performed there. My first role on Broadway was
in Sidney Kingsley's *Dead End*. I played Jesus twice, once under the direction of Reinhardt and then in another play by Maxwell Anderson. In 1939
I played in William Saroyan's first play, *My Heart's in the Highlands*,
directed by Bobby Lewis of the Group Theater, which was a phenome-
non because it incorporated poetry in a theater dominated by realism.
That same year I appeared in a film, *One Third of a Nation*, with Sylvia
Sidney whose brother I played, under the direction of Dudley Murphy.

Being a part of the Group Theater was a great experience. I was fourteen or fifteen years old when we went to the country in the summer of
1939 with the entire troupe, where we studied and prepared the staging
for the next season. That's what they did when they had earned enough
money, which was the case after the great success of the revival of
Awake and Sing and the production of *The Gentle People* by Irwin Shaw.
Everyone was there (except for Lee Strasberg who had already left): Elia
Kazan, Bobby Lewis, Stella Adler, Harold Clurman, Lee J. Cobb, Maurice
Carnovsky. It was during this "summer school" that I really learned the
acting trade. It was very exciting for the young man that I was. They
began by rehearsing the first Chekhov, *Three Sisters*, under the direction

---

2. On Max Reinhardt, and his work in America in particular, a great reference is the fascinating book by his son, the screenwriter and author Gottfried Reinhardt, titled *A Genius*
(Alfred Knopf, New York, 1979) (M.C.).

of Harold Clurman, without ever performing it in the end. Stella Adler played Masha and Luther Adler played Chebutykin. I didn't perform in any other plays staged by the Group because there were no children's roles for me, but I was dating Helen Adler, Stella's daughter, and I remained in contact with them until I joined the army.[3]

MC: *You didn't go to college?*
SL: No, I went to Columbia for one semester, where I took some French literature courses before I enlisted. As a child actor, I went to professional children's schools from ten in the morning until three in the afternoon, and when I was on the road, I took correspondence courses. What a terrible education I got that way, but I was able to receive all my diplomas! For example, I knew nothing about science, but I discovered later when I was in the army that I loved it.

MC: *At the age of seventeen, why did you enlist?*
SL: Because of my political convictions. I was very left wing. I remember when I was twelve or thirteen, I wanted to join the International Brigades and go fight in Spain. So when the War broke out, I wanted to join the Marines. You could enlist at seventeen, whereas you had to wait to be eighteen to join the Army. But they rejected me because of my poor eyesight. So I took a one-year training course in order to work in the radar service that the British had just developed. And I found myself on the Burmese front. I stayed in the army for five years. The experience that I gained was not worth the time that I spent there! Two years would have been enough, but I have no regrets because I wouldn't have liked to do what my friends from the Group Theater were doing, which was to perform on the road in military camps. I would have preferred to be in Europe fighting Hitler, but during all this time I learned what was important and also what I could do without. My encounter with India and her religions, Buddhism and Hinduism, was also a fundamental life experience. My stay on the front was somewhat helpful in *The Hill*, although, even though it takes place in the army, it's just a

---

3. The best reference on the Group Theater remains the memoirs of Harold Clurman, *The Fervent Years* (Alfred Knopf, New York, 1945) (M.C.).

film like any other that I have made that deals with the relationship between justice and "the system." On the other hand, I would like to make a real war movie, because I have never seen one that I found convincing. I have always wanted to adapt to the screen the best novel on the subject, *The Thin Red Line* by James Jones, but today it would be impossible because it would be too costly.[4]

MC: *When you came back from the War, what path did you choose initially?*
SL: I started again with acting. I performed in three plays, and then I helped found the Actors Studio. Kazan, Robert Lewis and Cheryl Crawford asked me to join the class for "experienced" actors, as opposed to a class for beginners. Very quickly I began to disagree with them. Kazan, Lewis and Crawford were extremely successful at the time, with directing in the case of the first two, and producing in the case of Crawford. And I had the impression that instead of performing really for yourself, you were auditioning for them. We were sticking to the realist tradition in which we all excelled. I wanted to try my hand at something different, play Ostrovsky, Sheridan, Farquhar, and not stage *Waiting for Lefty* for the umpteenth time, not to mention all the social theater from the 1930s that I could have played perfectly fine even if I had been woken up by surprise at four in the morning without any preparation! Some of us discussed this orientation, and we were thrown out. I was so angry that I started my own acting "school," The Actor's Workshop in Greenwich Village, with a dozen other "rejects." We rented a loft, built a stage, and sketched out a three year teaching program. There was Richard Kiley, Ann Jackson and Yul Brynner. The curriculum was very interesting. For two to three months we did modern realist theater which was what we knew best, in order to set down a "common language." Then we would go back in time, to Chekhov and Ibsen, and their opposites, Shaw and Wilde, then Restoration comedy, then Shakespeare's comedies, his tragedies, and then finally, Greek tragedy. Each step required a totally different style and technique. We hired the English choreographer Anthony Tudor to teach body movement, and

---

4. Andrew Morton brought the James Jones novel to the screen in 1964 under the same title (M.C.).

Marianne Rich to give us some vocal training. Since there was nobody to direct the scenes on which we were working, I took the plunge and started doing theater directing. At the same time, I was teaching at the High School for Performing Arts that had just started a theater department. During that time, Yul Brynner began working in television, which was emerging then (this was 1950–1951), and he convinced me to join him because aside from him, nobody knew anything about acting! So that's how I became his assistant, and I must say that he was a very good director. Then I became a director.

MC: *This was the golden age of American television.*
SL: Yes, those were marvelous years, when you think about how many screenwriters, directors, and actors emerged then. It proves one thing: that we were not all that exceptional but their talent was always there. You just need to give them the means to express it. The work pace was incredible. I directed two half-hour dramas every week during three years! I needed to have eight shows in my head all the time. While I rehearsed the two dramas of the week, I also had to take care of the casting for the following week, and of the sets and the costumes for two weeks after that. So at CBS I worked on the series *Danger* and on a fascinating series called *You Are There* that consisted of "covering" historical events using a TV news style. For example reporters "filmed" the death of Joan of Arc at the stake, the assassination of Julius Caesar, Washington at Valley Forge, the poisoning of Socrates, Lincoln's assassination. It may seem naïve now, but it was fascinating. And all the scripts were performed by unknown actors like James Dean or Paul Newman and written especially for the show by people like Paddy Chayefsky and Reginald Rose. Then I did longer TV dramas, they were called "Big Specials," for Studio One, Philco Playhouse, Kraft Television Theater. They were one or two hours long and had a little more time between each airing but not much more! Some were adaptations; some were original plays. I directed *The Philadelphia Story* and *Twenty Grand*, based on the Hemingway short story, one act plays by Tennessee Williams, etc. I had an affinity for certain screenwriters, and we often worked together, such as Walter Bernstein and Abe Polonsky, who were blacklisted and wrote most of the *You Are There* episodes under an assumed name. I collaborated only once with Paddy Chayefsky who worked for

NBC. It was on the adaptation of a Nelson Algren short story about a police officer. I suppose that I must have directed five hundred dramas in five years all together! Then Reginald Rose, the author of the televised drama *12 Angry Men*, that I hadn't seen, suggested that I make a movie of it, which is how I got started in film. But I continued working in television, because I liked it so much, like the adaptation of O'Neill's play *The Iceman Cometh*, and *Dibbouk* and even *Rashomon*!

I have to say that at the beginning of the 1950s, during the witch-hunt and after, television was far more politically engaged than film. I directed a two-part series on Sacco and Vanzetti that made a lot of waves in the U.S. And one week after Ed Murrow attacked McCarthy,[5] we followed up with Galileo's repent and the Salem witch trials in the *You Are There* series. All this of course was intentional. One of the great changes at the time was the arrival in Hollywood in the mid-fifties of people from television with Delbert Mann whose *Marty* took away all the Oscars, then Robert Mulligan, Franklin Schaffner, Frankenheimer, Ritt, Penn and myself. Schaffner and Mulligan were working with me at CBS, and we were all hired the same day, and Frankenheimer was my assistant—an excellent one at that![6]

My experience in television was irreplaceable, because the law of optics is constant, and it gave me a very fine visual training, not to mention everything that I learned about editing, rhythm and acting. And also psychologically I learned a precious lesson. The production that you're working on right now is not everything. There is another one waiting for you the following week. It's only a movie. The ephemeral nature of television taught me that in a positive way, because I have seen many of my colleagues become pretentious. In their conversations I hear the words "grandeur" and "masterpiece." For me, that is the beginning of the end. Each time you get started on another film, you cannot think in terms of a masterpiece, because at the very least, chance plays a role in every production. I don't want to

5. To read further about Murrow, consult the biography by Alexander Kendrick, *Prime Time* (Little, Brown and Co, New York, 1969) (M.C.).

6. Franklin Schaffner, John Frankenheimer and Robert Mulligan spoke of their television years at CBS in interviews they gave to *Positif* (numbers 117, June 1970, 122 in December of 1970 and 146 in January of 1973) (M.C.).

sound falsely modest, and it is true that chance, luck I mean, exists for some and not for others. But basically all one can do is to set the stage and hope for the best. When this happens, the film takes on a life all its own that one could have never predicted. I have made it a rule never to wait eternally for a project that I am dying to do, but to go on to something else, as long as I am motivated one way or the other. What matters most is to continue to make films, because there are a million reasons to make a film. The "old school" did not have this pretense of making only masterpieces, to make a movie only every four years. You remember thirty films by John Ford, but he made over a hundred! I love fifteen films by Cukor, but he just finished his sixty-fifth one! Films like *The Anderson Tapes* or *Deathtrap*, my latest one, I am not sorry to have made them. A movie is a movie, and you can learn something from every single shoot. For example, I shot *The Appointment* because I was having a lot of trouble going from black and white to color, and I wanted to work with Carlo di Palma, Antonioni's cinematographer, whom I hoped would help me get rid of this mental block. That was crucial for me. It was useful to direct that film for that reason at the very least.

MC: *Nevertheless, in your first color feature,* The Group, *you had achieved some rather brilliant results with Boris Kaufman.*
SL: No, I wasn't at all satisfied! I had trouble using color in a dramatic way. Boris has never made the transition from black and white to color; that is one of the tragedies of his life. We had innumerable battles, and I think that Kazan will tell you the same thing about *Splendor in the Grass*. We had to force him to make it simpler. Color is not like black and white, where the cinematographer has to do everything. The problems one encounters in color films are often resolved when you're lighting the set, and the cinematographer hardly has to intervene. This implies a whole philosophical attitude that Boris was not willing to adopt, which made him very bitter.

MC: *When you went from television to cinema, what was the greatest change for you?*
SL: The size of the image. And one of the more depressing things for me is the disappearance of the big screen movie theaters. In the multiplexes, the audience is looking at movie screens that are almost as small

as TV screens. It took me a while to get used to the bigger image, which explains why my early films had such a closed sense of staging. My dramatic style had developed on a twelve-inch screen, and suddenly I was hitting the emotions too hard on a thirty-foot screen. Also in the theater I had been trained to exaggerate the feelings in order to touch the audience seated in the second balcony. It took me years before I understood that I didn't have to do so much. Everything becomes clearer faster on a big screen. Also time flows differently on film than on television.

MC: *In your adaptations of plays to the screen, like* The Fugitive Kind, A View From the Bridge, *and* Long Day's Journey Into Night, *you respect theatrical convention, the unity of place, the absence of an establishing shot.*
SL: I have always led that fight. The press accused one of my best films, *Long Day's Journey Into Night*, of simply being a filmed play. Today, at UCLA they study film for its cinematographic technique, its use of editing, of different lenses and of lighting. This initial error stems from the tendency of many critics to confuse filmmaking with multiple set changes. If you put a face in front of a mountain backdrop, that's film. If you put it in front of a wall, it no longer is! There are four main characters in *Long Day's Journey Into Night*. If you make a film, there is one more, namely the camera. For me, the definition of a film is that thing that can reveal something about something or someone with the help of a camera, without which those revelations would not exist. People forget that when Griffith began making movies audiences thought that that would be the end of the theater. Not because you could go into the wilderness and shoot animal herds or train chases but simply because of the close-up shot. That was the instrument that was going to kill the stage because it could frame a behavior in a way the theater couldn't. But I understood that immediately; I was never tempted "to open" a play by putting it on the screen. When I filmed *12 Angry Men*, the fact that the entire action took place in one room was never a problem for me; it actually became an advantage. I wanted a smaller room, a lower ceiling, narrower walls; in a way, I made the space even more confined than it had been on the stage.

MC: *At the beginning of your film career, what drove you to do so many play adaptations?*
SL: Because they offered what so few film scripts had to offer, namely strong written expression. There were still people who believed in the

1950s that the movies had died with the talkies. You can argue anything if you want. For me, the sound is there; it's only a matter of using it as well as possible. O'Neill and Tennessee Williams had a prose style whose quality the screenwriters of the time could not replicate. *Long Day's Journey Into Night* is the first of my "human" films; I mean the films where I don't judge my characters. The same goes for *The Seagull*, *Dog Day Afternoon*, and *Prince of the City*. In O'Neill's plays, there are no good guys or bad guys, everyone is flawed in some way or another. He is the tragic side of Chekhov's gentleness, with more psychology but as much compassion. As for Williams, he only writes about one thing, and that is how destructive modern life can be. That idea has a profound effect on me, and I would have liked for *The Fugitive Kind*, which is a good film, to be even better. Brando is extraordinary in it. It is probably one of his best performances on the screen, and I think that Williams wrote the part for him. I also like Joanne Woodward very much. The only problem was Anna Magnani who was going through a personal crisis and hated being in America and in a film studio. This actress, so honest, authentic, sincere, had reached an age where her sole preoccupation was her appearance. She almost gave Boris Kaufman an ulcer. She would stop concentrating if the camera was not aimed on her left profile. It was as though all the hardships in her life had taken away all her tenderness, and when she gets mad in the film, she is brilliant! The rest of the time she rings false, looks spiritless. But despite the frustrations on the set, the film has turned out to be an important one for me, with a texture that I like. On the other hand, I don't have any qualms about *Long Day's Journey Into Night*, which is one of the films that I like the most, with four exceptional actors and a complex visual conception.

MC: *You also directed a film,* The Last of the Mobile Hot-shots, *based on a Tennessee Williams play.*

SL: Yes, it's an adaptation of *The Seven Descents of Myrtle*, which I shot partly in New York for the interiors and partly in Louisiana. It's not one of Tennessee's best plays, but I prefer to devote myself to his lower quality work rather than the best work of some other playwrights! I have never seen this film a second time and would be afraid to hate it, but, on the other hand, there is a certain humor, a richness, and there are such interesting characters, that maybe I wouldn't dislike it that much!

That play was a bit more extravagant than the others, without the usual lyricism.

MC: *Williams and O'Neill were preparing you to deal with ambiguity in your later films, more so than Arthur Miller's* A View From the Bridge.
SL: For me, *A View From the Bridge* was a very good story above all, but what I found irritating about Miller—with all the respect that I have for him—is that he belongs to that category of artist who becomes a prisoner of his own pretensions. The article that he published before the premiere of his play in which he compared it to a Greek tragedy attests to that. Who needs these parallels? That's what I said to Arthur: "All you need is a good drama about a character who is incapable of adapting to a new situation; you are hurting your play when you try to make it pass for Euripides."

MC: The Seagull *is one of your best films.*
SL: Yes, and my best adaptation of a play along with *Long Day's Journey Into Night*. I had long dreamt about it, but I needed a perfect cast, and in the case of a great play, you really have to be patient and wait. I was filming *The Deadly Affair* in London with Simone Signoret and James Mason. And because it was part of the plot of the film, we were shooting a scene from Marlowe's *Edward II* with the Royal Shakespeare Company with David Warner in the principal role. Between two takes, while waiting for a lighting adjustment, all of a sudden I realized that I had my ideal cast: James Mason as Trigorin, Simone Signoret in the role of Arkadina, and David Warner as Konstantin. Only Nina was missing. I telephoned Vanessa Redgrave who lived just a few streets away. She came right over to the Hammersmith Studio where we were filming, and we agreed right away to film *The Seagull*. Since I would have never gotten a clearance to shoot in the Soviet Union, I looked for a place near the sea that would be more or less at the same latitude, and right away I found a shooting location outside of Stockholm.

MC: *It's beautiful the way you shoot outdoors while preserving the theatrical character, with a dissolve separating each act.*
SL: We were faithful to Chekhov's play whose first two acts take place in a garden and then on a croquet lawn. It's only in the third act that you

enter the house. Simone Signoret was the perfect actress for Arkadina. And I felt justified in using her because of something that I had noticed. On Broadway there was a time when all the great actresses performed with a British accent, which showed what an inferiority complex we had vis-à-vis the British theater. At the end of the last century, in Russia, the French language and French culture had a certain prestige. My choice of Signoret was a rational one, to play the part of a Russian actress affecting a French accent. And the way she plays it is remarkable.

MC: *You have also adapted other plays to the screen, like* Child's Play, The Wiz, The Offence, Equus.

SL: *Child's Play* was a complete mistake. You know, from time to time, you end up convincing yourself to make such and such a film, and after four days of rehearsing, you realize that you've made a big mistake. But you can't tell anyone; it's too late! I had liked the play in the theater, but suddenly it seemed false and superficial, and I would prefer to forget it. On the other hand, despite its flaws, I like *The Wiz*, which the New York critics tore apart. I have always loved musicals, and I had always wanted to direct one. I opened up the play with an all black cast, which made more sense with an urban setting, rather than a rural one like in the original *Wizard of Oz*. That film is about knowing yourself, and the last song is "There's No Place Like Home." I wanted the story of Dorothy to be the odyssey of a young black girl who was afraid of crossing 125th Street, the border of Harlem, and who discovers New York. I was also interested in mixing realism with fantasy, although I did not succeed. *The Offence*, produced by Sean Connery, is not very satisfying. You come out feeling frustrated, but it's a fascinating story based on a play by John Hopkins, *This Story is Yours*. It was the psychological exploration of a cop's nervous breakdown. Aside from the first scenes, all the action takes place in a police precinct.

As for *Equus*, that was also my choice, but I should have never wanted to make it into a film. On the stage, it was a really poetic experience. But in fact, I disagree with the philosophy of the play. Although I am interested in psychoanalysis, I don't believe in the problems of Dr. Martin Dysart played by Richard Burton. The author, Peter Schaefer, a remarkable and wonderful writer, had never been pleased with the films made from his plays. He asked me to film *Equus*, which I did for him. He knew that I had issues about the play. We worked together on the adaptation. I am still not satisfied with the film, but the experience was well worth it because I had to work outside of realism. In my work with screenwriters and actors, I always use psychoanalysis in order to uncover the sub-text, what is not said, what is signified as opposed to what is outwardly said. You see it clearly in *Prince of the City*, when Daniel decides to side with the administration, with the power structure; he starts to wear a cross again, which he hadn't done at the beginning. I like those little details that often go unnoticed but have a great deal of meaning.

MC: The Anderson Tapes *surprised you—a well-constructed thriller.*
SL: It was very refreshing! For someone like me, with a tendency to be introverted, every four or five films, it's important simply to film an action-packed story, just for fun. My latest film, *Deathtrap*, falls into that category, a crime story with a tight plot, one of the best I have ever read, based on a Broadway play. Everything takes place in an enclosed space, after a first sequence that takes place in a theater. For me, these films (and I include *Murder on the Orient Express*) are like the parallel bars in gymnastics. They are for practicing and maintaining your technique.

MC: *How do you work with your actors?*
SL: Depending on the complexity of the scripts, I rehearse with them between two to four weeks. I gather them together, and we perform all the scenes, including the chases and the fights. Two to three days before the actual filming, they perform the entire film in sequence. For me, it's real, and it brings back the method that I used to get ready for the live TV dramas.

MC: *Were you conscious of a more fluid, better balanced and less insistent directing style in the mid-sixties, with your first color films, like* The Group *and* The Seagull?
SL: I only realized it when I began shooting *Prince of the City*! I really tried not to judge anyone and to show compassion for all my characters. When I finished the film, I wondered where this was coming from,

and then I remembered the filming of *The Seagull* and what it had entailed. When you participate in events as much as I do, when you are engaged politically, you tend to judge people and things, and it hurts your work. When I was editing *Prince of the City*, I suddenly noticed this evolution.

MC: *You also tried something more comical with* Lovin' Molly.

SL: Yes, but there were so many problems with that film! First, I should have taken a year to prepare it, because I wasn't at all familiar with life down South. I should have researched it more. It was an independent film, with little financing, so we had to shoot quickly, and that's why the makeup, for example, is not all that convincing. Anyway, it was a failure, due in great part to my haste. On the other hand, I think that *Just Tell Me What You Want* is more of a success, even though the press panned it. It's a mean film, a stylized comedy about hypocrisy, yet funny in my opinion, with a lightness that I am often seeking. It's the story of a vulgar and wealthy Jew who thinks that he owns the world and manipulates everyone around him. He has a beautiful mistress who refuses to satisfy his every whim, and who realizes that she too is manipulating everyone just as much as he is.

MC: *Do you work a great deal on the editing?*

SL: I edit the movie in my head during the filming. That comes from my training in the theater and live television where I had to make choices ahead of time. I use very little film. For *12 Angry Men*, we only used seventy-five thousand feet of film. I work very closely with the cinematographer. I plan every camera movement and choose the angles ahead of time. For *Prince of the City*, I decided to shoot the entire film at an aperture of 2.8 in order to give it a certain visual style. I told Andrzej Bartkowiak, my cinematographer, whose first film it was, that I did not want any normal lenses, like a 32 or a 36 mm, 50 mm at the most. In order to create an atmosphere of deceit, and false appearances, we only used wide angle and zoom lenses. The lighting in the first half was never on the actors but rather on the background. In the middle of the film, the lighting had to alternate between the foreground and the background, and at the end, on the contrary, the lighting was aimed on the foreground only. Visually we were trying to achieve something very simple and very clear, with very few sets and neutral colors. And one thing that I don't want is for the camera movements to be noticeable. A shot that you pay attention to is a bad shot. I was very lucky to have Boris Kaufman as cinematographer. He understood the relationship between lighting and drama, which is priceless. That's why I told you earlier that he had never successfully made the transition to color. He used too much light; he worked too much in detail without taking into account that the color that you are photographing is already an element in itself. But in black and white, he is one of the greatest aces in the history of cinema because he was so concerned about the content. First we would discuss the script, and then later we would start talking about angles and lighting. Oswald Morris works the same way and so does Gerry Fischer. Geoffrey Unsworth didn't worry about the meaning; he was more concerned with the aesthetics, and since that's what I wanted for *Murder on the Orient Express*, he was perfect! In fact, you have to choose your cinematographers the same way you choose your actors, depending on the style of the film.

MC: *Having been an actor yourself from a very young age, was that experience useful to you later on?*

SL: To perform as an actor is a process of self-discovery. Actors use themselves in order to give life to a character. It's that difficult aspect of the profession that made me abandon it when I was still young. I did not want to have my innermost self revealed to fifteen hundred people every night. That's why I understand the vulnerability of actors. As soon as they get to work, they bare themselves, and I don't want to violate them or exploit them. After having written the adaptation of *The Seagull*, we all got together, as usual, to read the script together. But this time, I didn't explain anything; I didn't try to explore its meaning. I began telling them about one of the most intimate events in my life, that until then, only my wife knew about. They understood what I was telling them, that they were going to have to live very intensely on an emotional level, and that I was the first one to "take off my clothes." I was revealing myself before asking them to do the same. When they have that assurance, when they feel that they are going to share an experience but that it will not turn against them, then they relax, and that's a good thing because, when you're tense, nothing good comes out.

Interview with Sidney Lumet

CHANTAL DE BÉCHADE/1982

CB: *Sidney Lumet, do you think your work in theater, both as an actor and a director, has led you to approach film from a theatrical perspective, for example in regard to your choices of themes, situations, and settings?*

SL: My background in theater gives me first of all a great love for literature. I use dialogue more than many other directors. There's a conflict among American filmmakers over this issue. Does pure cinema begin before speech? I've always thought it was a completely stupid argument and a futile one. Sound is here, and it's here to stay. And if we have to have sound, we should have the best sound possible, and the best sound possible is words. That's why I've often worked with plays written by Arthur Miller, Tennessee Williams, Eugene O'Neill, among others. The second influence from the theater concerns my choice of themes. I'm always very interested in people's individual relationships. It's a sort of film tradition to de-emphasize the human face. It used to be considered typical of film to have a face with a mountain in the background, for example, but not just to have a face against a wall. Now for me, what's important is the face, not at all what's behind it. So I think my background in theater makes me focus mainly on human relationships, and that will always fascinate me, because it's always changing; it's always different.

CB: *You've filmed nonstop since 1957. There's no other director who can claim to make a movie every year, sometimes more. Why this need to film at all costs? Is it a physical need? Is it a mission you feel committed to?*

From La *Revue du Cinéma*. February 1982: 71–78. Translated from French by Margaret Ciavarella.

SL: You should never take yourself too seriously. I think directors take themselves terribly seriously and try to make every film a masterpiece. For any director with a little lucidity, masterpieces are films that come to you by accident. I don't believe in false modesty, and there are reasons why these accidents happen to some people and not others. The best you can do is set a good foundation, and then as the film takes on its own life and becomes something you weren't expecting, that's an accident.

CB: *In much of your work, there is a critical look at things, a desire to denounce the instability in our social structure, for example in* Serpico, *in* The Anderson Tapes, *or also in* Dog Day Afternoon *or* Prince of the City. *Could we say that* Prince of the City *is a culmination of an urban series, or rather is it a desire to continue in that vein?*
SL: I'm not trying to plan out the work. In fact, I often don't really know where I'm going with a film until about five years afterwards! I only understand things from a distance. But sometimes there's something in me, as a man, something that makes me always want to question everything. So, at the risk of appearing cynical, I'll say that I like questioning things, people, institutions and in general, everything that passes for "good behavior."

CB: *Just so, institutions . . . does the fact that you film according to Hollywood super-production norms, that you don't deny yourself any of the means the American system provides you with, seem a little contrary to that affirmation, that approach, because in the end you decide to use those resources to create very polemical, even very anti-establishment movies?*
SL: The thing about greedy people is that they love money. That creates a sort of continuity. So as long as my movies make money from time to time, they leave me alone. It doesn't really bother them if people criticize their institutions. They aren't that insecure.

CB: *Overall, do you consider yourself a total outsider, an anarchist?*
SL: Not at all. I like order, and my work is very organized. I don't allow anarchy on the set. People don't just do what they want. Everything has to be focused on the film. What interests me is exploring, almost just for myself, things that have always fascinated me, that make life

not exactly what it should be. I know that seems a little banal, but you can't imagine how long it takes to realize that.

CB: *But isn't it also a pretext to use themes and sets that journalists would-n't be able to show from the slant of fiction?*
SL: Yes. But there are also things journalists can show that we can't. We all have our advantages and disadvantages. We filmmakers are totally free in terms of imagination, but for example, in *Prince of the City*, it would have been wonderful to be able to use people's real names. But there's a law in the United States: films as well as newspaper articles can be accused of defamation, and also, for the films, there's the law concerning private life. That means that if you use someone's real name on the screen, besides the fact that the production team can be accused of defamation, it can also be accused of violating the "invasion of private life" law. A journalist wouldn't have that problem. So again, both sides have their advantages and their inconveniences.

CB: *Isn't there a warning behind your social attacks against fragility and the possibility of manipulation? Isn't it a bit too easy, as a filmmaker, to depict social phenomena from the point of view of fiction rather than a TV documentary, for example?*
SL: In a certain way, the fact that it's true frees us up. There are things that happen in reality that you would never allow yourself to put into a work of fiction. For example, at the end of *Prince of the City*, two of the most important times of the character's life are two trials. The two trials happen in the same week and the two decisions are handed down the same day. If I were working on a complete fiction, and the screenwriter brought me this kind of conclusion, I'd tell him it was ridiculous, it was too neat and perfect to be true. I wouldn't believe it.

CB: *Is that why you decided to co-write the screenplay for your twenty-seventh film?*
SL: Yes. But the writing of the screenplay happened almost by acci-dent. In fact, I worked from documents concerning real trials, real

recordings. I don't think of myself as a screenwriter, I have too much respect for screenwriters and writers in general.

CB: *Was the story of Bob Leucci, the policeman who was the focal point of the book and the screenplay, exactly like you show it, or do you depart from reality a little bit?*

SL: In terms of those people, that group of detectives especially, it's not fiction, but for example, it's common to exchange sexual favors for drugs. Whether Leucci himself actually went in for that kind of thing, I don't know; I didn't ask. The reason this scene is in the film is completely different. I knew that at that point in the film the audience would start to establish an emotional relationship with the character. It's been almost an hour that we've been watching him go through an incomprehensible experience and I didn't want there to be a sort of easy identification between him and the audience. I wanted us to be able to judge him by his actions and not for sentimental reasons, so I had to add in some extra unpleasantness.

CB: *Is that to say that the length of* Prince of the City *is a necessity, a deliberate choice to put the spectator in a certain state of mind, and then finally create such a violent atmosphere that it could have a therapeutic value?*

SL: Absolutely. That's even one of the main reasons. It was very important that the spectator live the same experience as Leucci, go through it with him. There is a second reason that for me is equally important: to convey the moral complexity of the problem. One of the fundamental themes of the film is that nothing is what it seems to be, and again, everything comes from a certain respect for reality, for the nature of people's behavior. Every situation, every character is, at the end of the film, completely different than at the beginning, except for the character of Gus Levy (who pushes the dresser onto the prosecutor's head), who behaves the same from the beginning to the end of the film. Now, this sort of reversal of behavior that takes place inside each of the characters is the very heart of the film for me. It's what interested me the most, because it was the most human element. And that's why the film is so long. It was important to show the whole path of this reversal for each of the characters.

CB: *It's a way of showing or proving that you can't predict human behavior. It's a question but also finally a form of anguish that you express.*
SL: Absolutely. Not knowing what each of us could do "under pressure" is the essential for me.

CB: *Can we say that in that sense you are also making a political film on top of this story of the policeman's corruption and urban drama?*
SL: I think that's only an extension of the real subject of the film. The political implication isn't the central intention. But, nothing that puts the individual in conflict with the society that surrounds and conditions him can be apolitical. It's political by its very nature.

CB: *Why did you choose practically unknown actors for* Prince of the City?
SL: I thought it was essential that the spectator not have a prior relationship with that character. If it had been Pacino or Redford or someone like that, everyone would have said as soon as he came onscreen, "Oh look, there's Pacino, there's De Niro, there's Redford." It was important, for a story like this, that there not be any heroes or bad guys, that the spectator discover who was who. A star would have completely defeated the purpose.

CB: *Isn't it a little excessive to film* Prince of the City *on a hundred and thirty different sets? It's a sort of performance. Maybe even perfectionism?*
SL: That depends on the film. You can do anything anywhere. You can make paradise look like hell and New York look like paradise. And this film, which can seem to you like very realistic photography, in fact is not. Everything is perfectly controlled and everything is turned toward a specific goal, hence the necessity for a hundred and thirty sets.

CB: *It must be very hard for the actors to adapt to such different surroundings. How do you organize the work?*
SL: Most of the work is done in rehearsal before the filming. I have the actors rehearse like in the theater. We work for three to four weeks before the filming; we read the text, we discuss it. Then we get up, and we start to put the film in place. By the end of the second week, the

actors are completely off book and know their text perfectly. They know where they are, in emotional terms, at every moment. We work in detail at that point, even for the fights, because if you know what you're doing you may not need stuntmen, and I don't like stuntmen. At the end of the rehearsal time, in the last three days, we run through the whole film. This gives the actors a sense of continuity and of the content of the film, whatever scene they're in. If all questions have been answered, there are no more problems. What the actors generally like about working with me is the freedom they have and the secure atmosphere they can exercise it in. All this preparatory work allows them to be freer. That might seem paradoxical, but it always works. If someone is afraid, if someone is tense, the emotions won't flow as easily. The only way to make the emotion flow freely and easily is to feel that you are on safe ground. Tension destroys emotion.

CB: *What still moves you, what are you passionate about?*
SL: Lots of things. Work, obviously . . . a sunset . . . my wife, my children . . . politics . . . conflict . . . effort . . . that's enough for now.

Sidney Lumet: The Reluctant Auteur

DON SHEWEY/1982

ASTORIA STUDIOS OCCUPIES a non-descript warehouse on a sleepy side street in Queens. Inside, past the security booth, lies a vast cavern, about half of which is taken up by what looks like a fortress of lumber lit from within. Closer inspection reveals a movie set built to resemble the Suffolk County Courthouse in Boston where several major scenes will be filmed for *The Verdict*, a 20th Century-Fox production starring Paul Newman and directed by Sidney Lumet. A month and a half into shooting, the film is nearly a week ahead of schedule, though you wouldn't know it at the moment. The lighting is being adjusted for a new camera setup, and filming has come to a standstill.

Lumet, not a patient man, plops down in his director's chair bristling with energy. Short, balding, and dressed in a blue work shirt, blue jeans, and blue sneakers, he pushes his aviator glasses up on his nose and looks around, signaling his willingness to talk. The unit publicist seizes her chance to collect some data on the director. What are his favorite movies? "*Greed,*" he says slowly, "*Intolerance, Potemkin.*" Warming to the task, he names *The Passion of Joan of Arc, The Bicycle Thief, The Seventh Seal*, film school classics all. A crowd of cast and crew members gathers, curious to hear this litany. "*Casablanca,*" he continues, "*Stagecoach, The Godfather*, parts one and two, *Amarcord.*"

He could go on, but someone interrupts—no Sidney Lumet movies?

"No," he says placidly. "None are good enough." Then he looks up, his eyes widening and his mind retracing his list of favorites. "Those are some *good movies!*"

Is this false modesty or honest self-assessment? Or a little of both? After all, Sidney Lumet is one of the busiest directors in the movie business today. This year alone he has accepted the New York Film Critics Circle's best director award for *Prince of the City*; seen the release of *Deathtrap*, his film adaptation of Ira Levin's long-running Broadway comedy; wrapped up *The Verdict*, Fox's "big picture" for Christmas; and launched production on his next film, based on E. L. Doctorow's *The Book of Daniel* and starring Tim Hutton and Ed Asner.

Since 1957, when he graduated from live television to film, Lumet has directed an extraordinary number of pictures, including *12 Angry Men, Long Day's Journey Into Night, The Fugitive Kind, Fail-Safe, The Pawnbroker, The Group, Serpico, Murder on the Orient Express, Dog Day Afternoon, Network, The Wiz,* and *Prince of the City*. He has worked with a dazzling array of movie stars: icons like Fonda, Hepburn, and Brando; international celebrities like Vanessa Redgrave, James Mason, Simone Signoret, Ingrid Bergman, and Albert Finney; fine contemporary actors like Al Pacino, Faye Dunaway, and Robert Duvall. He has been nominated for an Academy Award three times, and he has a solid reputation in the business for bringing pictures in on time and under budget. He has the rare if not unprecedented distinction of becoming a successful movie director without ever having to abandon his New York base for the hills of Hollywood.

Still, Lumet is caught in a paradox. Though he is well respected, he knows the public will not line up at the box office for movies with his name on them the way they will for those of, say, Woody Allen. Though he controls the final cut of his films and can command $1.5 million per picture, his interest in a property doesn't guarantee that a studio will finance it. As for the critics, Lumet's crazy-quilt career has earned him a dubious honor: he is one director that Pauline Kael and Andrew Sarris agree on—they both dislike his films.

A veteran of twenty-five years of filmmaking, Lumet still considers himself, at fifty-eight, a student. "There are so many different reasons for doing movies," he says one day in his office behind Carnegie Hall. "Maybe the most fundamental reason is that I just believe in working. I don't believe in waiting for the masterpiece. Masterful subject matter only comes up rarely. The point is, there's something to advance your technique in every movie you do."

The Verdict is his thirtieth picture. Adapted for the screen from Barry
Reed's novel by playwright David Mamet, it portrays a broken-down,
alcoholic Irish-Catholic lawyer (Paul Newman) who stumbles upon one
last chance to redeem himself, both professionally—through a clear-cut
but difficult-to-prove medical malpractice suit against a large Catholic
hospital in Boston—and personally—with a mysterious beauty played
by Charlotte Rampling. Its courtroom setting hearkens back to *12 Angry
Men*, Lumet's first picture, and the character played by Newman (brilliantly, it must be said), wrapped in a blanket of furious, self-ordained
solitude, recalls similar little-guy-against-the-system characters in
Serpico, Dog Day Afternoon, and *Prince of the City*. As usual for Lumet, the
film is studded with strong performances, even in the small roles—
Lindsay Crouse and Julie Bovasso have several memorable scenes—and
suffused with social commentary, exposing the subtle ways in which an
insensitive institution corrupts the individuals who do its bidding and
attempts to crush those who won't.

For his part, Newman is playing down the film's implicit social commentary, partly because the *role* intrigues him so much. "I don't see this
as a film about malpractice. It's not anti-hospital, or anti-Catholic, or
anti-lawyer. It's the story of how a man redeems himself. He becomes
unglued not because he's bad—he's no worse than most people—but
because he can't help himself and he can't be helped by those who see
what's happening to him. It's such a relief to play something like this
instead of those strong, stalwart guys. This guy is ordinary; he's no better than he should be."

Visually, *The Verdict* is unlike anything Lumet's done before. "It's
very highly stylized," he says, "largely as a result of two decisions.
Because it's about people, especially Paul's character, who are trapped
in the past, there's nothing new in it. There isn't a modern building or
a modern piece of furniture in it. Everything is old, from another time,
as if time stopped for them a long while ago. And from a lighting point
of view, we worked on the basis of great warmth, highly directional
lighting.

"It sounds pretentious, but it's really very simple: we sat down
with Caravaggio's paintings, a $500 Rizzoli edition of prints, and I
asked Andrzej Bartkowiak—who shot *Prince of the City*, too—to break it
down for me. We spent a whole day analyzing the way he was treating
background, the way he was treating foreground, where light came

from, the way he was treating surfaces. Then we applied that to the picture, and the result is just extraordinary. Now, I could have done *The Verdict* totally realistically, naturalistically, if I wanted to. But I wanted something fresh for myself. I think that's why"—he knocks on the underside of his desk—"in total the work is slowly getting better, because I don't settle for one way of doing it."

Although Lumet disparages the notion of the director as auteur ("It embarrasses me, and I also think it's pretentious"), he still asserts the same creative control over his work that a Truffaut or Fassbinder would. I mention this to him, using his description of *The Verdict*'s visual scheme as an example of something that distinguishes an artistic director from an indifferent one. "My point is that everybody who does decent work does that automatically," counters Lumet. "So I don't know what the big *geshrei* is about, the big noise. Everybody who's good has been doing that for years anyway. So all the auteur theory did was make what had been natural self-conscious."

To Lumet, the term "auteur" is only a justification of directorial self-indulgence, or worse. "It's had a bad effect critically, because it's trained critics to look for the wrong things. It's had a bad effect on the young movie people. You see, I can't even use the words 'film' or 'cinema'. They stick in my throat because it's all become so precious." Lumet rejects auteurism as artificial and self-conscious. But his stylized approach to *The Verdict* is nothing if not self-conscious. Doesn't that make Sidney Lumet, however reluctantly, an auteur?

"You wanna go to work or you wanna fuck around all day?" Lumet whispers in Charlotte Rampling's ear. They kiss and laugh—and go to work, of course. It is a chilly March morning, and *The Verdict* is shooting on location at the Tweed Building, an old New York State office complex in Lower Manhattan. Its corridors will serve as those of the courthouse; most of the exteriors will later be filmed at the studio. This morning is devoted to shooting a short scene of Newman leaving the courtroom and glaring at Rampling across a grand second-floor rotunda.

Lumet is in his element. Wearing his customary blue work shirt and jeans and smoking Camels, he sparks activity in everyone on the set. One minute he is talking about lenses with the technicians ("Lemme see the 150") and the next he is kibitzing with the actors. Rampling's stand-in spends twenty minutes being lit while Rampling has a tête-à-tête with her director and her co-star. Lumet gives a little speech about anger. Newman, looking supernaturally handsome in a black suit setting off his silver hair, flips through a *Webster's New Collegiate Dictionary*, looking for some variation of "Get off my back!" Lumet gives a lot of personal attention to these actors, listening to them, touching them. Later, he and Newman sit on a bench secluded from the main corridor; the actor has his shoes off, and they're discussing the scene at hand.

NEWMAN: "I don't know if I like this girl. I wanna say fuck her, shit on her."
LUMET: "It's OK if you go one way and she goes another."

The actors walk through their scenes before the camera rolls. The unit manager strolls among the extras saying, "Lock it up, kids, please." Lumet usually shoots one take, two at most. "I call him Speedy Gonzales, the only man I know who'll double-park in front of a whorehouse," quips Paul Newman privately. "He's arrogant about not shooting more than he has to. He doesn't give himself any protection. I know I would." Newman has not worked with Lumet since the early fifties, when he appeared in a half-dozen shows Lumet directed for the live television series *You Are There*. But when the director was offered *The Verdict* by David Brown at Fox after a package developed by Robert Redford and writer-director James Bridges fell apart, one of his conditions for accepting was that Newman be cast in the leading role. Lumet suspects that a primary reason producers hire him to direct certain major movies is that stars like to work with him.

"He knows how to speak a variety of languages, whereas an insecure or tyrannical director often fails to communicate with anybody who doesn't understand him immediately," says Christopher Reeve, who played the young writer in *Deathtrap*. "He knows how to talk technical language—if you want to work that way—he knows how to talk Method, he knows how to improvise, and he does it all equally well. Michael Caine had his part nailed from day one, so Sidney left him alone; they just cracked jokes and had a good time. Irene Worth brought a lot of ideas; Sidney's job was to refine and edit the wealth of material she brought him. My way is improvisation as a process of finding out what I *don't* want in order to get what I *do* want. Then during shooting Sidney would often come up at the last minute and give me a new idea I'd never thought of—not a major change, but something fresh to put on my plate. That, combined with the work we'd done in rehearsal, made for spontaneous work."

Not every actor considers Lumet's pace invigorating. One actress who has worked with Lumet complains, "You've got to be so prepared because he shoots fast. Nobody in the history of show business has ever done faster setups, which is why you don't always look real well in Sidney's films. There's not a lot of time devoted to lighting." Some of Lumet's detractors have speculated that his films might look better if he worked at a slower pace.

Lumet doesn't defend his breakneck pace on grounds of cost-effectiveness—that shooting forty takes of every scene and using up millions of feet of film can create production nightmares on the order of a *Heaven's Gate*. "I do it because it's my own personal tempo," he says. "The only advantage to it is that the actors stay hot. The thing that exhausts them and kills them is waiting. Otherwise, there is no advantage. Because of my theater and TV background, I'm trained to make the dramatic selection in advance. So I rehearse, and then com-mit to one attack. It's neither good nor bad. It's just the way I work."

Most of Lumet's productions can be called interesting, even the ones that aren't very good. For example, *Bye, Bye Braverman*—a crudely made, garishly photographed, limply written black comedy about Jewish intellectuals gathering to mourn a dead colleague—is also a fas-cinating time-capsule travelogue of New York City. It's not a glamorous postcard like Woody Allen's *Manhattan* or Paul Mazursky's *An Unmarried Woman*, but a record of the grubby terrain traveled by a "street Jew" (as Lumet calls himself) of a particular time. During a long scene that takes place in Sheridan Square, for instance, the alert observer can spot in the background the original storefront office of the then-fledgling *Village Voice* a few doors down from the darkly tinted windows of the Stonewall Inn, where riots launched the gay liberation movement in 1969—two landmarks of sixties New York that no longer exist.

When Lumet began making movies in the fifties, he *had* to shoot on the streets, since almost no studio space existed in Manhattan. Elia Kazan was the only major director who filmed in New York at that time, and, as Lumet recalls, "We had no equipment. The crews weren't trained. The first time I brought a crane into the city, the guys didn't know what to do with the goddamned thing. They were Local 52 guys who worked on the docks when there weren't enough movies around. We had a lot of freedom, we were improvising all the time, and I guess that kind of stuff was finally very valuable. But as you make greater technical demands, you want that equipment."

Now, of course, the movie industry in New York City is flourishing enough to keep three equipment houses in business. And Lumet himself was instrumental in bringing Astoria Studios, where he spent a year and a half making *The Wiz*, back into use after years of dormancy. Along with the improvements made to lure moviemakers to New York, Lumet points out the advantages he has enjoyed all along: "No studio supervision. The use of the city itself. And better actors."

Lumet began his show business career as a child actor in the Yiddish theater—both his parents were performers—and as an adolescent he appeared on Broadway in Sidney Kingsley's *Dead End* and William Saroyan's *My Heart's in the Highlands*, among other shows. Like most New York directors, he appreciates the value of theater-trained actors; his pictures are filled with them. And, in fact, a large percentage of his work consists of play adaptations, including *A View From the Bridge*, *Long Day's Journey Into Night*, *The Seagull*, *Equus*, and *Deathrap*.

Despite Lumet's affection for theater, however, his films are not particularly "theatrical" in the sense of working within a consistent visual frame or utilizing ritualistic staging or acknowledging the artifice of "the play." Just about the only way Lumet's theater background is reflected in his work is in his penchant for a certain kind of broad, hammy acting traceable to the Yiddish theater.

This style can be excruciating at times; memory has transformed *Just Tell Me What You Want* into one long, shrieking temper tantrum. On the other hand, the hyperthyroid approach has helped salvage a number of the director's lesser movies. In *The Fugitive Kind*, Anna Magnani's endless overemoting both contributes to and compensates for the accent that renders her dialogue unintelligible (there's poetry in the way her excessiveness matches the ridiculousness of the script), and Marlon Brando plays a stud so sexually hot that the townsmen have to come in with a fire hose to put him out.

Besides the intense, flamboyant performances and New York City settings, Lumet's films reveal consistent personal preoccupations that,
after style, are the sine qua non of auteurism. In 1966, he wrote, "While
the goal of all movies is to entertain, the kind of film in which I believe
goes one step further. It compels the spectator to examine one facet or
another of his own conscience." Reminded of this statement, Lumet
says, with a chuckle, "It's worded a little pretentiously, but it's well
meant, and it's probably still true. Although I'm all for 'movies' as
opposed to 'cinema' and 'film,' the pictures I've done that I'm proudest
of have something to say about the human condition. I don't think *The
Anderson Tapes*, which is a first-rate caper movie, can matter as much as
Long Day's Journey Into Night."

Lumet's politics are liberal in the most general sense and derive from
personal experience. Growing up in a working-class Jewish neighborhood, Lumet was exposed to the kinds of leftist ideas that thrived in the
thirties; he was politically active as an adolescent in groups like the
Young Communist League. By the fifties, "communism" had metamor-
phosed from a vision of hope for working people into the enemy of
American motherhood and apple pie. Although Lumet, a director for
CBS-TV during the fifties, was never called on to testify about his
political background, his one informal encounter with the House
Un-American Activities Committee scared him.

Lumet, the father of two children from an interracial marriage (to
Gail Jones, the daughter of singer Lena Horne), takes a civil libertarian's
approach to politics rather than an ideological one. He is one of fifty
charter members of the Performing Arts Committee for Civil Liberties,
formed by Woody Allen this year to combat threats to free expression.
Many of his movies that actively engage in social commentary—*The
Pawnbroker, Fail-Safe*, the documentary *King*—reflect this admirable, if
rather unadventurous, political stance.

There is a subset of Lumet's socially conscious films, however, that is
harder edged and perhaps more personal. The plight of the informer in
Prince of the City, he admits, directly reflects his memories of the panic
and moral ambivalence of the McCarthy era. *Serpico, Dog Day Afternoon,
Prince of the City*, and *The Verdict* all concern men who summon great
courage to challenge the system and in doing so make themselves social
pariahs. In each case the central character is isolated in a pool of silence

throughout much of the story, apparently alone in believing his cause is just. Significantly, these four films also rank among Lumet's best in every way, from the directing to the acting, editing, photography, and writing. Lumet seems to be gradually lifting the veil on his radical past. His forthcoming production of *The Book of Daniel*, a fictional account of the life and death of Julius and Ethel Rosenberg, is apparently another step in this direction.

Like the chanteuse who sings best when conveying the emotion closest to her heart, Lumet returns to this little-guy-against-the-system theme again and again because it apparently expresses his own self-image: the New York filmmaker in an industry dominated by Hollywood, the successful director snubbed by the critics, the teller of truths no one wants to hear.

This is exactly the kind of notion Lumet is loath to discuss. He claims that he doesn't go in for self-analysis, and he denounces as "bullshit" and "gossip" what he calls "the personal movie," which he describes as opening "with a copy of Dostoevsky, on the coffee table so you know that Dostoevski means something to the moviemaker." But after much bluster he finally admits to an autobiographical element in his work. "For me," he says slowly, choosing each word carefully, "that personal struggle toward self-knowledge in a world that doesn't help you to it is there all the time."

For someone so outspoken, Lumet sometimes has an odd tendency to make direct and personal statements but then back away from them or cover them up. When it affects his work, this tendency is most unfortunate. For instance, *The Verdict* seems to contemplate big ideas like self-redemption and faith, yet in conversation Lumet plays down the religious implications of the term "self-redemption" and the political value the movie ascribes to "faith." The film seems to question the trustworthiness of doctors, judges, and priests, and to come down in favor of "the people." Yet not much is made of this; both in the film and in conversation, Lumet appears more eager to concentrate on the obligatory love interest, the weakest part of the story.

This is, perhaps, his hedge against pretentiousness. "I don't want to pour ten quarts of water into a two-quart pail," he likes to say. It could simply come from the fact that Lumet is not a literary man; he's an actor by instinct rather than a scholar skilled in sophisticated discourse. Or could it be a function of his unresolved conflict—a "personal struggle toward self-knowledge"—about expressing bluntly radical politics?

Lumet's politics have irritated critics on the lookout for sentimental leftism, and may partially explain their animus. In a review of *Dog Day Afternoon*, Andrew Sarris complained that bank robbers Al Pacino and John Cazale are sympathetically treated. "The crooks are cuddly, and the honest citizens are boobs and bores and bullies," wrote Sarris. "Lumet has crossed the line between compassion and complicity."

One critic who consistently pans Lumet's films is Pauline Kael, who painted a personally devastating portrait of Lumet in her notorious account of the making of *The Group*. Among her comments: "Lumet is a man with a bad ear for dialogue and no eye. . . . He seems to have almost no intellectual curiosity. . . . He hears what he wants to . . . he doesn't respond to what doesn't immediately relate to his own interests. . . . Lumet, after nine movies, still directs one-dimensionally."

"I antagonize them both," Lumet says of Sarris and Kael. "I think it's that I won't be put into the mold of their expectations. I have seen more good talent ruined by trying to live up to an idea of itself. That's why Pauline Kael and I are such enemies. She was wonderful to me in the beginning, but she had some idea of me I wasn't very interested in."

The real rift between Lumet and Kael came on "a very difficult evening" when the two of them got involved in one of those boring conversations about the function of a critic. "There were two other people present," Lumet recalls, "and she said to them, 'My job is to show him'—pointing at me—'which direction to go in.' I looked at her and said, 'You've got to be kidding.' She said, 'No, I'm not.' I said, 'In other words, you want the creative experience without the creative risk.' And that was it. She's never written a good word about me since."

Sarris, according to Lumet, expects from him "an identifiable piece of work. He would like to be able to sit in a room, see forty pictures of which four are mine, and without knowing who directed them be able to say, 'Those four were Lumet's pictures.' Well, you could not put together the director of *Prince of the City* and *Murder on the Orient Express*. You'd never say they came from the same man! The point is, I have a million reasons for doing different movies. I once did a movie because I was having trouble making the transition from black and white to color and had a chance to work with a cameraman who I knew could get me past my block. I did *Murder on the Orient Express* because I love melodrama. That's all. I wanted to have fun. It turned out to be some of the hardest work I've every done, because the piece was highly stylized, but *Network* would never have been as good as it was if I hadn't done *Murder on the Orient Express*."

Lumet props his feet up on his desk and lights another Camel. "I consider my career—and this could be the most pretentious thing of all, I don't know—an ongoing process. I don't know how good I am. I know I'm good, but I don't know how good. And I'm not going to find out unless I keep pushing against the borders. The borders are my borders. They can't be Andrew Sarris's borders, they can't be Pauline Kael's borders. They can't belong to anyone but me."

A more practical obstacle (than the critics) to getting Lumet's kinds of movies made is Hollywood's apparent reluctance right now to finance serious dramatic films. "Last year," Lumet points out, "*Prince* did not make money, *True Confessions* did not make money, *Reds* did not, *Ragtime* did not, *Whose Life Is It Anyway*? did not. There's some good work there; *True Confessions* is a hell of a movie. So I think they're going to shy away from dramatic material. In many ways, there's a lot more going on in TV than in movies. I can't see any movie company having done *Roots* or *Holocaust*. I don't know, we may have to resort to a kind of off-Broadway movie."

How would that work? "Nobody would take anything, you'd distribute it yourselves, and you wouldn't go to the majors for financing. Their distribution is lousy anyway, and their advertising is worse. The bookkeeping makes percentages almost meaningless, which means that above-the-line people want it up front, including myself. I did a picture once that cost $3.2 million and grossed $17 million; I had 10 percent of the profits and my first check was for $10,000. The company was telling me, 'You're a schmuck.' They're not interested in longevity, you see. They're just interested in this year's report to the stockholders. I'm very pessimistic."

You would never guess that by looking at his immediate future. On his desk is a first draft of David Mamet's screenplay about Malcolm X, which Lumet hopes to direct for Warner Bros. with Richard Pryor in the lead. Before that, he will do a picture called *Kingdom* about television evangelism. The project at hand, *Daniel,* Lumet submitted thirty-seven times to various studios before finally getting backing last spring. "It's something I've been trying to do for twelve years," he says. "It's the best screenplay I've ever had—Doctorow did it—and it's the best cast I've ever had." He grins. "The only one who can fuck it up now is me."

Are there any other pet projects that may come to fruition within the next ten or twelve years? "Listen," says Lumet, "if I can get these three done, I may just take my pension."

Somehow, that doesn't sound very likely. Lumet's favorite play is Chekhov's *The Seagull*—he ranks his film of it among his best—and he says he identifies with each character. Presumably that means there's a little bit in him of Trigorin, the successful hack novelist; Constantine, the earnest, uncertainly talented young playwright who yearns to make Art; Arkadina, the famous actress who, oblivious to her own affectations, rails against pretentiousness; and Medvedenko, the schoolteacher who's such a mediocrity that no one takes him seriously. But Lumet's attitude toward making movies probably comes closest to the sentiment expressed by Nina, the young actress who refuses to become a symbolic victim, like the seagull is. "I understand now," she says at the end of the play, "that in our work what's important is not fame, not glory, not the things I used to dream of, but the ability to endure." One can imagine that in ten or twenty years, when all the moguls Lumet disdains have retired with their fortunes, he will still be working, still making movies that matter.

Sidney Lumet: An Interview

KENNETH M. CHANKO / 1984

"GOOD ACTING IS REALLY SELF-REVELATION, and that's a very painful, complicated and frightening process. And it takes time to get people free enough to do that."

That's director Sidney Lumet talking about one of his favorite subjects—acting, and how to best get actors to realize their full potential in a given role.

In a recent interview after a day's work on his new film, *Garbo Talks*, at his unpretentious office on West 57th Street, Lumet continued, "That self-revelation process is done much better, and better nurtured, off the set, away from strangers and in a private atmosphere, where you can try things and not feel foolish. There isn't the pressure of the sun going down, or the 'Oh my God' of airplane noise or any of that. So it's a much more concentrated time than you ever get on the set, and therefore you can use the time much better—both for me and the actor. I think I spend more time in pre-production rehearsals with the cast than most directors.

"There's no real difference in terms of acting between theater and film. Well, there's one difference—you can get away with more in the theater; you can fake it easier than you can in film. But that cliché about how you have to reduce the performance, make it smaller on film, isn't true. You just have to work more honestly. In the old days Lana Turner had to keep her voice small, keep her 'expressions' small, because if she did anything big it would be like a hollow bell. If you have a full actor who's doing no more than he feels but feeling a great

From *Films in Review*. October 1984: 451–56. Reprinted by permission.

deal, there's no limit to how far you can go. Witness Pacino in *Dog Day*. A totally manic performance, and yet there isn't a dishonest moment on film."

After listening to Lumet matter-of-factly expound on the many aspects of acting, it's easy to see why he is referred to as the "actor's director."

"I like being described as the actor's director because it comes primarily from the fact that they open up with me more than they do with most directors."

Lumet, having turned sixty this year but looking much closer to fifty, made his professional debut in New York (he was born in Philadelphia) on radio when he was four years old. That, combined with the fact that he started a professional acting career in the Yiddish theater in his pre-teens (his father, Baruch, was a Yiddish stage star), and by the time he was twelve was acting on Broadway (one of his first roles was as one of the original Dead End Kids in Sidney Kingsley's *Dead End*), undoubtedly has a lot to do with his affinity for acting and actors.

Lumet appeared in such stage productions as *The Eternal Road*, *A Flag Is Born* and *Brooklyn, U.S.A.* and in two films as an actor, *Street Scene* and *One Third of a Nation*, before serving in World War Two.

"I was a kid actor and in those days Hollywood was a place where you'd make a lot of money and get corrupted," he recalls with a big smile.

After returning home in 1946, Lumet organized an Off-Broadway company with himself as director. He also taught acting in the High School of Performing Arts in the late 1940s before joining CBS in the early fifties where he was assistant director and later director for 250 live programs, quickly winning recognition as a talented director of television drama (*The Alcoa Hour*, *Best of Broadway*, *Goodyear Playhouse* etc.). Lumet hired hundreds of actors for what was termed his Revolving Stock Company, which included many roles for such young actors as Paul Newman, James Mason, Ed Asner, Jack Warden and Ed Binns, many of whom went on to star in his movies.

Lumet recalls how film came to mean something special to him. "The first inkling I got about the potential of movies was from the director Carl Dreyer. I think he's only done four movies or so (he actually made close to a dozen feature-length films.) I saw his *Joan of Arc* and *Day of Wrath*, and I couldn't believe what I was looking at. It was an enormous emotional experience.

"Also the French pictures of the '30s, Jean Renoir and Robert Bresson in particular, as well as Jean Vigo. The fact that movies could mean something was a revelation. I saw some of these movies in my mid-teens and then a lot more after returning from the war in my early and mid-twenties. I had no idea about directing at that time. I didn't start directing until 1949. I fell into directing by accident. It was luck— a gathering of knowledge and circumstance. Being at the right age when television came along was an incredible piece of luck. I don't think I would have had the sheer *chutzpah* to go fight for what it takes to get into pictures—to make a picture—today."

Lumet also considers getting his first feature movie assignment as "a lucky break. I had been doing a lot of work with Reginald Rose in television, and he and Henry Fonda wanted to make a movie of 12 *Angry Men*. Rose needed a director and Fonda—bless him—had seen something I had directed off-Broadway two or three years before when he was in New York with *Mr. Roberts,* and he had no problems trying me out as director. It was as easy as that."

Lumet, whose critically acclaimed early films include 12 *Angry Men, Long Day's Journey Into Night* and *The Pawnbroker,* feels he doesn't have an immediately discernable directorial style, and, what's more, he considers that something very positive.

"You couldn't describe the Sidney Lumet directorial style. I think that I always subjugate myself to the material, which, to me, is the proper way in which to approach a film. I'm not of the school of the directorial stamp. Some people tell me there's one on my movies anyway, but I'm not going for it. My style shifts from movie to movie depending on the subject matter and the way it's written. *The Verdict* is a drama and *The Deadly Affair* is a drama. They're shot totally differently. I would like to think that if you saw them you couldn't recognize that they were directed by the same person. I think that's very important.

"Whatever of myself is in those movies, and there's a great deal of myself in those movies, I don't like doing it on the level of dollying in on a copy of Dostoyevsky on the coffee table to show you I read Dostoyevsky when I was seventeen. I want to concentrate on what they're about, what I hope is the humanity in them. That's quite enough. Beyond that it's my job to serve the writer. I have a great respect for writers. I don't think directors should write. They're two separate tasks."

However, just because Lumet says he eschews a set directorial style, that doesn't mean he doesn't have theories on such things as camera movement.

"Camera work is principally composed of what the camera is contributing and what it is doing that the actor is not doing. It's all got to add up to a cohesive whole. For example, if the actor needs enormous freedom for a scene, you work it out stylistically in advance to put that freedom the actor needs to work for you visually. I know in *Dog Day Afternoon*, because I had worked with Al (Pacino) before on *Serpico*, that playing a character like that demanded mobility on my part. I integrated that into the style of the movie, and it made a great deal of difference. I had wheelchairs. I had rollerskates. Anything that was necessary to move the camera. Rather than tell Al to slow down I'd rather put the cameramen on rollerskates and have them pulled. Then make that part of the style of the movies. So the camera movement in this thoroughly naturalistic movie makes it look like it's actually happening right then and there. It looks like it was shot by television cameramen, fighting their way through crowds, and so on. Everything's got to work toward the same objective."

An explanation for the wildly different subject matter of many of Lumet's films (*Murder on the Orient Express, Dog Day Afternoon, The Wiz, Prince of the City*—thirty two films in twenty seven years) can be found in his comment, "I like to take vacations, but I also like to work, so I take a vacation in my work. That doesn't mean that I work any less hard. It's just that emotionally I like to find subject matter that works a completely different set of muscles. Usually after I've finished a very intense picture I try to get something very far away from that. So, for example, everything that I was thinking and reading about after *Daniel* just seemed pallid, so I figured that the only way to get back to work was to do something completely different.

"Also, *Garbo* was physically a very easy picture to make. And that's another way of changing the pace, because *Daniel* was as complex a production as could be. I did *Deathtrap* right after *Prince of the City*. So I switch reels, and you do that even in terms of physical production."

Surprisingly, Lumet said he doesn't go out of his way to seek out projects that lend themselves to New York shoots. "There was a time when I did that years ago—a deliberate search on my part to film in

New York. But that hasn't been so for many years now. Obviously, I'm clearly drawn to films that are set in New York, but I think that's just because I'm lazy and don't like to move around a lot. I wouldn't turn down material that would take me to elsewhere in this country or to Europe."

Lumet has a reputation—one that is getting more and more rare these days—of bringing a movie in under budget and often under schedule. Lumet directly attributes this to two things:

"I'm thoroughly trained technically, and I take time in preproduction for rehearsals. No technician can say 'I can't do that' because I know how it can be done. And the actors get the entire sweep of their characterizations during preproduction, so shooting sequence doesn't matter, and we can skip right through it. They know just where they are at any given time. Also, I'm sure coming out of live television helped."

The reason Lumet finds himself drawn to adapting stage work is very simple. "The writing is better in the theater. I love language. When I first began in television and early in my film directing career there used to be arguments—in the forties and fifties—that there had been no real cinema art since sound came in. Well, since sound is here, I want the best in sound. If words are going to be used, I want the best in words. Playwrights tend to write better language, more revelatory language, more profound language, than most screenwriters.

"I don't have any particular theory on adapting stage works to film. I take them one at a time. I didn't 'open up' *Long Day's Journey* at all, except for that scene on the porch, which was important, given the title. I don't believe in opening it up if you lose tension, lose characterizations or lose the story. I opened up *Deathtrap* very, very little because it would have let the tension out. It's a psychological thing. Confinement can work for you."

Lumet believes that he, and a few of his peers, are among a vanishing breed of directors who don't cater to a pre-teen or teen-aged audience. He also thinks that there is a vivid difference between directors of his generation and those of the younger generation.

"Directors today—the younger ones—are very different. Not better or worse, mind you. I think that Steven Spielberg is as sensitive as I am, as aware as I am—probably more so. The primary difference is a subtle yet profound one. I think you can draw a solid line between the directors who were brought up on television—who spent their childhood watching television—and those who didn't. That reflects the film's content and how the film is shot. Two totally different types of directors and two totally different types of movies.

"The number of pictures out today that don't trust their audience's attention span is amazing. Every seven seconds there's a cut—another cut—another cut. But then I realized something. It's not that these directors don't trust their audience's attention span, it's that they don't trust their *own* attention span. And this is the exact thing that they saw when they were watching a cartoon on Saturday morning—and I don't mean cartoon in a pejorative sense, like it can't have any meaning and it has to be shallow. But from a strict technical point of view, it was cut to this, cut to that, cut over there. See the roadrunner, cut to the wolf, cut back to the roadrunner, cut to the tree, runs into the tree, bang!, falls to the ground, cut. And that's what they think a movie is. Well, that's one kind of movie, sure.

"It's not a question of better or worse. There's no particular *kind* of movie that's better than another *kind* of movie. Hell, I loved *Indiana Jones*. If everybody did my kind of movie, I'd be so bored that I'd never go into another movie theater in my life."

Lumet's Morning Dawns

MAUREEN BURKE/1987

SIDNEY LUMET SWUNG ROUND IN HIS CHAIR and looked out of the window of his Upper West Side office in New York City. He considered the question carefully before answering: "I've never intentionally set out to educate people through my films," he says. "They have often made a social statement, which of course is good, but it would be wrong of me to say I carry a sense of responsibility. I'm generally moved more by the characters in a script than by their circumstances."

It was the characters in his latest film *The Morning After*, together with the determination of the lead actress, Jane Fonda, to get the movie produced that initially interested Lumet. *The Morning After* is a mystery thriller about a down-at-heel alcoholic actress who wakes up one morning to discover the body of a stranger with a knife through his heart lying beside her. Has she murdered him in a drunken stupor or has she been framed is the question posed by this $14 million Lorimar production.

Sidney Lumet and Jane Fonda first met in 1957 after the filming of 12 *Angry Men*. Produced and starring Henry Fonda in one of his finest roles, the picture was Lumet's debut as a director.

Lumet was determined to cast Jeff Bridges in the lead male role as the red-neck ex-cop who falls in love with the actress and tries to help her. "I could visualise him so clearly opposite Jane that I had absolutely no one else in mind for the role. This film was one of those rare occasions where I managed to get all the lead players I wanted."

From *Stills*. February 1987: 14–15.

The Morning After was the first time Lumet had shot a picture in
Los Angeles, and he made full use of his new backdrop. He claims to
have looked at the city through the eyes of a foreigner, using its natural
colours as a palette to enhance the look and atmosphere of the film.
"The quality of light is very strange in L.A. I wanted to use great blocks
of colour in the film to depict the feel of the city. Anywhere else the
colours in the sky change in a very subtle fashion. Not so in L.A. where
a relentless blue sky suddenly changes to orange and gold and red in
the evening. The colours are so rich, so vivid."

He is quick to credit his cinematographer, Andrzej Bartkowiak, with
the overall polished look of the film, praising his "understanding and
interpretation of the use of colour for dramatic reasons." Lumet originally
gave Bartkowiak his first break with *Prince of the City*. Since then, they
have worked together on every film made by Lumet, including
Deathtrap, *The Verdict*, and *Daniel*.

Since meeting in 1957, Lumet and Jane Fonda have tried
unsuccessfully several times to collaborate on a movie. "We've
been wanting to work together on something, and we just kept missing
each other," says Lumet. "When Jane initially sent me a copy of
The Morning After in 1982, I remember telling her the characters are
great, but if you make this as it stands, you must be out of your
fucking mind. "It was a terrible script. So she went away, had the script
rewritten and handed it back to me fifteen months ago, a very different
proposition. The film is sheer melodrama and that immediately
appealed to me. I love it."

Lumet's predilection for melodrama has manifested itself in such
classic films as Eugene O'Neill's *Long Day's Journey Into Night*, the highly
acclaimed *Network*, Peter Shaffer's *Equus*, *Fail-Safe* (which in 1964 was
one of the first mainstream films to sound the alarm about nuclear
power), and the comic melodrama, *Murder on the Orient Express*.

Although Lumet has never won an Academy Award, he has been
nominated four times for Best Director. In 1985 he was honoured by the
American Civil Liberties Union of Southern California "for his personal
commitment to justice . . . portrayed through his craft."

Jeff Bridges co-stars with Jane Fonda in *The Morning After*. Ironically,
Lumet also worked with Bridges's father, Lloyd, more than thirty years
ago on a TV drama, *Tragedy of a Temporary Town*.

Nominated for an Oscar in 1984 for *Terms of Endearment*, Bartkowiak also received considerable acclaim for his work on John Huston's *Prizzi's Honor*.

Despite the advantages of Los Angeles, the city still presented some problems, according to Lumet. "The attitude of the Beverly Hills police was abominable. They actually tried to interfere and place obstacles in our way, despite the fact that all our licences and permits were in order," he said.

The Morning After is the second film Lumet has made for Lorimar. The other, *Power*, with Richard Gere, Gene Hackman and Julie Christie, flopped at the box office. His next picture will be *Running on Empty*. As yet uncast, it is the story of two sixties radicals, now middle-aged and living underground. Lumet also hopes that a film based on Norman Mailer's *The Deer Park* will be produced in 1988.

Of more long-term projects, he says: "I get a little nervous about long-range views. Most of the results are usually pretentious. At the end of the day, you do your work to the best of your ability; hopefully it turns out to be of value to people."

Sidney Lumet: The Lion on the Left

GAVIN SMITH / 1988

SIDNEY LUMET is one of the only surviving political filmmakers in American cinema. Lumet began his career at the height of
McCarthyism. In the thirties, he recalls attending a single Communist
party meeting and was asked to leave after he pointed out that Soviet
society was not classless because the artists lived better than the masses.
Yet Lumet had a particularly close shave with the blacklist via the informal "Red Papers." In retrospect, *12 Angry Men* was a definitive rebuttal
to the lynch mob hysteria of the McCarthy era, and his 1960 adaptation of Tennessee Williams's *Orpheus Descending* added a postscript.
The Fugitive Kind foreshadowed the turmoil of the South in the sixties.
Far from being well-meaning liberal-humanist melodramas, along with
Fail-Safe and *The Pawnbroker*, these films are sophisticated ideological
critiques of postwar American society, shot through with an emotionally potent and socially acute leftism that did not sacrifice dramatic situation and acting performance. It is for the latter that he was initially
hailed in the early sixties as heir to Elia Kazan, as he himself agrees.

Lumet's output, in terms of quality and quantity, is phenomenal—
thirty-eight films in thirty years. He looks to be a workaholic and a perfectionist with hands-on control of everything that goes into a film, from
the choice of lens to the design of sets, from where the teamsters park
their trucks on location to the selection of a sound effect in the mix.

Scathingly dismissive of *auteurism*, Lumet might nevertheless be one
of its prime American exemplars, if not consistently at a thematic level,
then certainly at a formal one. His specific shaping of the look and style

From *Film Comment*. August 1988: 32–38. Reprinted by permission of the author.

of each film is at once very dependent on regular collaborators, notably cinematographers Andrzej Bartkowiak and Boris Kaufman, and yet rigorously conceptualized at a thematic level by Lumet himself in preproduction. For instance, the sky was never shown in *Prince of the City; Dog Day Afternoon* was shot with only natural available light; *The Morning After* was saturated in bright, garish primary color, and so on.

Amidst the mushiness of eighties' filmmaking with its televisual vocabulary and zoom lens aesthetics, Lumet is one of the few filmmakers who commands the medium and understands form and style. He carries an aesthetic torch that goes back to the height of Hollywood classicism in the fifties (*12 Angry Men*) and yet is responsive to sleek eighties modernism (best exemplified in the stark minimalist narrative and visual formalism of *Prince of the City*). Long dismissed as a director alternating between portentous play-adaptions and under-reaching political dramas, by Andrew Sarris on the one hand and Pauline Kael on the other, his critical cachet is inversely proportional to his filmmaking talent. Ask any filmmaker.

The key to Lumet's talent is his having been originally an actor. He was born in 1924, his parents were in theater, and he began acting for stage and radio as a child—in fact, he was a child member of the Group Theater. (Lumet had a copy of Elia Kazan's autobiography on his desk.) During World War II, he was in the signal corps in the Far East, as a film cameraman. On his return to New York, he formed his own theater group and studied with Sanford Meisner at the Neighborhood Playhouse. (Meisner's very practical and specifics-oriented technique is one of Lumet's formative influences.)

In the early fifties, he began to work for CBS in the heyday of live TV. It was a baptism of fire and taught him his craft—the ability to work very fast and yet obtain high quality results. Lumet, Franklin Schaffner (who directed the original *12 Angry Men* for TV), John Frankenheimer (Lumet's successor helming the *You Are There* show), and Arthur Penn together constitute a Fifties New York new wave generated by TV and shaped by leftist politics and method acting. Lumet reflects that perhaps he and his generation of film directors were thus seen as upstarts by the old guard of classical Hollywood. Fitting, now that his generation looks doubtfully at eighties' filmmakers who have cut their teeth on the anything-goes aesthetic incoherence of music video and commercials.

After the prestige success of the early part of the decade, in the second half of the sixties Lumet went on an international trajectory, making films in France, North Africa, Italy, England and Sweden. It was a period of consolidation and transition. Lumet moved away from black and white classicism (that started to go modernist with *The Pawnbroker*), to a fluid, mosaic style of gritty urban alienation and psychological detail: *The Anderson Tapes, Serpico* and *Dog Day Afternoon*. It culminated in 1976's *Network*, which confirmed the mature Lumet style.

Ironically, *Network*'s defeat by *Rocky* for the Best Film Oscar marks the end of seventies mainstream film's period of modernism; the tide turned back toward the bankrupt, emotionally fake triumphalism and reductive soap-opera sentiments that Stallone has come to embody. Lumet never looked back and so spent some time out in the box-office cold, almost up until his and frequent collaborator, screenwriter Jay Presson Allen's *The Morning After*. A determinedly commercial excursion into *Jagged Edge* territory (and his first film shot in L.A.), a year later it reads peversely like an ironic critique of the Reaganite eighties, just as *Prince of the City* now seems to be more about the movie business than law and order. Lumet chuckles at the idea.

Among still unrealized projects are *Malcolm X*, a David Mamet script which Lumet believes has been difficult to finance because it is "too radical," and a film about TV evangelism that foreshadowed the Jim Bakker/PTL scandal by several years.

For avowedly political filmmakers, the eighties has been a tough decade—look at the stalling of Arthur Penn, Michael Ritchie, and Robert Altman. But somehow against the grain, Lumet has done some of his best work—*Prince of the City* and *Daniel*—in this period, and even something as flawed as *Power* is still better than most everything else surrounding it.

So why does *Running on Empty* surface now, at the end of a decade that has attempted to obliterate, coerce or marginalize the politics and culture of the late sixties? Is it merely because the film's surface appeal (a coming of age story with River Phoenix as an eighties teen son of sixties radicals) is unthreatening and marketable? Or is it because demographics has made the sixties hip again?

The Big Chill was the self-satisfied expression of a generation that time forgot, living proof that instant history could be converted into instant nostalgia—with a little help from the people who thought they were changing the system from within, but were actually being swallowed whole. By contrast, *Running on Empty*'s ideological project is a rehabilitation of sixties values and objectives.

Judd Hirsch and Christine Lahti play two sixties radicals living permanently underground since sabotaging an MIT napalm lab in 1970. Forced to raise their two sons under a life of false identities and enforced marginality, they aren't waving but drowning. They've transmitted their sixties values intact to their kids, but now they're going everywhere and nowhere, in a state of continuous transition. Their paralysis is emblematic of the inadequacy of sixties values in the eighties, of the political exhaustion of a generation that tried to unite pleasure and politics and was scared off by the economic crises of the seventies.

Their seventeen-year-old son Danny (River Phoenix) is tired of living in limbo and longs for stability and the opportunity to pursue a career in classical music (Hirsch wishes he'd get hip and listen to more rock 'n' roll). He's also in love with a girl (Martha Plimpton) at his new school whose parents are the kind of stuffy Norman Rockwell–types that seem to populate small towns in Movieworld. Naturally she adores Danny's mellow, groovy parents, while Danny sees a mentor in her father, the music teacher (complete with bow-tie, natch). The film's script is based on a succession of expectation-reversals of this kind, since it's Danny's story and he's used to a life based on centripedal motion.

Danny's rejection of his parents way of life is not a rejection of their values however. We're never left feeling this film is an epitaph for the sixties, or a bash-the-hippies exercise, because it's ultimately about the durability and relevance of sixties values, and the political struggle they imply—at the level of personal relations. Progressive politics are situated in the characters' lived experience, which is itself an ideological realm. That's just another way of saying that personal relationships are political. The family is the basic unit of the economic and political apparatus. To begin to disengage the family from this institutionalism, and for a new set of family relations to develop, is practically impossible—unless the family's normal relationship to society is altered, which is precisely the case in *Running on Empty*, albeit with a certain suspension of disbelief.

If the family in *Empty* is trapped in a pattern of relations—patriarchal, based on subordination and denial—that are impossible to erase, despite the transformation of the surface conditions of family life, then at least the film affords the possibility of politically meaningful struggle being worked out in that context. Hirsch may be paternalistic, but his family's central governing principle is skepticism, and the lifestyle he has led them into only functions via a doctrine of questioning "natural" perceptions and searching for the symptoms of a normally hidden but definable order—i.e., in the first scene, Danny's view of an ordinary suburban street reveals the undercover FBI agents surrounding the house.

As such, the film is about the conflict between sixties values and normative culture, and about common sense perceptions vs. political imperatives. That conflict *endures*. (There are also striking parallels between this film and Kathryn Bigelow's *Near Dark*. Lumet cringed when I pointed them out: "I have some trouble with those kinds of films.") Anyway, shaky Marxist theory about the relation of the family to ideology aside, the film does use the Pope family as a vessel to contain the contradictions and conflicts of the sixties, not only to rehearse them, but to vindicate them through the vigor with which they work themselves through to emotional resolution. And it is an emotionally loaded film, depending, as usual with Lumet, the consumate actor's director, upon the performances that Hirsch, Lahti, Phoenix and Plimpton decidedly deliver.

—G.S.

GS: Running on Empty *is about locating the political in the personal and the personal in the political. In a number of your films the politics are given emotional fuel by the characters' relationships.*
SL: If you're brought up in a New York, Jewish, left-wing background, a Depression baby, being brought up in the thirties, I think it's almost automatic. It's just woven into you, warp and woof. There is no separation. And so, I guess, that's why it's there in so many pictures.

GS: *In* Running on Empty, *the twist is that the idea of questioning authority is turned back on the sixties children, who now "rule" their own families.*
SL: I never thought of it in terms of a reversal of Arthur's [Judd Hirsch] basic political position where he started as one thing but became another. It always struck me that his tight controlling of the family was because he was so unsure about the life he had led them into. He

thought of his control as a kind of discipline without which they were all going to collapse, but he was holding onto himself more than anything else. Well, at one point, in that last scene with the girl, the kid says, "He needs us to hold him up."

GS: *Do you think that Gus, a fellow radical who's still fighting the revolution, with guns, has a point in accusing them of becoming middle-class?*
SL: For my politics, I don't think he's justified. I'm very touched by his politics, because that is really running on empty. Oh, boy, is that hopeless. He's never going to reach anybody, and he's not reachable. And he's isolated. He's not the Red Brigade; he's not a terrorist in that sense. It is hopeless for him and others like him, because this is a country without a left wing. Europe has a left wing; England has a left wing. Even Russia has a right wing; we don't. We've got variations on the center, with some very right-wing people.

GS: *Do you consider yourself left-wing? Is* Running on Empty *a left-wing film?*
SL: I think it's a left-wing film. I'm not nearly as left-wing as it's possible to be now. I don't know where that would be in the political spectrum in America. I was a Jackson supporter during the primaries but will happily vote for Dukakis.

GS: *It's interesting that you chose a lyrical style. There's no sense of jeopardy or tension.*
SL: That was a deliberate choice. I wanted no false melodrama, I didn't want a sense of the pursuit, that their lives are liable to be wrecked any moment, and they could be dragged off in chains and so on. None of that. It's a very calm movie, deliberately calm. No substitution of energy to hop things up. It's there in the score. It's very important to be honest about what's going on with these people. In that sense the damage has been done.

GS: *It's as if the sixties and the seventies hadn't happened and that town was straight out of the fifties.*
SL: Even further back. I picked a town that I wanted to be super-idealized, clean, not a speck of dirt in the street. The high school was so

perfect—the classes look as if there's never been a moment of adolescent pain in them. Everything—from the son Danny's point of view—is ideal as anything he's ever gotten. Finally, of course, it is ironic, that what he sees as this perfect little refuge is something that his girlfriend, Lorna, finds totally stultifying.

GS: *There's no political discussion within the family, and so the film never directly addresses Reaganism and the eighties.*
SL: When you've had exposure over a long period, it's assumed. It was never in the script, we were never tempted to it, but it springs alive when Gus [L. M. Kit Carson, former underground filmmaker and screenwriter] comes into the picture. That's where the politics got so mixed up with the fucking.

GS: *Gus embodies what can go wrong with radical ideals.*
SL: It's over. That's the main thing. We shot a final scene between him and Arthur in which Arthur gets into his truck and finds Gus wounded. And Gus says, "You've got to shelter me; you've got to take me home with you." Arthur says, "No. I can't. My family comes first. I can't expose them to this." And after they have a sort of sentimental reconciliation, Gus crawls off to the bushes, wounded.

I cut the scene, because the original intention was to provide the motivating moment for Arthur to realize that he's got to let his son go—what's he going to do, open him up to a life of running? When I saw that the transition could be made without it, just between Arthur and Danny, I cut the scene. Otherwise, I thought it would sentimentalize the mood.

GS: *Tell me about the title,* Running on Empty.
SL: It's that state of loss of energy, which is as critical a thing as can happen in your life, and we all have it. You just get worn down finally, from continual fights. It's a fight to get the picture done, it's a fight to cast the picture properly, it's a fight when they change the cut on you. For directors who don't have final cut, I'm fortunate, I do have final cut, but it took me a long time to get it—I don't know how they survive. Then you start with the advertising and the distribution. There are very

few people in movies who do their job well. Most distributing companies do not do their job well.

GS: *How much influence can you exert on the way a film of yours is marketed?*
SL: Only if you come off a big hit. You'd never get any contractual control. That they simply will not give. You may have final cut in terms of the artistic product, but they will never give you control of advertising. That I know. But usually what happens is that if you've come off a big hit, they're very anxious to keep a good working relationship with you, so they listen to you and may even try to accommodate you to some degree. But it's only a question of that kind of muscle. And you certainly never have any legal rights to it. [Prior to this interview, Lumet put in a call to the New Jersey film commission in an effort to send a message to Congressman Peter Rodino (D., New Jersey) regarding the upcoming colorization-busting bill: "This guy Rodino is getting all the pressure from a lot of Democrat backers, like Jack Valenti and the theater owners and so on, who are backing Ted Turner, because they deal with him financially all the time. Colorization doesn't mean a damn thing to them. And so we'll do the only thing we can, which is to try to hit them in the pocketbook. I won't shoot in Jersey if Rodino goes against us. It's the only pressure I've got. It's a lot of money we're talking about. I once sat down with the mayor's Office for Motion Pictures and TV in New York, and we figured out just from my pictures, I brought about $400–450 million into the New York City economy. Woody Allen shot his last picture in Jersey. I shot *Running on Empty* in Jersey. And I could have shot it in Long Island. . . ."] So it's that continual struggle, struggle, struggle that just exhausts you finally. Whenever I get tired, I kind of refuel for a little while. But some people don't. And they get exhausted and fall by the wayside.

GS: *Like in* Running on Empty?
SL: Yeah. And it's not out of a loss of belief. That sort of thing happens usually very early, if it's going to happen, and then it isn't really fatigue, it's corruption. But the sixties generation succeeded at something very romantic. And then when it all didn't go their way, they ran out of gas. Certainly politically they did. First came exhaustion and then a refusal to re-engage.

GS: *What was your stance towards the sixties upheavals?*

SL: I had ambivalent feelings. I had tremendous admiration for something that was uniquely achieved, which was the stopping of a major war without overthrowing our own government in a revolution—which is I think maybe historically the first time it's ever happened. Because it was a young movement and coincided with the normal adolescent revolt, it also revolted against its own father, which was the old Left. And laughed at it, dismissed it. What little it knew of it. Didn't even bother really to learn about it to any great extent.

All the anti-war movement knew about the old Left were some generalized things about the Communist party. But there's a hell of a lot more in the history of the Left in the United States than the Communist party. That's a fairly recent development. The agrarian and labor movements at the end of the nineteenth century were wonderfully moving, touching things, and of great importance. And by cutting themselves off from the Left, they made themselves a one-action generation. The war, but after that, nothing—those people grew up, a lot of them voted for Reagan.

GS: *Did sixties thinking liberate you as a filmmaker? Did you feel, during or after that you could take more risks?*

SL: Absolutely not. In fact, I felt that the societal elements were rather naive and laughable. I'm just not thrilled by a rock 'n' roll drug culture. It doesn't seem to be enormously contributive to a way of living. It's a great way of enjoyment, but it has nothing to do with what one does about economics, about sociology, about very important forces in our lives.

The sixties "rebels" united with the blacks and then abandoned them. As soon as blacks got secure enough to say fuck off, they got frightened and did fuck off. Instead of fighting it out on an ideological ground and refusing to be pushed away no matter what, which is what I think the behavior should have been. So as a social movement within the United States, I think there was very little contribution. There was a tremendous international contribution in the sense of stopping the war.

The only lasting influence was the black liberation, which came about largely through the efforts of blacks themselves, and mostly among southern whites. You'll find that most black people involved in the civil rights struggle had far more confidence in the change in white behavior in the south than they did in white behavior in the north. That was largely black-achieved, black-led, and white-supported at the beginning, but as soon as the situation got a little sticky they pulled in their horns. God knows, it's as racially a divided country now. . . .

GS: *With all that happening, you were in Europe. Did you wish you could come back and participate?*
SL: Absolutely. I was in Rome when King was shot, and then I was in London when Bobby Kennedy was shot, and I had a picture to do in Sweden, but I had seriously been considering settling in Europe to work and decided then that I couldn't, that I really did belong here, and came back.

GS: *Were there projects that you felt needed to be made, for instance, about the civil rights movement?*
SL: No. I never feel that. As far as I can see, art has never changed anything. It's wonderful to have around, but we're sort of like terrific camp followers. Life develops and then we make some sort of reflection of it. I don't think we're ever in the forefront of anything. [Lumet's one foray into documentary was the 1970 *King: A Filmed Record. . . . Montgomery to Memphis* co-directed with Joseph L. Mankiewicz.]

GS: *In* Daniel, *the stark, harsh visual presentation of the sixties is set against a nostalgic, warm thirties. That seems to be against the received wisdom about the golden era of the sixties.*
SL: In *Daniel*, the golden era was the thirties, clearly, and the parent's generation. And that wasn't a political commentary on my part, that wasn't intended to say I felt this way about the Left in the thirties and that way about the Left in the sixties. It came about really because, from a creative point of view, the story of *Daniel*—I'm not talking about its meaning—is that a boy sets out to try to find out why his sister really died. What killed her. Emotionally. And, therefore, everything emotionally associated with the sixties, I felt should be treated in a very distant way, rather than an emotional way. And we even break the fourth wall—every once in a while Daniel stops and talks to us directly on camera. We broke it to that degree.

GS: *When did you discover that the style of a film, the look of the film,*
could embody the consciousness of the film's protagonist?
SL: I never understood it. I never did that consciously. I realized that's
what I was doing after I'd done a large number of movies. Especially as I
got more tired of realism and felt that I wanted to get greater stylization
in the work. And therefore the point of view—Whose picture is it?—
became a much more trenchant question for me.

GS: *Some of your recent films seem as though they're conventional narratives*
but aren't at all, because they're so often elliptical. Like Prince of the City.
SL: I don't like technique to show. I think it's an interruption for an
audience, it certainly is for me: when I see the wheels working, that's
when I cut out. But that doesn't mean that I'm against stylization. But I
want it to be done with such subtlety that you can't see it happening.
Prince of the City seems like a completely naturalistic movie. It is highly
stylized. The only one I ever knew who really spotted it and could talk
to me about it in great detail was Akira Kurosawa.

When he came over to the United States, we got along famously,
because I think he's the greatest living director in movies and maybe
that has ever lived, and he liked my work. So right away that was a
good basis for a friendship. And he talked to me at great length about
it, because it would take another director or possibly a cameraman to
see the subtle levels of stylization in that—and very extreme. They finally
wound up very extreme, but they were introduced over such a gradual
period of time that you don't realize how highly stylized that movie is.

GS: *Apart from* Prince of the City, Daniel, *and* Running on Empty,
what films meant the most to you?
SL: *The Seagull, Long Day's Journey into Night, Network, Dog Day
Afternoon, Fugitive Kind.* It's hard to tell about *12 Angry Men* because it
was the first one. Not many have been initiated by me.

GS: *The idea of being worn down and straying from your own ideals comes
up in the difference between* Al Pacino *in* Serpico *and* Treat Williams *in*
Prince of the City.
SL: Right. But Danny, the Treat Williams character, thought he could
manipulate. He thought, "Okay, they think they're using me. I'm going

to use them." They were very different men in that sense. Both in reality and in the movies that we did about them.

Serpico was a professional rebel. He happened to be a cop. He was a romantic, essentially. Danny, in *Prince of the City*, isn't that. Hardly. He's very realistic, but when you're an SIU—Special Investigations Unit—detective, you think you are on top of the world, that you can handle anything.

I am constantly amazed by the fact that these men can exist at all. It's the most extraordinary job in the world. It's such a peculiar job: there you are, living in a society that promotes freedom, and you're a cop, and the first thing you say is, "Oh, no you don't." You're the first line of reality.

I once did a picture in London with Sean Connery called *The Offence*. It was a failure, but it's a very interesting movie about the line between the most psychotic criminal possible—the child molester—and a policeman. The line was not that distinct, not in terms of behavior. The emotional identification between them, however, was so enormous that they understood each other totally. So all of those elements come into it. In *Prince of the City*, he's a tremendous egotist, the actual guy.

GS: *How did he feel about the film?*
SL: He loved it.

GS: *Did that surprise you?*
SL: Not at all. I wanted him to like it. He is bright enough not to want to be played by Robert Redford—he wanted an honest portrayal of it. That's his greatest vindication, in fact.

GS: *What influences shaped you politically?*
SL: The Depression. As simple as that. None of you can imagine now, but we were a country then of, I think about one hundred and thirty million. We had twelve or thirteen million unemployed. That's one out of every ten people. So you can imagine what proportion of the working force that was. Because women weren't working.

And veterans demonstrating in Washington encamped on the Potomac River and the army coming in and burning their camps down. And demonstrations—literally, about food, not to mention a job—and police coming along with horses and riding people down. It was a volatile situation. If I'm not mistaken, in 1920 Eugene Debs got I don't know how many million votes in the presidential election. He was a socialist. The radio station in New York City, WEVD, is for Eugene V. Debs.

GS: *Were you personally a witness to political events or were you made aware of them by your parents?*
SL: Both. My father, not my mother. But largely a witness, and also because I was a child actor. I was in the New York theater—I was therefore opened up to a great many experiences. I was in a play at one point, called *The Eternal Road* in 1936 and '37, and it was a gigantic production and many of the young kids in that play were going off to Spain to fight with the Lincoln Brigade.

GS: Daniel's *thirties sequences seemed to be a very personal attempt to recreate your own childhood.*
SL: Absolutely true. In the camp sequence where the Communist Party speaker is speaking, the clothes and so on, the choice of that house, the way the little boy was dressed, the poultry store downstairs. . . .

GS: *Do you see it as a golden era?*
SL: Not at all. Painful. But rich. Only those of us who lived through it and survived it came out with something that provided us with something very positive over the rest of our lives.

GS: *With all that's happened since, have you ever succumbed to leftist cynicism?*
SL: No, because the nature of it is that you push forward inch by inch. If you look at American history, you'll see that about every thirty years or so there's an enormously progressive president, and there's an enormously progressive time in the country. But a very short time. Usually centered about a president. And then he lasts for four years or eight years or something like that, and the remaining twenty-two years is just trying to push it back where it came from. Thomas Jefferson in the beginning of the nineteenth century, then Andrew Jackson in 1832, Abraham Lincoln in 1860. In a certain sense, certainly domestically, Theodore Roosevelt in 1902. Then Franklin Roosevelt in 1932, Kennedy in 1960—and I think we're coming up on it again.

GS: *That kind of cyclical optimism, though, runs against the thesis of* Power, *which saw the political process as terminally compromised and false.*
SL: Well, there's a whole new ballgame now. And I have no idea where it's going to go, and I don't think anybody does, and I don't know whether anybody's even judging it yet or trying to estimate its impact. That is what's happened since television began, because television really has taken over our lives, from the mid-seventies on, when we first had a generation that had never lived without television. Which is what *Network's* about. And that does frighten me. It doesn't dishearten me, but, boy, it scares the shit out of me. Because the nature of human experience is shifting rapidly, rapidly.

The Law According to Lumet

TERRY DIGGS/1995

TERRY DIGGS: *Is there any difference in the way you approach films that are fictional, and others that arise from real-life events, like* Serpico, Dog Day Afternoon, *or* Prince of the City?

SIDNEY LUMET: Fictional narratives, movies, take a lot of liberties with the law. I'm quite aware that in *The Verdict* the nurse who went to New York and was the "surprise witness" at the trial, if her testimony had been allowed at all, it probably would have been over-turned on appeal because she was a surprise witness and the defendants never had been notified of her appearance. So those kinds of liberties that make the story work beautifully are not, as we know, correct legally.

But that is in a fictional piece. On something like *Serpico* or *Prince of the City*, I'm very careful because they are true stories. Therefore I feel an obligation, first, to let the audience know that this really happened; second, that because it really happened, not to violate any legal premise at all. We were extremely careful in those pictures to make sure—and in *Dog Day Afternoon*—to make sure that we were not violating any legality at all.

So, for me, there is an initial separation. If it's a fictional piece like *The Verdict*, I certainly feel the dramatic right to take some liberties. But in a true story, I never would.

Posted 1995 on www.lectlaw.com/files/curo6.html. Reprinted with permission of *The Recorder* and the author.

DIGGS: *It seems as if you always come back to the subject of law, whether you're dealing with an outlaw, a lawyer or a police officer. Why do you find this metaphor of law to be such an expressive one?*
LUMET: Let's start with a very simple statement: if the law doesn't work, nothing can work in a democracy. It's the basis of everything. Then you come to that separation between law and justice. As every lawyer knows, sometimes they don't go together. Lawyers find themselves using literal legalities to, in a sense, evade the justice of the situation. It's that kind of complexity, where there is a separation between the law and what justice actually is that fascinates me so.

DIGGS: *In your films there is sometimes a separation between finding truth and finding justice. A survey of your films suggests that our present legal system works many times to crush truth, and if truth is revealed, it's at a really kind of terrible price, as in* Prince of the City *or* Serpico. *If we do find the truth, it's a kind of a miracle, as in* The Verdict—*which was the answer to a prayer. Is that an accurate statement of your films?*
LUMET: I think it's completely accurate, and all of this within the framework of, as far as I know, one of the best legal systems in the world. I've served on a jury three times. It was a great experience, by the way. What I found was that it was a miracle that it worked as well as it did.

DIGGS: *How did these jury experiences fit on a time continuum between* 12 Angry Men *and* The Verdict?
LUMET: It was all after *12 Angry Men* and all before *The Verdict*. Interestingly enough, I got summoned for jury duty after *The Verdict*, and I was turned down, because it was something that involved drugs and I said that I would have a very tough time dealing with anybody accused of pushing drugs. Just out of my own moral basis, I would assume guilt.

At that point in the *voir dire* where the judge says, if any of you have any internal reservations, would you stand up and articulate those now, I raised my hand and stood up and said I would find it very difficult in my own heart and mind to start with a presumption of innocence, simply out of my own reaction to what drugs mean in the world.

DIGGS: *One of the things that's overwhelming in terms of watching 12* Angry Men *is that jurors in that film were not as forthcoming with their biases as you were in your* voir dire *experience. Were you so forthcoming about what your role should be because of the extent about which you'd thought about the subject for 12* Angry Men?
LUMET: I don't know. I just knew it was an immediate, instinctive reaction and, needless to say, I was excused right on the spot.

DIGGS: *One of the key points of 12* Angry Men *seems to be that the jury doesn't really exist for the purpose of exposing the truth. What the jury system exists to do is interrogate—and to set up a scheme by which interrogation takes place—so that the biases we have in society don't block the truth. Does that seem an accurate statement of what 12* Angry Men *is about?*
LUMET: Yes, it does.

DIGGS: *There is a movement now in California to allow juries in criminal cases to convict on less-than-unanimous verdicts. Given the goals that you set out in terms of 12* Angry Men, *what do you think are the ramifications of legislation like that?*
LUMET: I think it's very dangerous, and especially in criminal cases where you're talking about changing a person's life forever. I'm still for the unanimous verdict. It may spring people. I think the chances are very good that O. J. Simpson is going to get a hung jury, but my own feeling is that it's one of those safeguards like our other constitutional safeguards of search and seizure and warrants and so on; Fourth, Fifth Amendment.

It may be a help to the criminal element. Undoubtedly people have gotten away with something because of those laws, but it's still better than innocent people being convicted because of the absence of those laws.

DIGGS: *Your work seems to be so explicit about some very, very troubling things, about the extent to which we really mask our own psychoses and neuroses, about the extent to which we tolerate racism, about our desire for expediency. You're so conscious of all of those things and how they impact on criminal justice. Where does that sensibility come from?*
LUMET: There's your instinct and then there's your life experience. I grew up very poor in the roughest sections in New York, and you

simply become very interested in justice because you see an awful lot of injustice around. I just know it's there and has been there from the beginning.

A picture I did called *Q & A* is a hell of a movie, and it's about that specifically, about the sort of built-in racism and assumed racism. Not even on a vicious level. It's just part of the normal behavior of anybody of that white, male world.

The interesting thing to me is that out of my own experience, it's not that I'm against the justice system as it exists in America. Hardly that. I not only have the greatest respect for it as I said before. I think it's a miracle that it works as well as it does. But I think it has to be constantly checked. It has to be constantly questioned because it has to be kept honest.

DIGGS: *Q & A makes one constantly aware of how unpleasant a system we have in operation and how terrible and oppressive the racial aspect of it is. I also come back to* The Verdict *over and over again because it seems to be such a relentless picture of how law silences women. Is that an accurate call about that film?*

LUMET: No. Every picture has its resonances, because the more resonances there are, the richer the film is. But primarily *The Verdict* was about a man looking for his own salvation, and it was a question of finding a way of achieving that salvation in, in this instance, law. It could have been in any other number of professions, but in this instance, the law was the instrument of finding that salvation.

DIGGS: *I have a classroom of twenty-four-year-old women law students who recently saw* The Verdict *and received it in one of two ways, as a film that denigrates women or a film that's about a system that marginalizes women.*

LUMET: It's the first I've ever heard that anyone thought that it in any way denigrated women. The women were to me such victims of male superiority, such victims of the kind of law that the James Mason character practices. There's a moment when he finds out that the expert witness for Paul Newman's side is black and he says, well, let's get a black guy sitting at the table with us.

I automatically reject any idea that because it's a woman or a black person or a Jewish character, that they can't have any faults. It seems to me the object should be the exact opposite. The whole point of equality is that so this character can be the same son of a bitch that every other character is without it being relegated to woman, black, Jew, etc. That's where equality lies. Talk about flawed characters, nobody begins this picture more flawed than the Paul Newman character. He's not even an ambulance chaser; he's a graveyard chaser.

DIGGS: *I can't talk to the director of* Network *and those fine films exploring the legal process without asking you about O. J. Simpson. You have really dealt with all of the components of this dog-and-pony show in one form or another: the reactionary frenzy that the media is capable of creating, the fallibility of the system when the media works on it in that particular kind of way. What's your take on the trial of the century?*

LUMET: The night of the white Bronco, that ride of the white Bronco, that night filled me with such horror. I don't know if you've ever read a novel of Nathanael West's called *The Day of the Locust,* but it was *The Day of the Locust* come true. Because what everybody was waiting for was for him to blow his brains out. That's what the attraction of the night was.

So I have not followed the trial. I don't read about it in the papers. I see what I see on the 6:30 news. I'm horrified at everything about it because I also, by the way, have come to the firm conclusion that television should not be allowed in courtrooms. I think half of the madness that we are looking at has to do with the fact of cameras being there.

I don't think cameras have left anyone's consciousness for one second. This includes Judge Ito. This includes the defense. This includes the prosecution and the witnesses.

From the most superficial knowledge of it, it seems to me (Simpson) probably did it. It seems to me that since the defense's job is so much simpler than the prosecution's, the prosecution has to prove everything beyond a reasonable doubt. The defense has to just set up a reasonable doubt in the mind of one person. So my instinct tells me that he's going to get off. And I know why people are so attracted to it. My God, it's got everything: race, sex, dope, a national hero.

DIGGS: *You seem to have a fear of the spectacle and of our love of spectacle. What does the camera do in the courtroom?*
LUMET: It makes everybody show off. As simple as that. There's a third presence there. There's not just prosecutor or defense and witness; there's prosecutor or defense and witness and camera. And I think it's finally going to be a very corrupt influence, an influence that will reduce the pain, the significance, the importance of what is going on, because it's going to become ordinary, because it's interrupted by commercials, because it is part of your sitcom, and it's going to trivialize it.

DIGGS: *In the celebrity trials that we have had in the last couple of years, do you see any of them as containing a kind of great narrative that would actually let us learn something about ourselves or our culture if we kind of paid attention to it?*
LUMET: I think that is happening, but in my view it's all happening on the negative side. We're debasing our culture. We're debasing our processes. It's all becoming more strident and therefore more insignificant.

DIGGS: *What do you feel about our capacity as a legal system to progress?*
LUMET: I feel it's retrogressing because of the introduction of television into it, making it part and parcel of trivialization. But I wouldn't presume to know anything about where the future of it might lie.

Sidney Lumet: Making Movies

HENRY TISCHLER/1995

IT WOULD BE EASY for Sidney Lumet to be mistaken for age
sixty instead of the seventy-one he actually is. His friendly manner and
unassuming smile make him seem like the favorite family uncle rather
than the high-powered Hollywood film director.

Yet, his life and career include a multitude of accomplishments.
12 Angry Men, The Pawnbroker, Serpico, Network, and *The Verdict* are just
some of the forty films Sidney Lumet has directed.

Lumet's films have received more than fifty Academy Award nomina-
tions. He has been nominated by the Director's Guild of America for
Best Director seven times. His most prestigious award is probably the
D. W. Griffith Award. In 1993 he received the Lifetime Achievement
Award from the National Arts Club.

In our interview about his book, *Making Movies*, he alludes to the tension between film as art and as business and shows that filmmaking is
ultimately a capricious, collective enterprise with no sure formulas.

HENRY TISCHLER: *Forty movies, fifty nominations for Academy Awards,
why would you want to write a book at this point in your life?*
SIDNEY LUMET: Two reasons. I had given two college lectures courses
some time ago: one at Yale, one at Columbia. I was really shocked at
the ignorance of the sheer moviemaking level. There was lots of discussion about aspects of "film." I don't mean to sound anti-intellectual,
but you know by the title of the book I call them movies. I was

---

Posted 1995 on www.authorsspeak.com/lumet_0995.html. Reprinted with permission of
the author.

astounded at how few people knew the sheer labor of making a movie. I also got bored after so many years of making movies of people coming by a location asking what are you all standing around for. Or the other reaction of seeing us work in the studio two days later and someone saying, "My God, I never knew movie making was that hard."

HT: *You called your book* Making Movies *as opposed to* Making Films. *Why did you do that?*
SL: There is an awful lot of pretentious nonsense gathered around movies like barnacles around a ship's hull. It really is and never has been anything but a mass entertainment medium. This is not to say it can't be art. Of course it can, but the motor that drives it is a lot of theaters and a lot of money and no matter what the scale is it doesn't matter whether it's Bergman working out of Svensk Film in Stockholm or Fellini.

No matter how great the artist is the problems are always the same, because the money spent on the film has to be gotten back in some way. For myself I prefer keeping it in the more realistic world of movies, rather than film, and as I said, God help us, cinema, which is a word I don't understand at all except at the top of Spanish movie houses.

HT: *Very often novelists who have optioned their books to the studios are unhappy because they have been shut out of the production process. Are they being disingenuous when they say that? Should they just assume that here is another business and they have bought my book and thrown some money my way, and I should get out of the way?*
SL: They are being completely disingenuous because they knew the rules. It's a jungle. It's a marketplace. It was never anything else, and if William Faulkner can be hired to write the screenplay for *Winter Holiday,* that picture's shot at Dartmouth, it can happen to anyone.[1]

It's happened to fine writers. Everyone knows the game, and if it's a book that matters to you, you have a choice. Don't sell the book at all or demand certain things, which may mean that you don't sell it. But you can get those things in your contract if you have enough clout, like

---

1. Editor's Note: it was, in fact, F. Scott Fitzgerald, and he was hired to write *Winter Carnival.*

anything else in the movies. It's like Claude Rains in that moment in *Casablanca* when he says, "Shocking, shocking."

HT: *What really is the director's job?*
SL: The job of the director in movies or television is basically the same. To take one hundred twenty people for example, in a small movie's production and make sure that everyone is going in the same direction. The expression we use is that we are all making the same movie. In other words, no department or costumes or camera or sound, should run off with ideas of its own. You want their ideas, obviously, but you want them all channeled into basic concepts of what the movie is about.

The director is the one who says "roll it," "cut," and most importantly "print." "Print" being take that negative, send it to the lab and have them make me a positive copy of it—that is what winds up on the screen.

Usually when you find writers who want to become directors and actors who want to become directors it very often comes from the fact that they have been so violated that they think that what has been their best work has been ignored by the director, and they feel, "I would like to do it myself, so I can get that all down."

HT: *Can you tell when a script is going to make a good movie?*
SL: You can only think that it is going to make a good movie. You never know. One of the things creative people are very nervous about admitting is that we don't know what is going to come out. I am not being falsely modest. There is a reason why the good accidents will happen to some of us and will never happen to other people. That's because we know how to prepare the ground for it. Good work comes out of a series of terrific accidents.

HT: *Over the years you have had many scripts to pick from, and you have chosen certain ones and for everyone you've picked you've rejected many. Something was happening there. What was it? Visually, you couldn't see them as a film?*
SL: No, no. It all had to do with an emotional connection with me. When I read a script, I am a blank page. I let it wash over me; it's a

totally instinctive reaction. I don't visualize it at all. I don't start work on it at all. I just sit back and if at the end I feel connected to it, very often for reasons I don't know at the time, then I am going to work on it.

HT: *Do you assume that the audience will respond as you did?*
SL: The truth of it is that none of us knows how an audience is going to feel. It is a continuous surprise to us. Comedy writers will tell you that they are always surprised that the joke they thought was the weakest is the one that gets the biggest laughs. The one that they thought was sure fire just dies there.

Anyone who says he knows what an audience is going to do is probably not telling the truth. I know of only two people who know how an audience is going to respond. Steven Spielberg knows. He's got some kind of magical connection with what an audience will respond to. The other is Walt Disney. His work is extraordinary. He could move an audience from terror to laughter. You look at those scores in the Disney movies; they're brilliant. It was all cold. He just had those numbers written, and it worked right from the beginning. Other than those two, I don't think anyone knows.

David Picker ran United Artists for a while, and it was his job to say "yes" to this picture and "no" to that because he was the guy signing the checks. We were talking about it many years later. I had done quite a few movies for David. He said, "If over the years I had said 'yes' to all the pictures I had said 'no' to, and 'no' to all the pictures I had said 'yes' to, the results would have been identical." I thought that was a very revelatory remark about American movies.

HT: *What about the actors? How much of difference do they make? If there is no science involved in picking a script, how much of a science is involved in picking the actors for a movie?*
SL: I don't know if you could call it a science, but the casting is about the most critical decision you'll make. You can prepare the ground work for the lucky accident, but miscasting will destroy and possibility of that glorious accident happening. When you have miscast there is never any way that actor is going to connect with the person he is playing. If that doesn't happen, you've got nothing.

HT: *You've worked with just about every well-known actor in Hollywood.*
Which have you really liked working with?
SL: Over the years there have been a lot of pictures. I have only had
two unpleasant times. I think that is because I have been an actor and
feel an automatic connection and I appreciate what they are doing
and I appreciate their courage. I loved working with Henry Fonda,
James Mason; they were two of the best actors in movies. Katie
Hepburn clearly, Marlon (Brando), (Al) Pacino.

There are so many actors I would still like to work with. I would
love to work with Michelle Pfeiffer. I have never worked with Bobby
DeNiro. I am very impressed with Winona Ryder. I think she has
something very special. I would love to work with Sissy Spacek. Tom
Hanks, I think he has become the best actor in America, I really do.
We are fortunate in this country because many of our stars are first
rate actors.

HT: *What makes it such a pleasure to work with some of the actors you*
appreciate?
SL: They are really actors. It is a process I don't really understand.
Becoming a star involves a combination of acting and a persona, who
that star really is. For example, I would not have had a very good time
working with Lana Turner, because there was all persona and no acting
talent. The common denominator about actors I've loved working with
is that they have been superb at their job.

HT: *Where does the producer figure into the process?*
SL: Today, they have almost no function. The studio provides the
financing. The marketing people decide on the campaign. There is no
secret anymore about distributing a movie. You make two thousand
four hundred prints, and it goes out. So you don't have the old process
that the producer used to be involved in of "let's open quietly in New
York, Boston, San Francisco, twelve theaters in all, three cities, and
slowly build it." All those options are gone now. You'll see in the ads
five, six—I've seen as many as eight—producers with different titles:
associate producer, executive producer, line producer, chief producer.
When you have that many producers, it means that there is no real
job there.

HT: *How is the studio different today than it was in the past?*

SL: It's different in the same way that the country is different. It is very easy to make fun of the studios. There has been a growing confluence of power. Studios buying up publishing houses and TV stations and cable stations. The amount of money at work now is enormous. I believe *The Lion King* will do a billion dollars. Now that is one movie! I don't know if people realize, but after armament, entertainment is the next biggest balance of payments factor in the world economy. That's how enormous it has become.

HT: *When you watch a movie like* Forrest Gump *or something else, do you see all the steps that a novice like me wouldn't notice?*

SL: No, I'm a terrific audience, unless I am bored by a movie. If I'm bored then I will start watching for the other things. Basically if it's a good movie, I am the best audience you could have.

Sidney Lumet: The Director Talks about Shooting in Snowstorms

HAROLD GOLDBERG/1997

PERHAPS WITH MORE LASTING EFFECT than any other director, Sidney Lumet has made New York City a superb supporting character in twenty-nine of his feature films. From New York as a stark, depressing backdrop for *The Pawnbroker*, to a schizophrenic look in *Dog Day Afternoon*, to the rich minutiae of his latest *Night Falls on Manhattan*, the award-winning director has captured New York on film in the same detail-filled way Picasso captured Barcelona in painting.

No doubt his trial-by-fire direction on TV's live *Studio One* in the early 1950s helped hone his instincts, but it was while directing the anthology series *Danger*—after director-turned-actor Yul Brynner left the show—that Lumet gained the taste for psychological drama and murder mystery that still shows up in his work. In 1995, Lumet shared his technique in *Making Movies*, a book he wrote about the craft of directing that became an instant best-seller. Recently plagued with a nagging sore throat, the master director nonetheless talked to writer Harold Goldberg for the *Hollywood Reporter* about his storied career and filmmaking in the city that never sleeps.

THE HOLLYWOOD REPORTER: *New York has been shot in so many ways, not only by you, but by nearly everyone of note. Are there still new ways to shoot New York?*
SIDNEY LUMET: Well, I don't know how many pictures I've done in New York. I've never duplicated a location even though some of the

From *The Hollywood Reporter*. New York Special Issue, June 10, 1997: N-14, N-48, N-50, N-52. Reprinted with permission of *The Hollywood Reporter*.

subject matters have been about the same areas in the justice system and so on. I can't think of anything richer than the city has to offer. It can be so many things. What's happening visually is so integrated into what the picture's about. The city can become whatever you want it to become. That's also really the reason I root myself here.

THR: *Why else do you choose to make New York your home?*
LUMET: It's a great city. I've been here all my life really. There's almost no choice. I almost can't imagine living anyplace else. I think it never stops. It's changing all the time, and it's so huge that you always have new things opening up to you.

THR: *Would you have any advice for filmmakers shooting in New York?*
LUMET: Never let your transportation go on the Cross Bronx Expressway or the BQE! You'll never get there on time. Those are my first words of advice. It sounds facetious, but I'm very serious. One of the first things I do when we're in preproduction is to make sure we don't route into those two places. One of the things you don't have to do anymore is sneak stuff. You can get official help. They're wonderful about that, and they have been since John Lindsay was mayor.

THR: *What was it like before John Lindsay?*
LUMET: It was murder. First of all, there were payoffs. What the city does officially now, it did unofficially then. You'd go into the local precinct and give so much money to the sergeant and so much to the patrolman. And with long movie schedules, you'd hit all three shifts. So there were three sets of payoffs you had to keep making. Secondly, nobody helped you in terms of traffic and moving from one location to another. I mean, on *Dog Day Afternoon*, they rerouted a bus line for me because buses cut into sound more than anything. So the logistics of making a movie are so much simpler now. More economical, too.

THR: *What's it like to shoot outdoors in New York? You shot* Stage Struck *with Henry Fonda in a New York winter.*
LUMET: It was in a snowstorm. But it's always a joy somehow. The bigger the obstacle, the more joyful it becomes to overcome, in a funny way. There have been times when I very well could have done without

it. We were shooting *A View From the Bridge* on the docks and—oh, the wind and the cold! When you got home, just the motion of your head turning literally left your shirt stuck to your neck, caked with blood, rubbed raw by the material in the cold. I remember I was lining up a shot and didn't realize I didn't have any gloves on and it was so bloody cold. It was unbelievable. I put my hand on the wheel and my finger froze. I had to get a doctor to peel me off. That kind of thrill is sometimes a solid pain in the ass. I hate night shooting and everyone does because it's exhausting. But there's a kind of visual beauty, amazing and thrilling, in seeing a city block lit up at night at two in the morning when everything else is still and quiet.

THR: *Does the fact that you were previously an actor yourself help you with directing actors in film?*
LUMET: Having been an actor, you know precisely why something is difficult. It makes your work with the actors very, very specific. Having been an actor leaves me open to their fears and their insecurities. I'm aware of them. It also gives me great consideration for their privacy. If they're good, they're not going to spare themselves or their emotions. Revealing them is a painful process. But I understand it and respect it. And I think that's why they start to trust me after a very short while.

THR: *Over the years, you've developed this mythic fascination with cops, lawyers and hoods in New York. What draws you to that combination?*
LUMET: In truth, I don't know. I know one generalized sociological answer, which is if a justice system isn't working, a democracy can't work. OK, but that's intellectual. Clearly, the question makes total sense because I keep coming to it again and again and again. There's something in that whole life that draws me in.

THR: *Have you ever wanted to be a cop or a lawyer?*
LUMET: Oh, God, no. I couldn't last three minutes. What those people go through in one tour of duty—I don't think I could make it. And a lawyer I certainly wouldn't have wanted to be. There are a whole bunch of things I don't understand about them. When I get angry, it usually is for life. I can't fake anger. I can't use anger as a tactic. They argue vehemently in a courtroom where it seems there is so much feeling involved, and then they go out and have lunch together. I don't get that.

THR: *Are there any movies you regret not having made?*

LUMET: Well, I had *The Last Temptation of Christ*, Nikos Kazantzakis's book, under option for about three years, then dropped it. I couldn't get a deal on it anywhere. Then, of course, Marty (Scorsese) did it wonderfully. And all I could think of, with the attacks on Marty, a Catholic fellow, was, thank God I didn't do it! That's all they needed was a Jew to have directed it. There would have been blood on the street.

THR: *Are there any scenes or other things that you regret having cut out of a film over the years?*

LUMET: I had a picture once that I thought had a brilliant score by a very modern composer. And I found that when we ran the picture, it was not only not working, but it was actively disturbing. I got a new score because it was interfering with the story. I always blame myself for that, for not being able to show this wonderfully talented composer how to hit closer—to subjugate himself more to the movie itself. Maybe I mixed it badly; I don't know. There is a scene in *Night Falls* where my brilliant DP David Sardi and I wanted to get an orientation of all the surrounding area. It took all day and practically all night to light, and was one of the most complex shots logistically that could possibly be done. I got in the cutting room and said, "My God, isn't that a marvelous shot . . . and I don't need it." When David saw the film, I said, "David, will you ever forgive me?" But he was gracious about it.

THR: *Do you have any favorite New York directors and are there any scenes that have moved you or you have learned from?*

LUMET: I always like being in Woody Allen's world. It's a very singular world, a very specific area of New York life. As far as learning, you never know really when something has entered the subconscious. I remember when I was doing live TV, and I had a show where this guy was standing before the desk sergeant being booked. And the sergeant wasn't paying any attention to him. He just kept scribbling away, scribbling away in his log. There was no dialogue. No music. Just the scratching of this pen. Finally, the guy breaks down [and asks], "How long are you gonna leave me standing here?" About five years later, I saw *The Informer* again and there was that same scene. I had seen it years before, and I was doing what John Ford had done.

THR: *Is there anyone you credit with giving you your big break?*

LUMET: Oh, without a doubt Reginald Rose and Henry Fonda. One of the things I talk about in the book is luck. I didn't have to go get that big job. Reggie came to me. I had done a lot of his scripts, including his first script, in live TV and we worked wonderfully together. Reggie came to me with *12 Angry Men*, and the co-producer—the muscle behind it— was Henry Fonda. That's the reason the money got put up. Talk about luck. I had a workshop for actors in a loft down on Irving Place in the Village, where I actually began directing. Just thirty of us studying body movement and voice and diction and scenes. At the end of each year, we would try to do a new American play. One of the kids in the play, Joe Gerard, was appearing in *Mr. Roberts* on Broadway. And Fonda was in it, too. So Fonda came down, always being the generous man he was to young people. Two years later, when Reggie proposed my name, Fonda recalled it and said: "I remember seeing something of his off-Broadway. Very interesting. Let's go with him." It was that simple. I didn't have to meet anybody. We didn't have to take breakfast, lunch, drinks or dinner. I didn't have to go in and discuss my ideas. I didn't have to audition for it. It just fell into my lap.

THR: *Your next project is* Critical Care.

LUMET: I shot it in Toronto and it will come out in late September or early October. It's an exciting and risky picture, and I hope we do for the health care system in the United States what *Network* did for television. It was hard to do, to keep a line between the comedy and the drama.

THR: *What was your best experience filming in New York?*

LUMET: I don't have a best experience, although *Prince of the City* was an extraordinary experience only because it was so mechanically complicated. We had thirty-five locations and a fifty-one day schedule. And we had budget restrictions so we had to manage three locations a day. It was miraculous to get it all done. Other than that, they're going to have to carry me out. I just hope I can keep getting jobs long enough, for as long as I last. Because there's nothing better than directing.

Critical Care and Collaboration

STEVEN SCHWARTZ/1997

CRITICAL CARE is the forty-first feature film directed by Sidney Lumet and my first produced screenplay. The film stars James Spader, Kyra Sedgwick, Helen Mirren, Anne Bancroft and Albert Brooks. Lumet and I share the producer credit on the movie, which is based on a novel by Richard Dooling, and begins a platform release in late October.

Collaboration between writer and director. We don't hear many celebrations of it, but it can be good. *Very* good.

On *Critical Care*, I was the first, last, and only screenwriter—present for rehearsals with the cast and on the set throughout filming, working with the director through post, including viewing all cuts and writing looped dialogue. Is this a miracle? It was a collaboration with Sidney Lumet.

Movies directed by Lumet have received more than fifty Academy Award nominations, including nine for Best Screenplay. He has five Academy Award nominations: four for Best Director and one for Best Screenplay (shared with Jay Presson Allen), and is the recipient of the Directors Guild's highest honor, the D. W. Griffith Award for Lifetime Achievement. Adding to the hundreds of awards given him from around the world, this year the WGA East made him the first film director honored with the Evelyn F. Burkey Award: "To one whose contribution has brought honor and dignity to writers everywhere."

As a child actor Sidney was a member of the legendary Group Theater, appeared in his first movie at age thirteen, and scored his first

From *Written By: The Journal of the Writers Guild of America*. October 1997: 40–44.
Reprinted with permission of the author.

Broadway hit before he was old enough to drive. After Army service in World War II, he returned to the theater and soon began directing. Moving to television, he directed literally hundreds of dramas during its "Golden Age."

A movie director since his 1957 debut with *12 Angry Men,* he's known for such now classic films as: *Long Day's Journey Into Night, The Pawnbroker, Fail-Safe, Serpico, Dog Day Afternoon, Network, Prince of the City* and *The Verdict.* Among the writers whose plays or screenplays he has brought to the screen are: Anton Chekov, Eugene O'Neill, Tennessee Williams, Arthur Miller, Reginald Rose, Walter Bernstein, Waldo Salt, Frank Pierson, Peter Shaffer, Paddy Chayefsky, Jay Presson Allen, E. L. Doctorow, and David Mamet. While Sidney has had final cut on all his movies since *Murder on the Orient Express* in 1974, he is one of those legendary directors who has always refused a possessory credit. In fact, his contracts expressly prohibit the use of the possessory or "A film by" credit on his movies and in their advertising and publicity.

Sidney is also the author of *Making Movies.* In his *New York Times* review of this book, Roger Ebert wrote: "I am sometimes asked if there is 'one book' a filmgoer could read to learn more about how movies are made and what to look for while watching them. This is the book."

I hope this is the first of many successful collaborations I will have with directors. I hope that for every writer. This conversation is my attempt to share my joy in working with Sidney.

ss: *At our first script meeting, you did something unprecedented. You began by asking me questions about the script. It was my first meeting that didn't start with someone telling me something about the script. [Sidney chuckles.] Do you always start with questions?*

sl: Always, always. It's an automatic process. I have to find what I'm going to do from what you wrote. So the first thing is to be certain: What do *you* want this movie to be about? What do you want an audience to feel? What do you want me to feel? It has to start with questions. Telling is for bad scripts.

ss: *Many of your questions were about the subtext. In early rehearsals, you also focused a great deal on the subtext in each scene. Is subtext essential to a good script?*

SL: Yes. Subtext has to be there. A good script presumes a life before the script began and a life that continues after the script ends. The subtext forms a psychological portrait of the characters and directly affects their action in the script. The same line spoken by different characters, or characters with different intentions, changes completely in performance and meaning, depending on the subtext.

SS: *Helen [Mirren] wrote to me, saying, "Thanks for the words, and especially, for the lack of words." Concerned I might misunderstand, she explained that I'd left a great deal unsaid, which allowed her to act, and that a lot of writers say everything and leave nothing for the actor to do. In your book* Making Movies *you write: "[David] Mamet always leaves a great deal unsaid. He wants the actor to flesh it out." Are you saying he gives the actors a subtext to play?*
SL: Exactly. I'm talking about the subtext.

SS: *So often readers lose the subtext. I understand how easily it can be missed, especially by people reading eight or ten scripts on a weekend. Over time I've received many comments about one scene—the scene between James [Spader] and Ed [Herrman]. "It's too long." "It's all exposition." That kind of thing. And it was full of exposition—that was one of its purposes. But I thought it was fine, and you thought it was fine. Ed wasn't at rehearsals and while other scenes took on life, that scene kept just being read. And I really started to worry about it . . .*
SL: I remember you even rewrote it and tried making it shorter.

SS: *Yes, but you stayed with the original. And then Ed arrived and played the scene with James, and it was terrific! There was a mano a mano between the characters in the subtext and Ed and James played the shit out of it! Nobody even notices all the exposition. I'm very proud of it technically; it's one of my favorite scenes now.*
SL: That kind of thing can happen, not just with writers but with all of us. Sometimes actors want changes made to the script when there's nothing wrong. The actor's nervous about his or her performance. He's still working into the role and not yet comfortable, so they start wanting to change the script. I'm not opposed to making script changes, and actors are often remarkably perceptive about changes that really should be made, but sometimes it's an actor avoiding their own hard work.

SS: *You know, people read a script and say, "This scene isn't funny" or "That scene won't play." That's one reason the first table reading was such a terrific experience. So much becomes clear immediately. If people laugh, it's funny. If they squirm in their seats, it's boring.*

SL: That's one of the values of a rehearsal period: finding out if any rewrites are necessary. Is all the information being clearly conveyed? Are we missing any plot or character transitions? How are we on the length? Does the dialogue crackle? The time to fix a script is before shooting starts.

SS: *What are the advantages and disadvantages for you, as the director, in having the writer around at rehearsals and during shooting?*

SL: There are no disadvantages unless the writer is resentful in turning his piece over to other people. This happens with some writers, even when people are doing exactly what the writer wanted them to do. It's an ego thing. That's the only disadvantage.

SS: *Your approach of starting by asking the writer questions reassured me as a writer: I knew you cared about and really understood what I was trying to achieve. You were taking my vision and making it your own. That made it much easier, emotionally, for me to turn the screenplay over to you and then, to serve your vision. It's an odd but wonderful thing. You were serving my vision, and I was serving yours.*

SL: Yes, and when that happens a third vision is reached which is different and better than would have been possible with either of us separately.

SS: *Many writers worry about being on the set. You once mentioned that a lot of writers don't like actors. I do like actors, but I didn't want to say or do something that might throw them off or disrupt your work with them. So tell me, can a writer interfere with what you're doing and what the actors are doing?*

SL: If a writer starts to operate on an independent level, he or she can screw up the most essential area. It would be destructive for me to be present when a writer is writing and as he wrote the lines, say, "Are you sure that's what you mean?" It can be equally destructive if a writer fails to understand the actor—and the director—are going through the exact same creative process as the writer.

I know most writers don't believe that. Some think—and there is a basic snobbism here—that acting is an *interpretive* art, whatever the hell that's supposed to mean, versus a *creative* art, which is writing, with directors somewhere in the middle. This is nonsense. It's *all* creative.

Do you want to sit and argue as to whether Vladimir Horowitz is as great an artist as the composer he's playing? You can argue that for a lifetime; it doesn't matter. The point is the composer wrote it to be played, and it does not spring to life until Mr. Horowitz plays it. The same thing is true of any dramatic piece that's been written. Yeah, you can leave it there on the library shelf, if that's what you want, but it doesn't fulfill its function.

There is no point in writing a play or screenplay *until it is performed*. And as long as performance is a necessary step, you might as well take pleasure in it. Otherwise, be a novelist. Obviously, some things are going to get lost in performance and some things are going to change. That's a very painful part of being a writer. I understand that.

But I have had magnificent writers tell me that watching a production of their work illuminated it for them in ways they never thought possible. They began to see values that not only weren't intended in the beginning, but of which they weren't even aware.

So, like everything else in life, there's a plus side and a minus side. The minus side is, it's not gonna be exactly the way you envisioned it. That's also the plus side. You may get something out of it that's *beyond* what you had in mind in the first place.

ss: *That was my experience. I felt my writing was strongest when the performance revealed something to me about what I'd written. Those moments came from a deeper place and were a truer, less manipulative writing.*

And the writing can be made stronger while working through the performance. There was that one scene where Helen's character discovers "Bed Two's" heart arrhythmia. We both knew the scene wasn't working right but didn't know why. Then Helen questioned why her character would point out the arrhythmia. We both knew instantly that was the problem. I rewrote the scene and then it was fine, but it was Helen who gave me the key. And in the mano a mano scene between James and Ed that I was talking about earlier, James suggested a line that really gave it extra juice.

That's why rehearsal was my favorite part of the whole process. It fascinated me to watch you and the actors trying different ways to approach a character, a transition, or a line.

SL: Do you remember that lovely rehearsal of the last scene between Helen [Mirren] and James [Spader]? It was so *desperately* moving, it was *beautiful*. And we looked at each other, knowing it had reached such a gentle incandescence. What was going on between them was so alive, and it was eminently satisfying. And that was lovely.

SS: *Yes, and there were many moments like that for me. But if an actor asked me: "What did you think of that?" or "How was that?," I felt very inhibited about talking openly for fear of throwing off their performance or your work with them.*

SL: You were quite right. The feeling was very valid. Other writers—especially when this ego thing comes into it—*want* to get away in a private corner with the actor, to give them their version, to create another intimacy. It's destructive because the basic process of movies is that all of the emotional connections channel into—and you know I'm not an egotist in this sense because you've seen me work and you know how I worked with you and you know how I've worked with others—but the communication has to lie between the person who says "Print" and the person who's performing, because that's where it happens.

SS: *Absolutely. Although at some point I realized I was avoiding saying hello to people in the morning . . . [Sidney laughs] . . . and there's a point between not disturbing the process and being outright unfriendly.*

SL: But you saw—because of your sensitivity and delicacy about specifically that problem—you saw how eventually welcomed you were. Within no time at all you were not the outsider or the writer watching; you were one of the company. And that's the best thing that can happen.

SS: *That's true. Several cast members remarked they'd never worked on a film where the writer—unless he was writer-director—was at rehearsals and shooting. Initially the actors may have been concerned my presence might inhibit them but that passed and then things were quite nice.*

Here's one of my warmest memories: one day when we were filming, one of the actors was discussing a line change with you. I was listening on the headset and it was fine with me, so I wasn't getting involved. Then James [Spader] came up to me, very concerned. He told me the line was fine as written and that I should fight for that line. It was a wonderful moment because I knew James was genuinely concerned about protecting me and my work. That really touched me.

Actually, there was a great deal of respect from everyone for the text. Is that something that emanates from you or is that something good actors automatically have?

SL: No. Not all good actors automatically have it. What happens is, a lot of talented people have to do a lot of junk, especially those working continually in series television. They get used to trying to fill those little gaps . . . the "uhs," the "wells." All those little handles, which are so destructive to good writing. I deal with that immediately. I knock out the handles, knock them out right away, because they're also bad for performance.

But with *Critical Care* everybody took the film because they loved the script. That's why everybody worked for less money—they felt there was something valuable in it. But generally—and certainly in movies—respect for the text is something the director has to establish because actors are used to being given a great deal of leeway.

SS: *We once discussed the possibility of doing* Critical Care *for pay cable. Much of that conversation was about image size. How does image size affect your work as a director, and how did it affect your choice of whether this project would be done for the large screen or small?*

SL: I don't know if television could ever be capable of doing a fictional tragedy. Many years ago, with a version of *Iceman Cometh,* I came as close to directing a genuine tragedy for television as I could achieve. It was quite extraordinary. Still, I never hit the grandeur the writing demanded and that I saw achieved onstage. I don't think it ever fulfilled O'Neill's real intention. With *Long Day's Journey,* I think we accomplished that intention—at least, as much as you can with a work that complex. It was an extraordinary movie and a genuine tragedy. But that was for the big screen. I don't think we would have achieved the same thing on television.

SS: *Why not?*

SL: The reason—and it has to do with *Critical Care*—is there are certain themes of a certain size that demand a physical representation of a certain size. The size of the theme has so much to do with it.

On the small piece of glass you lose the instrument of distinction between the wide shot and the close-up. The close-up is the only thing that really registers on television. Yet, if you use the close-up incessantly, you use it up. You have no relief from it, so it starts losing its value as a point of visual emphasis.

You're caught between a rock and a hard place. You can't get a genuine sense of composition in a long, wide shot that, from an image point of view, makes a statement, because you don't have the definition and you don't have the scale. You can't see what's going on. And by losing the wide shot and the medium shot, you are destroying the emphasis and value of the close-up.

So I don't think you can do a movie where the theme is of a certain size on television. That's precisely why I didn't want to do *Critical Care* on the box. It's an important piece of writing and I think we would've been reduced—I, as a director, would have had my tools much more limited in trying to tell that story.

SS: *When you were preparing to do that television production of* Iceman, *a critic asked you, "What are you going to do with all those long dull passages?" In* Network's *evolution there were the same concerns. Why do executives and critics often seem to have problems with words?*

SL: That criticism was thrown at O'Neill his whole life. And it's wrong, because those so-called "long dull passages" are not repetitions. Here's an analogy: it's like using an awl in a piece of wood. With every turn of the awl, it goes deeper and deeper into the wood. These are not repetitions, they are *deepening* the process.

Because I was brought up in the theater, words were never an enemy. In fact, I love them. So when you come to Peter Finch's four-page speech in *Network* or James's two-page speech in our picture, you do a very simple thing—you act the shit out of it! You come in loaded for bear! If the speech is justified, then you've got the room to act the bejesus out of it. And so you gear the performance—and also preserve a certain kind of camera work and a certain kind of editing process—specifically for those "long dull passages" and the result is they're not long and they're not dull.

SS: *In a 1960 interview you were asked, "Would you someday like to write your own scripts?" You answered, "I can't write." Since then you've written three produced screenplays, receiving an Academy Award nomination [shared] for one of them. What happened?*

SL: The first script [*Prince of the City*, written with Jay Presson Allen] came about out of pressure. Jay was doing a script and, as so often happens to Jay, she had a couple of irons in the fire. She said "Sidney, why don't we divide up the work? You do the nuts and bolts. You break the book down and set it up structurally." Which I did, since she was literally off working on another picture. When I went over it with her, she was delighted. Then we had the lucky instance that some of the dialogue was actually in transcription, from the wire Treat Williams's character was wearing. So she said "Why don't you take the scenes where he's got the wire on?" So I wound up writing about half the dialogue.

It was also a world in which I felt completely comfortable, as were the worlds of *Q & A* and *Night Falls on Manhattan*.

But I still don't think I'm a writer, in the sense that I know I could not have written *Critical Care*. No way. The language, the sounds—it's not something I would have been able to do.

SS: *On all your films you've avoided the team approach to writing and multiple writers—is that true?*

SL: Absolutely. I go with what attracted me originally. You know, when you're hot you always receive every script from the studios, the last line of which is: "By the way, we know it needs work and you can put on anybody you want." That, to me, means the studio doesn't know what it wants. I have gone to a second writer on rare occasions—very rare—and certainly the idea of a stable of writers is nuts.

SS: *Many of your films are famed for their "naturalism," even when they're actually very stylized. One thing about you that surprised me is that you're not a big believer in research.*

SL: Not any more, though I once was. I've learned something: If you're telling the truth, it doesn't have to be factual. Because you're telling the emotional . . . the psychological truth. What I'm saying is, "truth" doesn't mean "real." The character may not be perfectly accurate but that doesn't matter. If you're telling the truth that's quite enough.

SS: *In* Making Movies *you tell a story about working on a scene with Brando that went for about thirty-seven takes before he finally got it. When it was over, you said you could have told him what to do but wanted him to discover it for himself.*
SL: I could have told him what was *blocking* him. He kept going off on the same line every time. And from a previous conversation between us, I knew what that was about.

SS: *And it was something that was personal to him that happened to relate to this scene?*
SL: *Very* personal. Right.

SS: *OK. And you chose to let him discover it rather than tell him . . . why?*
SL: It would have been a violation. I'm not a doctor; I'm not an analyst; I'm not a father figure; I'm none of those things. I'm the director. And if the actor and I have shared something in our personal lives, I have no right to use that or misuse it in terms of the work.

SS: *I remember complaining to you once about how hard it was to deal with all the . . . stuff . . . one has to deal with and still keep some kind of honesty and passion about the work. You listened politely and then said something like, "But Steven, that's the whole secret to filmmaking."*
    It made me aware that's a struggle in which we're all engaged. I really admire how savvy you are about the business and yet, artistically, you have great integrity and high productivity. How did you learn to put the business side together with the artistic?
SL: I don't know. I swear to God, I don't know. In one sense, I think of myself as the luckiest man in the world. At the same time as I was doing *Pawnbroker* for union minimum, I was signing with Twentieth Century-Fox to do a picture for $250,000—which in those days was

a helluva lot of money—and they accepted the double standard. They never said: "Oh look, you just did *The Pawnbroker* for scale." It was something that got established early in my career and people—the studios—accepted it. How I got away with it, I don't know. Generally, I'm terrible with business. I don't know how to invest. I don't know how money can earn money. I don't know any of those things.

ss: *And yet you know how the business works.*
sl: Oh yes. The way the business works is very simple: the business is about making money. I've never kidded myself it's about anything else. It's not about letting you and me do what we want. Nobody here is Lorenzo de Medici.

An Interview with Sidney Lumet

ANTHONY KAUFMAN/1998

"WHEN YOU GET OLDER, they give an award to you just for surviving," said Sidney Lumet, on the eve of his Lifetime Achievement Award at this year's Gothams. But that, of course, is just a lot of bunk. More than a gritty New York survivor, the seventy-four-year-old director has achieved more than most American directors could ever dream of—forty-two completed feature films in forty-one years.

Ever since his directorial debut in 1957, with the Oscar-nominated courtroom classic *12 Angry Men*, Lumet has given us lasting images of the twentieth century: Rod Steiger's haunting portrayal of the Holocaust-plagued Pawnbroker; Al Pacino's flamboyant portrait of a gay bank robber in *Dog Day Afternoon*, and Peter Finch's unforgettable rant in *Network*—"I'm mad as hell and I'm not going to take it anymore!"

It's no surprise that the Gothams are making Lumet the toast of the town. He's a New York director through and through, and his presence predates many of the directors we think of as New Yorkers—Woody Allen, Martin Scorsese and even the late John Cassavetes who gave Lumet his first job as an actor. [Editor's note: This is not in fact true.]

From Columbia and Warner Bros. to United Artists and Paramount, Lumet might not be the first director that comes to mind when you think of independents, but his ability to maintain autonomy in his filmmaking has never flagged, whether working for twenty-five thousand dollars or six figures. He recently spoke to Anthony Kaufman on behalf of IFC [Independent Film Channel].

Posted 1998 on www.ifctv.com/events/iffm/coverage/daily_21b.html. Reprinted with permission of the author.

IFC: *What has New York City, as a set, as a place, given to your movies?*
SL: It's capable of telling any kind of story, from the most lyrical and romantic to the most desolate and alone. Just within the city itself, New York has any atmosphere you could ever imagine to tell a story. Plus, interestingly enough, with the kind of file cards I've got in my head, if I had shot a picture in Russia or Italy and suddenly found that I needed one more shot, I know a couple of places where the façades of the building can be Moscow . . . or sixteenth-century France. It's that kind of architectural richness that I love about New York. It isn't like most cities, which kind of look the same, rich and poor, period.

IFC: *What about the community of New York filmmaking?*
SL: I don't really know about any community. When I first started, there was nobody here except Kazan and me. But he was just occasionally here and mostly out in California. As a community developed and Mazursky started making movies here and Woody, we all just stayed separate. There wasn't any particular pride or boosterism about doing movies in New York. It's simply where we wanted to do movies, for the acting talent and for what it gave us visually.

IFC: *At some point in your career, there must have been a decision not to go to Los Angeles?*
SL: It wasn't a clear-cut decision. The first few pictures (I did) needed to be done here, just out of their subject matter. Then it turned into the fact that my kids were in school and I didn't want to uproot them. So there was the practical part of it. There was also the other area—my reluctance to go to L.A. because the studio system was in effect and fairly powerful. If you did a picture out there, you were being thrown in at a production meeting. It wouldn't be just your art director there; it would be the head of the studio's art department. And that didn't seem to me like a very sensible way to work. Going to L.A. seemed to be asking for a lot of aggravation and argument.

IFC: *Still, you worked a lot within the "studio system," but there's also a certain amount of independence that you've retained. How have you balanced the two?*
SL: It's been tough but very rewarding. It has happened, for example, that I've been working for a studio at my normal commercial rate, and

at the same time, a studio was financing or distributing what I would call my "off-Broadway movies"—the ones that were independently financed—where I'd be working for minimum. And what I found was that I never got penalized for that. When it came time for a normal commercial movie, the business affairs departments never said to my agents, "But he did this pictures for twenty-five thousand, what do you mean he's asking for this?" They never tried to penalize me, and I've always liked them for that. It was very gentlemanly of them. I've got no bitches. Nobody who's done over forty movies can have a complaint.

IFC: *How did it feel to go, probably within a year's time, from one set where you had a fifty thousand dollar budget to one where you had a million-dollar budget?*
SL: It felt terrific. It was always a relief to get a larger budget, so you didn't have to kid yourself. Although I'm very responsible, even with my commercial budgets, I'm very grateful when someone's given me umpteenth dollars to make a movie, and I don't have to raise the money individually.

IFC: *Yet was it also a relief to go back to smaller budgets and have more freedoms?*
SL: Here's an interesting thing, and it'll come as a bit of a shock. I've been very free when I worked with the studios. I've had final cut for a very long time, since *Murder on the Orient Express.* Certainly when I began—I think it's possibly true today—there were problems with "independent financing," because number one, there really is no such thing. For instance, when this process began originally of selling off foreign territories and raising your financing that way, it was a big pain in the ass. Because the Italian distributor wanted an Italian star, the French and the German, the same, and you'd wind up with this polyglot casting, with seven different actors floating around and everybody putting his two cents in. So there wasn't that much freedom, and for whatever reason, I didn't find that much attempt by the studios to throttle me. Maybe it was just the fact that I wasn't physically there.

IFC: *But over time, I'd bet your earlier studio films would have been financed independently. For instance Warner Bros. financed* Dog Day Afternoon, *and I don't think that would happen today.*

SL: No, I don't think so. Today, the market has been totally devoted to star power and the star is the main financial item. There are a million reasons for this. Since the foreign market has become so important, the stars are critical. Obviously, action movies do better in India than dialogue movies. All I'm saying is that I don't think independent financing is the panacea that everybody thinks it is, and I don't think studios are as bestial as everybody thinks they are.

IFC: *You've been making movies since 1957 with 12* Angry Men. *What other changes have you seen over the years?*
SL: I think the biggest change is what we just started talking about. There is a head of a studio, whom I have immense respect for, Sherry Lansing. Sherry said to me one day, "Sidney, I can sit you down and show you by the books why we are better off in most instances spending a hundred million dollars on one picture with one international star than we are doing ten ten-million dollar movies." And that's an enormous change, because Hollywood began by making its money on volume. And that's no longer true. I don't know if you've noticed, but Disney is cutting back its production next year and a number of studios are reducing their number of movies. The reason for that is twofold. The international market is one of them. The star-driven action picture does better. Also the distribution costs are so enormous, with advertising. When we were doing *Dog Day*, Warners was going to take a thirty-second ad during the Superbowl. And it was $250,000. And we were saying, "Boy, they must really believe in the movie to spend that kind of money." Now, I think $250,000 is about what you pay for a double or triple truck ad in the Sunday *Times*. So when you start relegating that kind of cost over ten pictures, as opposed to just pouring it into one picture, Sherry's statement starts to make a lot of sense.

IFC: *You're quite in tune with the business aspects of making movies. . . .*
SL: I think a director has to be. There is no Lorenzo Medici who's going to give you some money and something to eat and say, "Go, paint what you want." It's a business, and we live and die by it.

An Interview with Sidney Lumet

JOANNA E. RAPF/2003

DIRECTOR SIDNEY LUMET and I met in his small office
on West 54th Street in New York City. He was dressed casually in jeans,
sneakers, and a sweater and fiddled with a roll of stamps and a small
gray elephant as we talked. Recording the session was Alex Eaton, my
son, who eased the awkwardness of a first-time meeting by revealing
that Lumet was, along with Buster Keaton and Orson Welles, one of my
idols, a "god." This interview was not a routine academic exercise, but a
high point in a life of loving movies.

JR: *I've been teaching your films for at least fifteen years . . .*
SL: Oh my god . . .

JR: *. . . so I really am profoundly moved to be here . . .*
ALEX: *You're her hero.*
SL: Oh, that's very sweet . . .

JR: *And I use your book in almost all of my film classes . . .*
SL: It's a good book . . . I re-read it about six months ago, because I
was trying to think if I wanted to work on another book. I don't think
of myself as a writer, but that is a good book; it's so simple, clear, direct,
so non-bullshit.

JR: *I want to ask you about several lines at the end of two of your films.
One is at the end of* The Verdict, *where Paul Newman says, "We doubt*

ourselves, our beliefs, our institutions . . . I believe there is justice in our
hearts." And the other line is from Running on Empty *where Judd Hirsch says*
to River Phoenix, "Go out there and make a difference. We tried." Do you feel
those lines express something of what you are about?
SL: I'll tell you the god's honest truth, Joanna, I'm not that introspective.

JR: *You always say that in your interviews.*
SL: And I really am not. I take a piece of material, because it appeals to
me. I don't analyze it. I don't look for certain kinds of material. I'm not
trying to make my work amount to a certain point of view. But I obviously
respond to certain subject matters, certain locales . . . but it's totally driven
by the subconscious. And I trust that. So, the lines are wonderful.

The one from *The Verdict*, as you know, is a line by David Mamet.
It's interesting because the book is total trash. If I'd ever read the book
first before I read the script I never would have done it. It's fascinating
to me that David drew that story from it; it obviously touched something in him in a way that is totally subconscious . . . except that David
works out of tremendous intellect. He really thinks it through. But it's
interesting because the lines express, literally, a religious belief. And
they were perfect for that character and for that denouement. I never
knew David was religious. But it turns out in the past five years or so
he's become very religious—he's become an orthodox Jew.

Judd's line to River Phoenix is very moving, spoken to somebody
that young, to somebody that pure. It's also very, to me, manufactured
in that I never believed that a father would say that to somebody. In
truth, let me put it this way—and I don't mean this pejoratively—it's a
sentimental line. There's sentiment that works and sentiment that's
moving and sentiment that doesn't. There's a difference between sentiment and sentimental, and that line borders on the sentimental. Let's
talk about sentimental for a minute, because it involves so much of the
word. To me, it's sentimental if it's earning its points for reasons other
than the movie. In other words, when you're looking at the little kid,
looking up at its mommy and saying, "Oh, but mommy, you can't
leave me alone," it's idiot sentimentality because what it is relying on is
the number of times that you have heard that in reality . . . when you
had your own kid, and it's the first time the child had to be alone in a
room at night, aware that it was going to sleep alone, the first time you

drop the kid off at school. . . . In other words, the emotion that that
evokes in you has nothing to do with that screenplay, that moment,
that piece of work. It's the resonance of all the other things, and that to
me is total sentimentality . . . and bad work.

JR: *But is that true of Judd Hirsch's line?*
SL: No, not quite . . . not quite. But it's borderline. *Running on Empty* is
a wonderful movie, and I'm not putting it down at all. I think Naomi
[Foner] is a sensational writer. But it's just that in that movie there is
not a chance of a snowball in hell that that couple, in those circumstances, would be schlepping around a keyboard for the kid to practice
on. When they leave an animal behind . . .

JR: *Was that shot where they leave the dog there, was that a deliberate
foreshadowing of them leaving the son at the end?*
SL: No, it never occurred to me, but the reason I like it is because it is
so unsentimental. It shows that they are tough people . . . that the only
way they could've survived these ten years or whatever the length of
time it is, is with that kind of toughness. And fuck the doggie (laughter), who cares? There are four lives at stake here. So, in that sense,
there are borderline realities that verge on the sentimental. This happens a lot and in a lot of good work.

   12 Angry Men is borderline sentimental because there is no way in the
world that a nice attractive guy is going to turn eleven people around.
It cannot happen. It is also certain, if one has any degree of honesty
about what one looks at, that there is no way that when a bigot starts
to talk at a table that eleven people are going to get up and walk away.
But because we are dramatists, not documentary filmmakers, you work
very hard to make those moments truthful on the deepest level you can
so that they do not turn out to be sentimental. And that's where your
craft comes in, and your technique, and you do enough work so that
people don't notice, if possible, the lack of 100 percent truth in those
kinds of moments. Now that doesn't make for bad work; in fact, getting
away with it is my idea of good work.

   High Noon is a perfect example: a director being skilled enough to
take a totally sentimental movie and make you not only believe it but
have your heart pounding and wishing—wishing for the end that

does happen. One of two things would've happened if they were really dealing with the American West in that situation in *High Noon*: they either would've shot that sheriff before the guys ever got off the train, or in the reverse, somebody would've hidden upstairs in an attic somewhere and shot one of those guys in the back. But they're not. It is the difference between good work and good movies, and great movies . . . the things that I'm talking about. . . .

JR: *So* Running on Empty *is a good movie, but because it is so close to that dangerous edge of sentimentality, it's not a great movie.*
SL: It tips over to that dangerous edge. I had to work hard to make sure that those moments didn't happen. You may remember in the book, *Making Movies*, I talk about that wonderful argument I had with Naomi about where the kid did the boogie-woogie after he played a Beethoven sonata, just to show that he was just as real as any kid on the block. But he's *not* as real as any kid on the block, his life experience is totally different you know . . . and it only got resolved because River questioned it.

JR: *At the end of* Running on Empty *you have a high-angle shot and the truck drives around River Phoenix . . .*
SL: Twice.

JR: *And one of my students suggested that the family is giving him a visual hug . . .*
SL: Dead on.

JR: *Isn't that sentimental?*
SL: No, because I think that is (actually/accurately) possible. I think that is realistic. They couldn't leave him, and they don't want to go. It just seemed to me a totally honest moment. I didn't think I was milking it at all.

JR: *What about using the James Taylor song from the party scene with the family singing its lyrics over that scene?*
SL: That's probably the best time they had had with each other at the party, in all of the horrible years that they've had. And that's the thing they would all be thinking of at that moment.

JR: *Sometimes students feel that Judd Hirsch's conversion, his decision to let his son go, is not motivated enough. And I've read in an interview with you that you cut a scene with Gus that was used to trigger that motivation. As the film stands, do you think it's motivated enough without that scene?*
SL: Well, to tell you a surprising thing, Joanna, I haven't seen it since I did it. I don't look at my work. When it's over, it's over.

JR: *You never go back and look at anything?*
SL: Nope. And I don't know, I can't remember when I saw the movie last . . . it was probably within a couple of weeks after it opened. My memory of it is that there are so many reasons that he would want to, just like there are so many reasons that he wouldn't want to, that it was never anything more than a 49/51 proposition to begin with. And it's motivated emotionally, it seems to me, maybe not in terms of him specifically, but I think the scene between Christine [Lahti] and Steve Hill—the scene between her and her father is one of the most powerful scenes I've ever seen in a movie. And so that emotionally, you are ready—you are begging—that kid to leave, for them to send him away, so that they don't wind up with that kind of sadness between them.

JR: *It's such a multi-layered film because of that . . .*
SL: It is. It is because of its subject matter. See, I don't know if I've ever said this publicly, but I've done three movies, *Daniel, Running of Empty,* and *Family Business,* that are thematically the same thing—the cost that others pay for one's passions—and I only recognized this afterwards. It really begins with *Daniel.* As I've said so often about *Daniel,* I wasn't ever denying its political nature, but I was not being disingenuous when I also said it's the exact same suffering that I'm talking about that kids have when their parents are artists. Any deep emotional commitment on the part of the parents is going to cost something . . . not just to the parents but also almost always to the children. Now, it can be a constructive cost or a destructive one. There are too many factors that go into it for me to try to label it one way or the other *but* there is no doubt that there is a cost. The positive side—one of the positive sides—is that the kids learn about passion, learn about commitment, learn about a million things that I personally admire. The destructive side is that nobody's home, even when they're home. If it's the father,

he's not really there. If it's the mother, she's not really there. Maybe there are geniuses who can do it all, but I don't know who they are. A lot of my friends for some reason are people who have worked in musical comedy, in the theater, and the big joke among the people who write the book and the lyrics and the music is there are two great secrets to doing it, there are two secrets to doing a great musical and nobody knows what they are. And I feel that way about child-raising. There are two great secrets for raising children and nobody knows what they are.

When Edgar [E. L. Doctorow] and I were being interviewed and talking to people about *Daniel* and explaining that passion and commitment doesn't have to be just about politics, that it can be about a stockbroker, about anybody who has a central source of passion outside of the family itself, people thought that we were trying to deny the political ramifications of the movie. Never! We were just saying that it's broader than the Communist Party, U.S.A. And I was very bothered by the reception that the picture got, first of all because I felt that the reception *was* political. I certainly know it was political as far as the *New York Times* went.

When you analyze the movie, when you really look at it from a filmma . . . moviemaking point of view, it's a brilliant movie. It's an extraordinary movie. And that was never acknowledged. So when Naomi's script for *Running of Empty* came along, in a way what I was subsequently to understand was that I was trying to do a less complex version of *Daniel*. The time was not fragmented the way Edgar [Doctorow] had fragmented it. The emotional issues were simpler. The guy that was killed in the lab, it was an accident, as opposed to the committed communists that the parents were in *Daniel*. And the children themselves were simpler. In *Daniel*, the girl is having a nervous breakdown and finally dies because of her mental state—literally her mental state. The boy's story is of a man who's just trying to dig himself out of a grave. And so if there were sentimental things in Naomi's script, in a way they were almost welcome because they simplified the very complex question. And again, it didn't work. It's interesting in terms of its reception. I don't remember what the reviews were like, but I don't think they were very good, although Naomi was nominated for an Academy Award. The movie certainly never found an audience.

And then third, I was just so angry (laughter), in my head . . . I just did a completely dopey movie . . . a really comedic version of the same thing . . . a silly, bad picture I did called *Family Business* with Sean Connery and Dustin Hoffman and Matthew Broderick.

JR: *What did you think of The* Book of Daniel *itself, the source of Daniel?*
SL: Magnificent. Magnificent. But Edgar did his own screenplay; he did it on spec. It arrived full-blown from the head of Zeus . . . we rewrote two scenes. That's about all. So, it sort of avoided the basic problem of adaptation.

JR: *The* Pawnbroker *was an adaptation. Would you talk about making that film?*
SL: It was a fascinating book. He was a wonderful writer (Edward Lewis Wallant)—but a very flawed novelist. He wrote two novels as I remember, both of which were totally arresting and totally flawed. Which is what made them good movies interestingly enough, because why do a great novel? You're never going to get it. At least 124 of you have to be as bright as one person was. It seems to me that Wallant's intention was to write almost a parable. He was really telling the Christ story over again. He was Jewish. I don't know how religious he was. I don't know whether he was trying to go back to the story of the resurrection in Jewish terms rather than Christian terms. But he certainly was bordering on a totally mystical book.

JR: *Is the puncturing of Nazerman's hand in the book?*
SL: No, I did that. But just the name Nazerman, which is so close to Nazareth, and then the story—the young boy gets sacrificed you know—there were just too many parallels. Young boy in love with a whore . . . so many parallels. And so it didn't seem like strictly a holocaust piece to me.

JR: *Did you have any special feelings about doing The* Pawnbroker *because of the subject matter?*
SL: Well, at that time I hadn't read Eli Weisel's piece in which he says that he didn't think anyone should do anything about the holocaust, that it should be left alone because it was a unique experience and no

creative or fictional work was going to come up to it. It is a position I basically agree with completely. The original script for *The Pawn-broker* said to use real footage of the concentration camps—newsreel footage—and I wouldn't do that because it seemed so totally exploitative. Those people didn't die so that we could use them in the movie. So the few incidents that we had I staged completely with actors. We didn't use any newsreel footage. And afterwards, certainly over the last years, since I read Eli's statement—and as I say I agree with it completely—I know if I had to do the movie over again I would not do it.

JR: *You wouldn't do the film at all?*

SL: No. No, even though it really isn't about the holocaust in the sense that it's just a traumatic incident. And I said what I did about Eli because I think there's a peculiar obligation here. I don't think people ought to work on the holocaust, but having said that, I'm very glad that Steven [Spielberg] did because I think *Schindler's List* a great movie, a real contribution forever. He did a magnificent piece. So I guess what I'm saying is, unless you can turn out a great piece, and I don't mean that in the *Variety* sense of the word "great," I mean unless you can turn out a great piece of work . . . stay away from it. And who's to judge if it is? There are conflicts in my position obviously. At the time, I didn't have them. I was very carried away by the script and the book.

JR: *What was it like working with your father in films like* The Pawnbroker *and* The Group?

SL: It was no problem. He was a professional actor and we'd worked together—I was a kid actor and he used me all the time in the shows that he was working on, and I'd been doing it for so long, as he had too, so it was just literally a professional relationship. It was no problem whatsoever—no special input, he didn't have to be handled in any way. Surprisingly easy.

JR: *As a young actor you were involved in the Actors Studio and of course you knew Elia Kazan. What are your feelings about him now?*

SL: They're not simple, Joanna. I was very moved at the Academy Award tribute when he seemed absolutely senile. It's as if he were saying, "Okay, does that do it? Is that what you want me to do?" Weird. And it seemed to me that both Marty [Scorsese] and Bobby [De Niro] were as embarrassed as could be. They were trying desperately to hide behind him, literally . . . it was the damnedest trio I've ever seen walk out there. It was very weird, the whole thing.

I don't think anybody knows what they're going to do when called before a Congressional committee like HUAC [the House on Un-American Activities Committee]. All the resolutions in the world disappear the minute you're face-to-face with it, as with any human situation. Now it is absolutely true that Kazan was in those years the most successful director on Broadway. He certainly wouldn't have had a problem making a living or doing work. The big question is—what if he wanted to do movies? What if that had become his passion and the thing he cared about most? To do that, he had to testify. To me, he was never—despite some fine films—he was never quite the movie director that he was stage director. He was a great stage director, and he was a very good moviemaker. So, what do you do? It's hard. For myself, I never came up before the Committee. My name came up when they tried to blacklist me in television. . . .

JR: *Yes. I've read your piece in* The Nation . . .[1]
SL: So you know about that. I didn't know what I was going to do. . . . I mean, I was hoping I would behave well. But I didn't know what I was going to do when I walked in the door. The only Communist Party meeting I'd ever been to in my life was when I was fourteen. My sister took me to one in Astoria, and I got thrown out (laughter).

JR: *So your accuser really did have you confused with someone else?*
SL: Yes, that was all. But in all honesty, I didn't know what I would do. I behaved well. On another day, who knows? I might have crawled. I don't know.

JR: *You have said in interviews that you did* Anderson Tapes *as a lark, kind of to lighten up, just a caper film. Do you think today, in light of what*

---

1. Sidney Lumet, "It Must Have Been . . ." *The Nation* (April 18, 1981): 469–70.

we're living under now, with its emphasis—almost to an extreme—on
surveillance—it's become quite topical?

SL: Absolutely. It's not that I wanted to lighten up, it's that it is just
that way in melodrama, which is delicious. I have no apologies for
doing it; I love melodrama. But it is—this is going to sound awful and
pretentious—it is a lesser form, lesser in the sense that it's easier. If
you've got a good story, that's all you need. And when they are really
superb is when you get a melodrama on the level of *Silence of the Lambs,*
which was not only brilliantly directed but marvelously acted. Jodie
Foster and Anthony Hopkins were sensational. And all of a sudden you
got into a world that was very, very terrific. You were not only, just like
that, on the edge of your seat, with your heart pounding every second,
but you were fascinated by those two people. So, that's the best that
melodrama can be. And *Anderson Tapes* was a caper movie. It's what
I'd call a caper movie with a gimmick. The gimmick, however, is
something that was prescient. It was true then, because it was right
after the HUAC time, so on and so on. Surveillance was not necessarily
unknown to Americans, especially if you were radical and black. There
were a number of shots there, as I remember, of the Black Panther
headquarters and so on. So, it's unfortunately a lucky accident about its
prescience because boy—it's back, isn't it?

JR: *It's uncanny. How prescient is* Network *today?*
SL: People have always said of that movie, "Oh, what a brilliant satire,"
and Paddy and I have the same response. We say, "That's not a satire;
that's reportage." The only thing that hasn't happened in that movie is
that we haven't shot anybody on the air . . . But, you know, you get
these reality series going a little bit further and it's going to happen.
But Paddy was always prescient. You remember *Hospital.*

JR: *How about* Critical Care?
SL: It's also a satire—and a delicious one. I love that movie. And it was
written by a wonderful guy by the name of Steve Schwartz, a sweet,
good, wonderful . . . terrific guy—and a wonderful writer. I don't know
what to tell you about it. I fell in love with the script the minute I read
it. Again, I don't think we did much work on the script at all. It was cat-
astrophically distributed by something called Artisan Films. The only

picture they ever made any money on was . . . what was *The Blair Witch Project* or whatever it's called. And that's what they should be releasing, that's all. They didn't know how to handle it. And I don't remember if the reception was particularly good. On pictures like that, unfortunately, you need the *Times* . . . and we didn't get the *Times*. So sometimes when I speak of the picture not being well reviewed, I'm relegating it to the *Times* because for pictures like that, and for a *Daniel* or *Running on Empty*, you need the *Times* to launch you.

JR: *Critical Care has a very tenuous balance between comedy and tragedy. And because of this, my students are sometimes unsure about how to react to it.*
SL: Well, then, I'm interested in that, Joanna, because that's my fault. The director should always be firmly enough in command so when he wants you to laugh, you pee in your pants, and then he cuts it off like that. God knows Robert Altman is brilliant with that. But I don't have a natural talent for comedy. So my command isn't quite as firm as it should be. I remember after I ran the picture the first time, and I realized that on the rough cut with the first shot you really didn't know if you were in a mortuary or what—it was so weird . . . It's a 360-degree camera move, all the way around the room, following this nurse. And I realized it was setting the picture off "grimly." It looked very forbidding. So I called Nora Ephron, who is a close friend and who I like enormously, and she saw the picture and I said, "Nora, what do I do here to let them know that it's going to be alright to laugh, because there are some laughs coming within the first five minutes of the movie, and I want those laughs?" And she said, "Oh, why don't you play 'Dry Bones' "? And she was absolutely right of course, because it gave you permission to take off. But still, within the body of the picture, my command wasn't quite firm enough, but it's still a very good movie.

JR: *It's also about a real issue, more and more real every day. On another subject, first and last shots of your movies . . . is it true they're not usually in the script?*
SL: Almost never. I can't remember one that was. And they're almost always the first things that occur to me. And, most of the time they're the only advance camera commitment I make. Because they do occur to me at a very early point.

JR: *So that long montage at the opening of* Dog Day Afternoon, *that's not in the script?*
SL: That *was* scripted. That was scripted.

JR: *. . . including the music that ends up coming from the car radio?*
SL: Well, see it's so funny . . . how things work out. When we first began the movie our editor, Dede Allen said, "Well there'll certainly be a score." And I said, "I dunno, Dede. I have the feeling that there may not be a score." And as you know there wasn't. And, she said, "Well there'll certainly be music over the opening titles." I said, "Probably, maybe . . ." So, because the shots were all stolen—there is no audio on them—she just threw in this Elton John record to cover the shots. And we just got attached to it—for no reason. I knew that stylistically I did not want music because one of the obligations of that movie is—"Hey folks, this really happened." You cannot therefore go ahead and do a score to it. So, I began looking for a way to motivate the music you're hearing at the beginning. We just took the Elton John record, and as we got nearer and nearer to Pacino and his friends in the car, kept adding the filter, filter, filter, until "Bang"—there it is on the radio.

JR: *Is it very common for you—and I sense it is—to have the writer of a film on the set?*
SL: All the time, whenever I can. Sometimes, it's interesting how the corruption has been so total among all of us. Sometimes I've asked the writer to do that and he says, "Well, talk to the studio and see if you can get me paid for that time." It's not unjustified. But considering how violated most of them have been and how often they complain about not being involved in the production, I've always been rather stunned that they would turn down an opportunity like that, and some have.

JR: *But you prefer it?*
SL: Yeah. Not necessarily on the set, but certainly for the two weeks of rehearsal—two or three weeks of rehearsal.

JR: *One of your favorite movies is* The Hill. *Why?*
SL: It's just so true, so unhooked, and the melodrama is not hokey. As I said, I don't really look at my movies afterwards, but I've seen it a

couple of times, oddly enough, because Ted Turner colorized it, and it's terrific. They are so terrible at this color work—this colorization—so all they did was make the sky blue and the sand brown and the clothes brown and the skins ruddy. There are just three colors in it, like a comic strip, and it looks marvelous, because that's the way it looked to the eye when we were there. I didn't feel it interfered with a thing because there was no attempt at gradation, and I did it, as you know, without any artificial light at all. As I say in the book [*Making Movies*] Ossie [cinematographer Oswald Morris] would say to me, "Sidney, you want to see eyes?" and I'd say, "Yeah." And he'd take out his handkerchief and hold it up as a reflector under the lens. So, the fact that there was no lighting in the movie, including in the prison cell, where all Ossie did was pour light through that window, and the floor was sort of light, and the walls were whitewashed, so that everything else was bounce light, and then he didn't add any light, that makes the colorization work. What makes colorization so atrocious in most Hollywood movies is the lighting. The process itself is not great. Electronic color is much truer, much better—I like it much better than film color. But, because there was no lighting in *The Hill*—it was not lit—it looked good. What also helped the colorization was that Ossie used a film stock made by a company called Ilford. I think they're out of business now. But anyway, it was extremely contrasty. And that's one of the reason they went out of business, because the film was too contrasty.

JR: *Speaking of black and white and color, you've said that you had a hard time going from black and white to color, which is why you made* The Appointment. *Can you explain a little more why you had trouble?*
SL: Well, I was brought up in black and white; every movie I saw was in black and white until after the war. Then, out of my first seven or eight movies, only one was in color, *Stage Struck*. After that, the next six or seven were all in black and white. What I'm talking about, literally, is your palette. And the black and white palette has another kind of definition. You're using shades of gray from pure white to pure black to tell a story. And I didn't know how to do that in color. Part of the problem was also that Boris Kaufman—whom I loved and we did many pictures together—wasn't terrific in color. He was a great black and white cameraman. But he was fighting color all the time. It wasn't natural to him.

And it wasn't natural to me either. So, I just had to get with somebody who could show me what it was about and how to use it. And I found the perfect person—Carlo Di Palma who had been photographing the Antonioni movies.

It was so simple. It was like all complicated questions: it had a very simple answer. Almost all of my black and white pictures were not studio pictures—they were all location pictures. He said, "Just pick the right place and then don't do anything about it." It was perfect. It made such sense. By "right place" he meant, a place that—in its color—helps you tell the story. Having said that, when I saw him in London next, he was making a picture with Antonioni. They were painting the grass green. (Laughter) The two of them . . . it was hilarious . . . great big paintbrushes . . . and all the grips making the grass a deeper green.

JR: *Have you ever done that, changed the color of your locations in any of your films?*
SL: Yeah, oh yeah. Largely because, for instance—the time of day matters. And sunlight or no sunlight matters. But not nearly as often as it would seem. Most of the time I took Di Palma at his word, and if the location wasn't the right color, try to find something else.

JR: *Now that you've worked in high definition 24 p., I gather that you love it.*
SL: It's true color. You see, we don't realize it because we've been so seduced by movie color. There have been close to one hundred years of brilliant color photography, going back to the Lumière brothers, who did color movies, believe it or not. But movie color has nothing to do with what the eye sees. It's not at all the same. And I'm not stupid. The reason is simple: there are only three forms of energy. There's thermal energy . . . you may remember this from your physics class . . .

JR: *I got a D in physics . . .*
SL: There's some good stuff there. . . . which is heat. There is electromagnetic energy. And there is chemical energy. Now those are the only forms of energy that exist in the universe. And when you go from one form of energy to another, you lose efficiency. For example, if you are working in thermal energy—which is heat—and it is turning the

generator, which is going to create electricity, if you put in one hundred pounds of steam, you would not be getting a one hundred pounds of electrical energy out. You would be getting ninety . . . eighty-five . . . seventy . . . it varies. So, when you're dealing with movies, as we now do them, you are dealing with electromagnetic light, converted . . . recorded on a chemical base—which is what film is. And then when it's projected, it's being reconverted back to electromagnetic light. (Looking out the window) You have never seen that color sky on film, ever. You've seen blue—but not *that* blue. You're talking about grass—you've seen green but not grass green. The first time I saw that HD Sony camera was a test reel they had made up, and one of the shots they did was when the Yankees won the pennant that year, and there was a camera on lower Broadway as they were shooting the ticker-tape parade, low— against a kind of hot building—with the sun hitting the building, but the street was in complete shadow. And Joe Torres's car was coming up the canyon, and it was surrounded on front and back by four black cops. And they marched right by the camera. And it was the first time I've ever seen black skin look like black skin. It was the first time I was ever able to say, "Oh this guy is a dark-skinned guy. This guy's light skinned." The texture, it was all there. And when I went out with the camera the first time, bang! I was able to capture whatever my eye first saw. Now, you can do anything you want to with it. You can get the movie Technicolor look. In the demo reel, Sony had some Hollywood cameraman light an interior set. And it wound up looking stupid. It wound up looking like 1940s Technicolor. You would've expected Doris Day to come in through the door. So you can create that because you've got tremendous control over each individual color. But what you cannot get with film is exactly what your eye sees—and that you can get on tape or digital disc because it's all electronic. It never changes its form. Its recording surface is electromagnetic.

JR: *So would you like to do a whole movie that way?*
SL: Everything. Everything. Everything.

JR: *No more film?*
SL: No. It's cumbersome. I don't know of a single director who isn't frustrated by the time it takes, the money it takes, the effort it takes . . .

JR: *Shooting in high definition video gets us to the subject of* 100 Centre Street. *You did all those shows that way?*
SL: Yeah. And with three cameras.

JR: *Did you deliberately echo the opening of* 12 Angry Men *with the opening shot of the* 100 Centre Street?
SL: No I wasn't aware of it, but the minute I saw it I said, "Oh! I recognize that." It was one block up. The other was 60 Centre Street and this was 100.

JR: *Was the Alan Arkin character based at all on Justice Edwin Torres?*[2]
SL: No, it wasn't at all. Eddie Torres is a wonderful writer by the way. His novels, such as *Carlito's Way* and *After Hours*, are terrific. They've all been made into movies . . . Torres is a real Puerto Rican. He's got the short-brimmed hat and the yellow silk tie . . . natty. No, Arkin's character came from the fact that I have always been fascinated . . . again, in terms of cost . . . what does it cost judges? What happens at five thirty when they go home? I mean, they ain't kiddin' around. They are dealing with "it." And the slightest decision changes lives, not just whoever is up in front of them, but whatever . . . like a pebble in a pond. And so I've often just wondered. I wanted to do a movie about that cost, but I never had a story idea for it. Anything I came up with seemed forced, seemed melodramatic. And then when the series came up, I thought, "This is perfect." First of all, we would have thirteen hours to talk about it. And how much better that would be than a two-hour movie. The only reason I'm sorry we didn't get a third year is because I was developing it as we were doing the series you know, and the first year had a wonderful dilemma for him. And then in the second year, dropping him in with his own kid. And then, when that resolved itself at the end of the second year, I thought, well, third year—he can't take it anymore. And then I was going to do a terrific thing with the other judge. He wasn't going to quit, but he was going to go off to another country just to get away and see what happened to him. And I would've had something good happen to him. And with the other judge, Queenie, in

---

2. Q & A is based on a novel by Torres.

the third year I was going to have her find out that someone she sentenced to death seven years ago turns out now to be innocent of it because of the DNA. It's a wonderful area to investigate. There are certain professions where if you are not great, you're a butcher. There's no such thing as a good surgeon. If you're not a great surgeon, you're a killer. If you're not a great teacher, you're a killer. And I'm starting to feel that way about newspaper people. And, certainly it's true of judges.

JR: *What do you mean by newspaper people who have to be "great"?*
SL: Most become either part of what's going on or are now sucked into cooperation with any administration, not just Republican. It seems to me there's been nobody since I. F. Stone. Paul Krugman seems to be doing some good work on the *Times* . . . he's wonderful. But for the rest of them, I don't believe what they accept.

JR: *You once called* Long Day's Journey Into Night *the first of your "human" films, and by that you meant it's a film where you don't judge your characters. And you made a list in 1982 that includes* The Seagull, Dog Day Afternoon, *and* Prince of the City. *What films would you add to that now?*
SL: I would put *Daniel* in there. But I would have to look over my list of movies, because I do forget them. I'd put *The Hill* in, funnily enough. I think any picture that doesn't sentimentalize, which is honest, which earns its own emotion is human.

JR: *I know* The Seagull *was a very personal film for you. In an interview with Michel Ciment you said it provided you with some of the strongest emotions you ever felt in your life. My sense was that those emotions had to do with something like the futility of our aspirations and our dreams. And I just wonder if, after all these years, you remember those emotions?*
SL: I certainly do. I certainly certainly do. I was rereading *The Seagull* over the weekend. It's interesting . . . I read it again. I haven't looked at the movie again. And all of the aspirations are noble, and it's wonderful to fall in love, and it's wonderful to ride a horse across the lake, and it's wonderful to see older people in love, and it's wonderful to pursue this one and pursue that one, and finally, it is so futile. And finally, it just flops over into tragic, not even intending to. And I think that's true about life. As I'm getting older, one of the things I find very

disheartening is that almost nobody I know is having a good old age—
either physically, or in a great many instances, emotionally—in terms
of satisfaction. Did I do my job? Did I do good work? Did I do the work
I could do? You know, we just buried Adolph Green and—mad nut—
and there he was, the last three years of his life, couldn't see—couldn't
hear. A man who loved music like Adolph needed to hear a piece
once—I'm talking about a symphony—and could sing it back to you.
He was some kind of genius in musical terms. That's how his friendship
with Lenny Bernstein happened. And for him to wind up not being
able to hear . . . He wrote certainly the best musical up until *Chicago*.
Have you seen *Chicago* yet?

JR: *No.*

SL: Brilliant. Marvelous. But *Singin' in the Rain* is the only musical I'd
call "great." So for him not be able to see and hear . . . awful, just awful.
So, *The Seagull* is about—if it is "about" anything, because it's such a
wonderful play, sometimes you can't pin it down to any one theme—
but if it's about anything, it's about the futility of. . . .

JR: *You don't feel your life has been futile.*

SL: No, no I don't feel it's been futile. I guess I wish a lot of things
were different, but so does everybody. Nothing more human than that
wish, is there? No, I don't feel it's been futile.

JR: *If you look back at your career, it's absolutely extraordinary.*

SL: You see, I never think in those terms . . .

JR: *No, but I do.*

SL: Thank you, Joanna.

INDEX

Actors Studio, 58, 93, 184
Actor's Workshop, The, 93, 161
Adler, Helen, 92
Adler, Luther, 92
Adler, Stella, 91–92
All About Eve, 58
All the King's Men, 3, 10
All the President's Men, 75
Allen, Dede, 188
Allen, Jay Presson, vii, 83–84, 88, 133, 162, 163, 170
Allen, Woody, vii, 111, 117, 138, 160, 173, 174; *Manhattan*, 115
Altman, Robert, 133, 187
Anderson, Maxwell, 91
Anderson Tapes, The, xii, 44, 46, 63, 81, 96, 101, 105, 117, 133, 185–86
Andrews, Harry, 27, 43, 61
Anne Frank, 9
Antonioni, Michelangelo, 96, 190
Appointment, The, 96
Arkin, Alan, 192
Asner, Ed, 111, 123
Awake and Sing, 91

Bacall, Lauren, xi
Bakker, Jim, 133
Ballad of a Soldier (Chukrai), 57
Bancroft, Anne, ix, xi, 162
Bannen, Ian, 48, 63
Bartkowiak, Andrzej, 112–13, 129–30, 132
Bergen, Candace, xi
Bergman, Ingmar, 6, 152; *Seventh Seal, The*, viii, 110

Bergman, Ingrid, xi, 55, 111
Bernstein, Leonard, 194
Bernstein, Walter, 94, 163
Big Chill, The, 133–34
Bigelow, Kathryn, *Near Dark*, 135
Binns, Ed, 123
Bitter Rice, 23
Black Monday, 8
Blair Witch Project, 187
Bobby Deerfield, 74
Bourgeois Gentleman, 40
Bovaso, Julie, 112
Boys in the Band, 53
Brando, Marlon, x, 4, 22, 57–58, 98, 111, 116, 155, 171
Bresson, Robert, 124
Bridge on the River Kwai, 8
Bridges, James, 114
Bridges, Jeff, 128–29
Bridges, Lloyd, 20, 129
Broderick, Matthew, xi, 183
Brooklyn, U.S.A., 123
Brooks, Albert, xi, 162
Brynner, Yul, 23, 93–94, 157
Bullins, Ed, 49
Burton, Richard, xi, 69, 74, 76–77, 100
Bye, Bye Braverman, 54, 55–56, 88–89, 115

Caine, Michael, xi, 114
Caligula (Camus), 3, 73
Call for the Dead (John le Carré), 62
Capote, Truman, *In Cold Blood*, 83
Carné, Marcel, 90
Carnovsky, Maurice, 91

Carson, L. M. Kit, 137
Casablanca, viii, 110, 153
Cassavetes, John, 20, 173
Cazale, John, 119
Chancellor, John, 68
Chayefsky, Pady, 70–71, 94, 163; *Hospital*, 68, 186
Chekov, Anton, 39–40, 42, 90, 91, 93, 98–100, 121, 163; *Three Sisters*, 91–92
Chicago, viii, 194
Child's Play, 100
Christie, Julie, xi, 130
Clair, René, 9
Clooney, George, xiii
Close, Glenn, xi
Clurman, Harold, 91–92
Cobb, Lee J., 91
Coburn, James, xi, 63
Connery, Sean, x, 27, 43, 48, 55, 61, 63, 100, 142, 183
Crawford, Cheryl, 93
Crime in the Streets, 20
Critical Care, xiii, 161, 162–72, 186–87
Cronkite, Walter, 68
Crouse, Lindsay, 112
Cukor, George, 96

Daley, Bob, 82
Danger, x, 17, 71, 94, 157
Daniel, viii, ix, 118, 120–21, 125, 129, 133, 140, 141, 143, 181–83, 187, 193
Davis, Desmond, 18
Davis, Ossie, x
Day, Doris, 191
De Niro, Robert, 108, 155, 185
De Sica, Vittorio, 9; *Bicycle Thief*, viii, 110
Deadly Affair, The, 46, 49–50, 62, 99, 124
Deathtrap, 96, 101, 111, 114–15, 116, 125, 126, 129
Dean, James, 94
Debs, Eugene, 143
Dehn, Paul, 55, 62
Dexter, John, 73, 77
Di Palma, Carlo, 96, 190
Dibbouk, 95
Diesel, Vin, xi
Disney, Walt, 154
Doctorow, E. L., 121, 163, 182–83; *Book of Daniel, The*, viii, 111, 118, 183
Dog Day Afternoon, vii, 53–54, 66–68, 69, 72, 73, 75, 81, 85, 86, 89, 98, 105, 111, 112,

117, 119, 123, 125, 132, 133, 141, 145, 157, 158, 163, 173, 175, 176, 188, 193
Dooling, Richard, 162
Dreyer, Carl, 9, 90; *Day of Wrath*, 123; *Passion de Jeanne d'Arc, Le*, viii, 110, 123
Dreyfus, Richard, xi
Dunaway, Faye, xi, 68, 111
Duvall, Robert, xi, 111

Ebert, Roger, 163
Eisenstein, Sergei, 90; *Potemkin*, 110
Elliot, Denholm, 43
Ephron, Nora, 187
Equus, 68, 69–70, 73–77, 100–1, 116, 129
Eternal Road, The, 3, 91, 123, 143
Executioner's Song, The, 83

Fail-Safe, xiii, 14, 26–27, 44, 60–61, 73, 81, 82, 111, 117, 129, 131, 163
Family Business, ix, 181, 183
Fassbinder, Rainer Werner, 113
Faulkner, William, 23, 152
Fellini, Federico, 152; *Amarcord*, 110
Finch, Peter, xi, 169, 173
Find Me Guilty, vii, xii
Finney, Albert, xi, 111
Firth, Peter, 68, 69, 73, 77
Fischer, Gerry, 103
Fitzgerald, F. Scott, 152n
Flag Is Born, A, 123
Fonda, Henry, x, 20, 48, 60, 111, 124, 155, 158, 161
Fonda, Jane, xi, 128–29
Foner, Naomi, 179, 180, 182
Ford, John, 16, 96; *Informer, The*, 57, 160; *Stagecoach*, 5, 110
Forrest Gump, 156
Fortunato, Ron, xiii–xiv
Foster, Jodie, 186
Frankenheimer, John, 16, 18, 19, 27, 82, 95, 132
Frears, Stephen, xiii
French New Wave, 8, 18
Front, The, 71
Fugitive Kind, The, 3–6, 8, 10, 18, 22–23, 39, 57–58, 73, 89, 97–98, 111, 116, 131, 141
Funny Girl, 70

Garbo, Greta, ix
Garbo Talks, ix, 122, 125
Garcia, Andy, xi

Gates of Hell, 49
Gerard, Joe, 161
Gere, Richard, xi, 130
Gielgud, John, xi
Gingold, Hermione, xi
Gloria, vii, xiii
Godfather II, 67, 110
Gordone, Charles, 51
Greed, 110
Green, Adolph, 194
Greenwood, Joan, x
Griffith, D. W., 97; *Intolerance*, 110
Griffith, Melanie, xi
Group, The, x, 27, 44, 56, 81, 96, 101, 111, 119, 184
Group Theater, 91–92, 132, 162

Hackman, Gene, xi, 130
Hall, Peter, 63
Hanks, Tom, 155
Harris, Burtt, 88
Hawks, Howard, *Red River*, 5
Heaven's Gate, 115
Hemingway, Ernest, 94
Hendry, Ian, 27
Hepburn, Katharine, x, 24–25, 31–32, 34–36, 38–39, 41, 58–60, 111, 155
Herrman, Ed, 164, 166
High Noon, 179–80
Hill, Steven, 181
Hill, The, 18, 27, 43, 44, 61–62, 63, 92–93, 188–89, 193
Hirsch, Judd, 134, 135, 178–79, 181
Hitchcock, Alfred: *Lady Vanishes, The*, 54; *39 Steps, The*, 62; *Torn Curtain*, 62
Hoffman, Dustin, xi, 183
Holden, William, xi, 68
Holocaust, 120
Hopkins, Anthony, 186
Hopkins, John, 45, 47, 51, 63, 100
Horne, Lena, xi, 117
Horowitz, Vladimir, 166
Howard, Trevor, 48
Hunter, Tab, 20, 59
Huston, John, 6, 22; *Prizzi's Honor*, 130
Hutton, Tim, 111

Ibsen, Henrik, 93
Iceman Cometh, The, 25, 28, 37, 74, 95, 168–69
Indiana Jones, 127

Jackson, Ann, 93
Jackson, Michael, xi, 78
Johnson, Don, xi
Jones, Gail (third wife), 117
Jones, James, *Thin Red Line*, 93
Jones, Quincy, 12, 79
Just Tell Me What You Want, 102, 116

Kael, Pauline, 111, 119, 120, 132
Kaufman, Boris, 6–7, 29, 32–33, 41, 57, 96, 98, 103, 132, 190
Kazan, Elia, 7, 9, 18, 22, 91, 93, 96, 115, 131, 132, 174, 184–85
Kazantzakis, Nikos, 45; *Last Temptation of Christ, The*, 160
Keaton, Buster, 177
Kennedy, John F., 143
Kiley, Richard, 93
King, Alan, xi
King, Martin Luther, 140
King: A Filmed Record . . . , 117, 140
Kingsley, Sidney, *Dead End* (the play), x, 3, 91, 116, 123
Krugman, Paul, 193
Kubrick, Stanley, 6; *Dr. Strangelove*, 26, 60–61
Kurosawa, Akira, 141; *Dreams*, xiv

Lahti, Christine, 134, 135, 181
Landau, Ely, 14, 25–26, 27, 36
Lansing, Sherry, 176
Last of the Mobile Hot-Shots, 63, 98–99
Last Year in Marienbad, 15
Lawrence, Carol, 23
Lenya, Lotte, xi
Levine, Joseph, 36
Lewis, Robert, 91, 93
Lindsay, John, 158
Lion King, The, 156
Living Theater, The, 67–68
Long Day's Journey Into Night, xi, 21, 24–26, 27, 28–43, 44, 47, 59–60, 69, 73, 77, 81, 91, 97–99, 111, 116, 117, 124, 126, 129, 141, 163, 168, 193
Loren, Sophia, x, 20, 59
Losey, Joseph, 91
Lovin' Molly, 53, 102
Loy, Myrna, xi
Lumet, Baruch (father), ix, 56, 89, 91, 123, 143, 184

Lumet, Sidney: on actors, 48–49, 101, 103, 109, 122–23, 155, 159, 171; on adaptation, xi, 22, 39–40, 47, 60, 73–78, 97–101, 104, 116, 126, 183; on the auteur theory, xi–xii, 113, 131, 163; on casting, 48, 84–85, 154; on Cinemascope, 9, 10; on color, 49–50, 75–76, 96, 103, 119–20, 129, 189–91; on comedy, ix, 55, 187; on development of his work, 45–46, 90, 101–2, 120; on editing, 102; final cut, viii, 111, 137, 163, 175; on HD video, xiii–xiv, 190–92; on Hollywood, 7–8, 80, 86–87; on independent production, 8, 174–76; influences on, 9, 110, 116, 123–24, 132, 143, 147–48, 160; on informing, 85, 117–18; on the law in his films, 145–50, 159; lens plots, xi, 34–35, 38–39, 43, 56–57; on melodrama, 46, 120, 129, 186; on New York, vii–viii, 21–22, 66, 80, 85–86, 88, 111–16, 125–26, 157–59, 174; politics, 92, 117–19, 131–33, 135–36, 139–40, 142–44, 182, 185; preproduction, x, 76, 126, 132; on producing, 87–88, 155; on psychoanalysis, 101; rehearsals, the importance of, x, 4, 48–49, 101, 108–9, 122, 126, 165; on reviews, 10, 70, 74; on screenwriting, 6, 46–47, 83–84, 106–7, 124, 126, 170; on scripts, 45, 51–52, 153–54, 163–66, 168–70; on self-revelation, 42–43, 103; on sentimentality, ix, 178–80; shooting style, 50–51, 102–3, 112–13, 115, 124–27, 131–33, 136, 141, 189; and television, x, xii–xiii, 4–5, 16, 17–21, 32, 37–38, 57, 70–71, 94–97, 102, 120, 123, 126–27, 132, 144, 150, 157, 168–69; on theater, 5, 9–10, 11, 80, 116; theatrical background, ix–xi, 56, 59, 89–94, 102, 104, 116, 123, 132, 143, 162–63; themes in his work, 51, 64, 104–6, 117–19, 128, 131, 135, 178, 181–82, 186, 193–94

Magnani, Anna, x, 4, 22, 57–58, 98, 116
Mailer, Norman, 83; *Deer Park, The*, 130
Making Movies, x, xv, 151–52, 157, 161, 163, 164, 171, 177, 180, 189
Malina, Judith, 67–68
Mamet, David, 112, 120, 133, 163, 164, 178
Mankiewicz, Joseph L., 11, 140
Mann, Delbert, 3; *Marty*, 95
March, Frederick, 29
Marlowe, Christopher, 62–63, 99

Mason, James, xi, 49, 99, 111, 123, 148, 155
Matthau, Walter, x
Mayer, Louis B., 8
Mazursky, Paul, 115, 174
McCarthy, Joseph, 95, 117, 131
McCarthy, Mary, 27, 56
McKellen, Ian, 63
Medea, 67
Meisner, Sanford, 132
Miller, Arthur, 23–24, 27, 73, 99, 104, 163
Mirren, Helen, xi, 162, 164, 166–67
Morning After, The, 128–30, 132, 133
Morning Glory, 20, 58–59
Morris, Oswald, 75, 103, 189
Mr. Roberts, 124, 161
Mulligan, Robert, 82, 95
Murder on the Orient Express, viii, 53, 54–55, 69, 70, 73, 74, 101, 103, 111, 119, 120, 125, 129, 163, 175
Murphy, Dudley, 91
Murrow, Edward R., 9

Network, vii, xii, 68, 69, 70–71, 73, 89, 111, 120, 129, 141, 144, 149, 151, 161, 163, 169, 173, 186
Newman, Paul, x, xi, 94, 110, 112–14, 123, 133, 148–49, 177
Nichols, Barbara, 20
Night Falls in Manhattan, xiii, 157, 160, 170
Nolte, Nick, ix, xi

Obler, Arch, *Night of the Auk*, 3
Offence, The, 44–45, 47, 63–64, 100, 142
100 Centre Street, ix, xiii–xiv, 192–93
One Third of a Nation, 91, 123
O'Neill, Eugene, xi, 24–26, 28–29, 31, 37, 42, 59–60, 70, 73, 95, 98–99, 104, 129, 163, 168, 169
Ophuls, Max, 22

Pacino, Al, xi, 53–54, 66–67, 74, 108, 111, 119, 123, 125, 141, 155, 173, 188
Pawnbroker, The, x, xii, 12–16, 27, 44, 47, 61, 65–66, 69, 73, 88, 90, 111, 117, 124, 131, 133, 151, 157, 163, 171–72, 183–84
Penn, Arthur, 95, 132, 133
Perkins, Anthony, xi, 74
Peters, Brock, 13, 15
Pfeiffer, Michelle, 155
Philadelphia Story, The (for TV), 94

Phoenix, River, xi, 133–35, 178, 180
Picker, David, 154
Pierson, Frank, 163
Plimpton, Martha, 134, 135
Plowright, Joan, xi, 69, 76
Polonsky, Abe, 94
Ponti, Carlo, 20
Power, xii, 130, 133, 144
Prince of the City, vii, xi, 81, 82–90, 98,
    101–3, 105, 106–8, 111, 112, 117, 119, 120,
    125, 129, 132, 133, 141–42, 145–46, 161,
    163, 170, 193
Production Code, 10
Pryor, Richard, 78, 120

Q & A, ix, 148, 170
Quintero, José, 29

Ragtime, 120
Rains, Claude, 153
Rampling, Charlotte, 112–14
Rashomon (for TV), 95
Reagan, Ronald, 139
Red Alert (Peter George), 60
Redford, Robert, 108, 114, 142
Redgrave, Colin, xi
Redgrave, Lynn, xi, 63
Redgrave, Vanessa, xi, 99, 111
Reds, 120
Reeve, Christopher, xi, 114–15
Reinhardt, Max, 91
Renoir, Jean, ix, 90, 124
Rich, Marianne, 93
Richardson, Ralph, x, 24–25, 30, 33, 34–35,
    38–39, 40, 60
Rigby, Ray, 27, 61
Ritchie, Michael, 133
Ritt, Martin, 3, 95
Robards, Jason, Jr., x, 24–25, 29, 31, 34–35,
    39, 60
Robbins, Jerome, 80
Roberts, Meade, 6
Roberts, Tony, xi
Rodino, Peter, 138
Romeo and Juliet, 40
Roots, 120
Rose, Billy, 22
Rose, Reginald, 8, 20, 94, 95, 124,
    161, 163
Rosenberg, Ethel and Julius, ix
Ross, Diana, xi, 78, 79

Ross, Ted, 78
Royal Shakespeare Company, 63, 99
Running on Empty, ix, 130, 133–41,
    178–82, 187
Russell, Nipsey, 78
Ryder, Winona, 155

Sabinson, Allen, xiii
Sacco-Vanzetti Case, The, 3, 95
Salt, Waldo, 163
Sanchez, Jaime, 14
Sanders, George, 20, 59
Sardi, David, 160
Sarris, Andrew, 70, 111, 119, 120, 132
Saroyan, William, *My Heart's in the
    Highlands*, 3, 91, 116
Schwartz, Steven, 186
Scorsese, Martin, 160, 173, 185
Seagull, The, 30, 32, 39, 40–41, 42–43, 44,
    47, 49, 69, 81, 88, 90, 98–100, 101–2,
    103, 116, 121, 141, 193–94
Sedgwick, Kyra, 162
Segal, George, 54
Serpico, 53, 64, 67, 69, 72, 75, 81, 82, 83, 85,
    86, 105, 111, 112, 117, 125, 133, 141,
    145–46, 151, 163
Schaffner, Franklin, 20, 95, 132; *Best Man,
    The*, 18; *Woman of Summer, A*, 18
Schell, Maximilian, xi
Shaffer, Peter, 68, 70, 73–76, 100–1, 129,
    163; *Royal Hunt of the Sun*, 75
Shanghai Express, 54
Sharif, Omar, xi
Shaw, Bernard, 93; *Doctor's Dilemma,
    The*, 3
Shaw, Irwin, *Gentle People, The*, 91
Shawn, Wallace, xi
Sidney, Sylvia, 91
Signoret, Simone, xi, 49, 62, 99–100, 111
Silence of the Lambs, 186
Simpson, O. J., 147, 149
Singin' in the Rain, 194
Spacek, Sissy, 155
Spader, James, xi, 162, 164, 166–69
Spiegel, Sam, 8
Spielberg, Steven, 126, 154; *Schindler's
    List*, 184
Splendor in the Grass, 96
Stage Struck, ix, 3, 6, 18, 20, 21, 58–59,
    158, 190
Stallone, Sylvester, *Rocky*, 133

Stapleton, Maureen, x, 23
Star Wars, 77
Steiger, Rod, x, 14, 61, 173
Stevens, George, 7, 9
Stockwell, Dean, 24, 30, 38–39, 60
Stone, I. F., 193
Stone, Sharon, xi
Straight, Beatrice, xi
Strasberg, Lee, 58, 67, 91
Strasberg, Susan, 20, 58–59
Street Scene, 123
Sunup to Sundown, 91
Sylbert, Richard, 34, 41

Television, the "Golden Age," x, 56, 70, 94, 163
Terms of Endearment, 130
That Kind of Woman, 3, 18, 20, 21, 59
Torres, Edwin: *After Hours*, 192; *Carlito's Way*, 192
Tragedy in a Temporary Town, 20, 129
True Confessions, 120
Truffaut, François, 113
Tudor, Anthony, 93
Turner, Lana, 122, 155
Turner, Ted, 138, 189
12 Angry Men, vii, 3, 6, 18, 19–20, 44, 45, 56–57, 59, 64, 69, 81, 95, 97, 102, 111, 112, 124, 128, 131, 132, 141, 146–47, 151, 161, 163, 173, 176, 179, 192
Twenty Grand (for TV), 94

Unmarried Woman, An, 115
Unsworth, Geoffrey, 103

Valenti, Jack, 138
Vallone, Raf, 23
Verdict, The, vii, xi, 110–14, 117–18, 124, 129, 145–46, 148–49, 151, 163, 177–78

View From the Bridge, 18, 23–24, 39, 44, 73, 86, 97, 99, 116, 159
Vigo, Jean, 9, 90, 124

Waiting for Lefty, 93
Wallant, Edward Lewis, 14, 61, 183
Walton, Tony, 75
Warden, Jack, 123
Warner, David, 39, 99
Weill, Kurt, 91
Weisel, Eli, 183–84
Welles, Orson, 6, 177
West, Nathanael, *Day of the Locust, The*, 149
Whitlock, Albert, 79
Whose Life Is It Anyway?, 120
Wilde, Oscar, 93; *Importance of Being Earnest, The*, 55
Wilder, Billy, 6
Williams, Tennessee, 3–4, 6, 22–23, 57–58, 63, 73, 94, 104, 131, 163; *Glass Menagerie, The*, 23; *Night of the Iguana*, 22; *Orpheus Descending*, 4, 22, 57, 73, 131; *Seven Descents of Myrtle, The*, 98–99
Williams, Treat, xi, 141, 170
Winter Carnival, 152n
Wiz, The, viii, 74, 77–80, 89, 100, 111, 116, 125
Wizard of Oz, The, 78, 100
Wojtowicz, John (Sonny), 67
Woodward, Joanne, x, 22, 98
Worth, Irene, 114
Wyler, William, 9, 10
Wynn, Keenan, 20

You Are There, 94–95, 114, 132
Young, Freddie, 49
Youngstein, Max, 26–27

Zinnemann, Fred, 7, 9

CONVERSATIONS WITH FILMMAKERS SERIES
PETER BRUNETTE, GENERAL EDITOR

The collected interviews with notable modern directors, including

Robert Aldrich • Pedro Almodóvar • Robert Altman • Theo Angelopolous • Bernardo Bertolucci • Tim Burton • Jane Campion • Frank Capra • Charlie Chaplin • Francis Ford Coppola • George Cukor • Brian De Palma • Clint Eastwood • John Ford • Terry Gilliam • Jean-Luc Godard • Peter Greenaway • Alfred Hitchcock • John Huston • Jim Jarmusch • Elia Kazan • Stanley Kubrick • Fritz Lang • Spike Lee • Mike Leigh • George Lucas • Roman Polanski • Michael Powell • Jean Renoir • Martin Ritt • Carlos Saura • John Sayles • Martin Scorsese • Ridley Scott • Steven Soderbergh • Steven Spielberg • George Stevens • Oliver Stone • Quentin Tarantino • Lars von Trier • Orson Welles • Billy Wilder • Zhang Yimou • Fred Zinnemann